THE UNOBSTRUCTED UNIVERSE

By

STEWART EDWARD WHITE

A Dutton  *Paperback*

NEW YORK

E. P. DUTTON & CO., INC.

THE UNOBSTRUCTED UNIVERSE

by
STEWART EDWARD WHITE

CONTENTS

PART I

PART II

PART III

PART IV

PART I

CHAPTER I

THE TWO CHINESE BOXES

ONE Thursday evening Joan returned from a trip to the city very much vexed with herself. I was visiting Darby and her over a long week-end, and so was present to hear her plaint.

"I hate to be a fool," was its gist, "and I hate doing silly things; and I like to plan things out and then do them; and I *am* a careful shopper, and I hate to buy things I don't want —"

"Tell us about it," Darby and I urged.

"Listen," said she. "I went to town this morning with a careful list of errands to do. The first one was at a shop over on Fifth Avenue; and to get there you take an Avenue bus from the Hudson Tube, near the Penn Station — right to the door."

"Well?" said we.

"I found myself on a *cross-town* bus," wailed Joan disgustedly. "I always take the Avenue bus — *never* the cross-town. Yet there I was! And they don't even leave the station from the same place. And that isn't the whole of it!"

"Go ahead," we encouraged.

"I went to the end of the cross-town line — I thought I might as well — prepared to walk the five blocks to my shop. At the end of the line there's a big department store — I almost *never* shop there. I hadn't been there for years. But I thought I'd walk through it to the Avenue instead of going around by the side street. I'd hardly got inside when I caught sight of a red box being trundled off on a floor truck along with a load of other stuff. No reason why I should be interested in red boxes, but I just *had* to chase after that one. And was I disappointed when the truck got away from me down an elevator! I even hunted up a floorman and shot a volley of questions at him. He told me the box must have been one of the Chinese chests they had been having a special sale on; and he directed me to what they had left. They were good-sized camphorwood chests, covered with pigskin and painted with various designs and colors. I went and bought one," said Joan bitterly.

"Weren't they attractive?" I asked, puzzled by the bitterness.

"They were most attractive," she admitted. "But I have camphorwood chests. And" — her voice rose in emphasis — "in all this house there's not a place where I could put another camphorwood chest — or any other piece of furniture for that matter — without everybody's falling over it every time he went from here to there. I have about as much use for a camphorwood chest as Tabs has for two tails!" Tabs being the family cat.

Darby and I shouted.

"That isn't the worst," said Joan.

We became quiet, in expectation.

"You see," said Joan, who was now beginning to enjoy her own narration, "none of the chests was red. The one I bought was yellow. And that red color — the color of the first one I saw, on the truck — somehow I couldn't get that particular shade of red out of my mind. No, said the salesman, the merchandise on the truck was all sold goods. No, there were no more red ones. You'd think that would have satisfied me, wouldn't you? Not at all. I insisted they must have a reserve; I insisted on seeing the department manager; and finally I elicited that there *was* a reserve, but I couldn't see it. Just the same, I kept at them, and I *did* see it — they must have thought me crazy! And there was a red one. And I bought that! I bought *two* of the dratted things! Now I ask you! And tomorrow they'll be out here in Orange Center cluttering up everything! Well, they'll go back bright and early Monday morning, I can tell you that! I can't *imagine* what got into me!"

Neither could we — not until the third evening.

Nor will you — not until the third chapter.

CHAPTER II

AGAIN I BEAR WITNESS

1.

ABOUT six months before Joan bought her two unwanted Chinese boxes in New York — at eight o'clock, on the fifth of April, 1939, in a little foothill town of California, my wife Betty died. And immediately I had gone out of the house to face the overhanging mountains and my own emotional and intellectual conflict.

Some twenty years of exploring with Betty beyond the known frontiers of present consciousness had lifted from me most of the conventional ideas as to death. I had come to have no faintest feeling of it as final and irrevocable separation. Nevertheless, I found on April 5, 1939, that the even greater number of years — thirty-five of them — spent with her close companionship in exploring the odd and wild corners of this, our earth, had sharpened rather than dulled my sense of the immediate separation. We had been more closely knit together than most. During those years of companionship, crammed as they were to the brim with journey and adventure, from then unknown Central Africa to the wildest of Alaska, we were apart only three times: twice when I was on African expeditions inadvisable for her, and throughout my service in the first World War.

Now, in the conventional phrase, I had become a man who had "lost his wife." The loss was more than that of personal companionship, close and warm as that had always been. It was also the loss of the one I had long recognized as the more important member of our working team. When I left that little house, in the California foothill town, to stand alone in the moonlight, beneath the stars, it seemed to me that my part of our greatest adventuring — that in the Unknown — had calamitously ended. For I honestly believed it impossible for me to carry it forward alone.

You see, in addition to our other, and richly abundant, activities, Betty and I, since March 17, 1919, had been exploring another land, that unseen land of mystery from which, it used to be said, "no traveler returns." We doubted that. Betty had visited that land, and had returned, many times. It was her reports of these, her explorations, which made up the body of the work I now felt so impossible without her, and so untimely broken off.

We had accomplished something, we thought; and what we had done had already found print in four books; but it had seemed to us both that there was still a strong lead onward to something culminating, something Betty had not yet reached. So she fought hard to stay; and I fought hard to keep her. And it had looked like a winning fight until the very last.

2.

The four books were these:

Credo, a preliminary volume issued in 1925, in which, without revealing its actual source, I presented the practical aspects of the philosophy received psychically through Betty from "the other side";

Why Be a Mud Turtle?, 1928, in which I reported further teachings of the same philosophy that seemed to me so applicable to modern living that it was actually unfair to withhold them from our growingly complicated world — but again without explaining the origin of the concepts;

The Betty Book, 1937, in which I threw my hat over the modern public's materialistic windmill and wrote frankly of "the excursions of 'Betty,' a psychic intimately known to me and of absolute integrity, into the world of 'other consciousness,' and of the communications received by her . . . in a condition of trance or otherwise . . . from forces which I have ventured to call 'the Invisibles.'*" But even so, it was only my own hat I threw. I refrained from stating in so many words that "Betty" was in reality Elizabeth Calvert Grant White, my own wife.†

Just after Christmas, 1938, the fourth book, *Across the Unknown*, was finished and the manuscript shipped to its publisher. Here there was no attempt to conceal the identity of Betty. Indeed, the flood of enthusiastic and demanding letters that increased rather than diminished month after month following publication of *The Betty Book* had at last convinced us of the truth of what the Invisibles had told us repeatedly, from the very beginning:

"The *message* is what is important . . . the *message* and the fact that we are able to give it: not you."

3.

Thus it was that communication with the Invisibles, disincarnate earth-entities, had been of daily occurrence

* From the introduction to *The Betty Book*.
† See Appendix I (*Who's Who in America* Reference Service, January 1940).

in Betty's and my home. I had taken down in my own brand of "shorthand," and then typed for record purposes, several thousand single-spaced pages of teachings so received. From these several thousand pages, containing well over a million words, I had written my four books acclaiming the intellectual reasonableness of the continuity of life — the going forward of the individual *I-Am* after natural death.

And then, very soon after the last proofs had received the author's corrections, Betty died. What happened out on the hillside under the trees that April night I have told elsewhere. That record still stands. While *Across the Unknown* was actually in press, I added one short chapter entitled "I Bear Witness." I repeat a portion of it here because I can tell it no better:

"You know the cozy, intimate feeling of companionship you get sometimes when you are in the same room; perhaps each reading a book; not speaking; not even looking at one another. It is tenuous, an evanescent thing — one that we too often fail to savor and appreciate. Sometimes, in fact, it takes an evening or two of empty solitude to make us realize how substantial and important it really is.

"Then, on the other hand, you know how you draw closer by means of things you do together. And still more through talk and such mental interchanges. And most of all, perhaps, in the various physical relationships of love and marriage.

"Now when you stop to think of it, all these latter material contacts, right through the whole of life, are at root and in essence aimed at really just one thing: that rare inner feeling of companionship suggested feebly in the sitting-by-the-fire idea. That is what we *really* are groping for in all friendly and loving human relations, hampered by the fact that we are different people more or less muffled from each other by the barriers of encasement in the body.

"Well, within a very few minutes that companionship flooded through my whole being from Betty, but in an intensity and purity of which I had previously had no conception. It was the same thing, but a hundred, a thousand times stronger. And I realized that it more than compensated for the little fact that she had stepped across, because it was the thing that all our physical activities together had striven for, but — compared with this — had gained only dimly and in part. Why not? Actually it was doing perfectly what all these other things had only groped for. So what use the other things? and why should I miss them?

"Does this sound fantastic? Maybe; but it is as real and solid as the chair I am sitting on. So much so that I have never in my life been so filled with pure happiness. No despair; no devastation; just a deeper happiness than I have experienced with her ever before, save in the brief moments when everything harmonized in fulfillment.

"And furthermore it has lasted, and is with me always."

Now, more than a year later, I can in all honesty repeat: "It has lasted, and is with me always." The experience of that night was charged neither with the exultation of emotional belief nor the quiet sureness of intellectual knowledge. There was just a quick dissolving of my conflict; for *Betty* had not gone — *she* was still with me. There was left me no doubt as to her Presence with me on the hillside.

That presence has continued, not all the time, but normally so. I go into a room; she may or may not be there. I stroll about her garden; she may or may not walk with me. But many times throughout each twenty-four-hour day she *is* there, her vivid personality enveloping me, and not only me but even strangers visiting in the house.

It was Betty who, when here, created easy, friendly hospitality in our home — not I. She it is who still creates it; for Betty is still living. This I know. Not as I live, but with me in "the one and only universe." She has given me a thousand proofs of it. And through another psychic — Joan of the Chinese boxes, about whom much more in the following pages — a whole new concept of possibly scientific thought including a unique, and I think illuminating, terminology.

Betty calls it a "divulgence." The few physicists or metaphysicians to whom I have submitted various portions are all agreed, with normally professional reservations, that it is "important." One, less normally professional than the rest, let himself go.

"I don't care how or where you get it," he said. "This is definitely a step forward — a system of anticipatory thought. At the very least it will give us laboratory fellows new premises to work from and new hypotheses to work toward."

Perhaps. Betty called it only a divulgence.

Divulgence of what? Of *The Unobstructed Universe* where Betty went after her body died and concerning which, its ways and means, methods, laws, habits, work, triumphs, failures — indeed, its very *place* — she, through Joan, has since reported back to me.

CHAPTER III

ONLY ONE CHINESE BOX

1.

FOR nearly six months, then, after her death, Betty and I continued living in "the one and only Universe" with, however, a barrier of verbal communication between us; she on her side and I on mine.

I hope I have made it clear that she had most decidedly "come back" in the most satisfying form possible, for me at least. Nor was my experience unique to myself. From all over the country I received letters, many of them puzzled, some of them even from people who had met Betty but casually and many years ago, trying to tell me about their feeling of her presence with them.

"I found myself happy and twinkling, for no reason at all. I had a merry sense of Betty — out of a clear sky — apropos of nothing. No heartache — just a merry and impudent nudge." — "I did not think I could stand it. But all evening I had a sense of Betty, and a feeling of peace that I had not thought possible." — "When I think of Betty I can't possibly *pump up* any feeling of desolation. She's just *there*" — this with a sense of amazement. —"It was an astonishing experience of amazing power.... I just called to her, and instantly she was there, and with a voltage that swept me right out of myself."

That sort of thing. And so much of it, and from such scattered sources, and from so many people who had no use for, or no knowledge of, "psychics." Explanation of fortuity and coincidence began to look rather absurd.

But Betty appeared as yet to have nothing to *say*, in

words. This might seem rather curious to anyone familiar with the type of work she had been doing for twenty years. That had involved her penetration into the higher consciousness, the state of being in which, presumably, she now dwelt; and her reporting back to me her experiences and findings. That was "communication from the other side." Also we had slowly come to know and trust a small group of friends who — incidentally to the friendship — were gifted, as Betty was gifted, with her peculiar sensitiveness or talent. If anyone could "come back," as they say — and by that they generally mean come back in conversation — it certainly should be Betty.

Furthermore, a good many people wrote me, or asked me, whether I had "heard from Betty," and were bothered when I told them I had not — not in the sense of their inquiry. I was not bothered. On the contrary, I came almost at once to appreciate the wisdom of her course. For the very moment the ordinary and customary "message" was offered, that moment the brightness of her present demonstration must be — even if ever so slightly — dimmed. Admit my conviction that it is actually Betty speaking; admit my acceptance of authenticity as respects the body of the "message" received, there must always remain in my mind some slight question as to detail — how much is Betty; how much is the subconscious of the psychic?

To be sure, it can be, and is, sorted out in time. We had found that to be true. But, *unless she had something important to say*, how could mere spoken words add to what, apparently, she was now trying so successfully to do?

2.

In this frame of mind I flew East, in the early part of September, 1939. It was my first visit for many years. Though I had crossed the continent nearly a hundred times, I had never ceased to consider it inordinately wide, and the journey inordinately time-consuming. Well, I reflected as the plane touched earth, we have at last done something about that! In 1884 it had taken me nearly a week to get to the Coast from Chicago. Here I was in Chicago for breakfast, and I had left San Francisco after dinner the night before! Time and space were no longer the barrier they had been. A trite enough reflection. But unknowingly I was hitting the keynote of my next big adventure.

My purpose had to do with a novel just written and in the process of publication, and with renewal in person of certain friendships that the said space and time had not been able to affect. These were many. Among them was that of a man and his wife who, twenty years ago, had published a book that has had a profound effect, in that it introduced certain new concepts that have become so integral with our body of thought that they are today used as building blocks in many an intellectual structure by people who have never heard of the book or its authors. The title of the book is *Our Unseen Guest*, and the concepts of which I speak will appear naturally in the course of what follows.

Now we get back to the Chinese boxes. For the Joan of that bizarre episode was the Joan of *Our Unseen Guest*. The authors had elected to call themselves Darby and Joan — and still so choose to conceal themselves.

Twenty years ago they were, and still are, both professional people. They could not — or thought they could not — risk the possibility of such controversy as, almost invariably, has raged about outstanding mediums. And theirs was no pseudo-anonymity. Even today there are, I suppose, not a score of persons who are aware that Joan possesses her special talent; and of that number not half have any first-hand experience. The privileged few realize that she is one of the greatest psychics, if not the greatest, in the world today.

Such a statement requires a moment to explain why I make it.

As to method: Joan works blindfolded from a state of trance, into which she enters instantly and completely at the signal of Darby's touch on her wrist. However, she is not "unconscious" in the sense of helplessness or immobility; she is not "asleep." At times she even moves about or does things apparently required of her. I have seen her, for the demonstration of some point being made, perform an intricate dance, accurately and surely, through a room crowded with furniture, though she was as usual heavily blindfolded. Invisible entities talk through her, and then her own personality is completely absent; but on occasion she also reports in her own right what is shown her or told her, in which case, of course, apparently she participates. Nevertheless, on returning to her normal state she never has the slightest recollection of anything that has been done or said, and she has no sense whatever of the passage of time. This latter was once amusingly illustrated to us. She had been "out" for perhaps five minutes when it became necessary to make certain arrangements before we could actually begin the work in hand, so Darby brought her back.

"How long has it been?" she asked.

Somebody in mischief told her "about three hours."

She accepted this so unquestioningly that she was much concerned because, as she supposed, she and Darby had missed their last train home! We had to show her the clock before she would be convinced that only five minutes had elapsed.

This perfection of abeyance, so to call it, is remarkable, but not unprecedented. But added to it are certain qualities that justify my estimate, such as honesty of character; total absence of egotism; an eager desire to help, to play the game; a fine mind and intelligence; and a fastidiousness of social selection in ordinary life which, we have been assured, is of enormous assistance to the Invisibles in keeping their channel clean and free of the extraneous that clutters up so much of this kind of effort.

"The point is this," we were told, "Joan is selective. She is so in her social and intellectual interests. So there are some individuals here whom Joan welcomes, and others she does not. Joan accepted Stephen,* who came to her out of the thin air, just as she would have accepted him if she had met him on earth."

Betty and I had first met Darby and Joan at the house of Margaret Cameron,† in 1922. With them, and Margaret, and another psychic, Mrs. John Palmer Gavit,‡ we conducted the remarkable series of experiments in demonstrating and verifying the "second body" — beta body, we called it — described in an appendix to *The Betty Book*. In the next seventeen years we had with

---

* The personality who gave most of the material for *Our Unseen Guest*.

† Author of *The Seven Purposes*.

‡ The "Mrs. Gaines" of *The Betty Book*.

Darby and Joan but two other contacts: once when Betty went East without me, and once when they visited us at Burlingame for two days. Nevertheless, in spite of so few meetings, and in spite of the fact that Betty and Joan were doing diametrically opposite kinds of work by different methods, the two of them had always "clicked." And they always felt that, somehow or another, they were destined to do more good work together. But they, no more than Darby or myself, realized how perfectly they were being trained, each in her own way, to combine their methods in one triumphant effort when the time came.

3.

These two were among the friendships I had come East to renew. Nevertheless, my interest was not in the possibility of getting in verbal touch with Betty. I must repeat, I did not *need* verbal touch with Betty. I would not seek it, unless I were convinced that she really had something to say beside greeting and chit chat; and my opinion then was that her serious work had been rounded out, had reached its culmination. So I wrote it down in the chapter "I Bear Witness," added to *Across the Unknown* after she had died. "This [the demonstration of her presence], I now believe, is the 'great blossom' of which the Invisibles spoke; the final significance to which all of Betty's twenty years of work was to lead. Here is her concrete proof of one reward that can come to those who follow in her footsteps, her final evidence that her instrument of twenty years' forging is strong enough to stand the supreme test." Unconsciously I think I was just a little afraid of weakening the perfection of that demonstration of her actual and continuing presence: I was inclined to let well enough alone.

My first evening with Darby and Joan swept that particular fog out of my head. Betty had something to say: and she said just enough to prove to us that all of her previous work, and all of Joan's previous work, and before that the work of Margaret Cameron — who was one of the first Americans to make a nation-wide psychical stir outside professional research circles — were really a necessary preliminary foundation to what she was going to be able to tell us now, from her present point of view.

In all this business of alleged communication across the border, the question of identification has always been the focus both of investigation and of opposition. When a man calls you up on the telephone, saying he is John Smith, and the matter is important, you want him first of all to prove to you that he is who he says he is. The best way he can do it is to tell you something that only you and he know. That, transferred to psychical research, is what is called evidential material, or simply "evidential."

So important it is, from the point of view of research, that the great bulk of psychic investigation has been in the direction of obtaining and analyzing evidential. The task has proved to be one of extraordinary difficulty; and, speaking by and large, your researcher is delighted if, out of a great mass of material, he can winnow an occasional bit which, with reasonable interpretation, can be considered air-tight. When he gets such a bit he publishes it in a *Journal* rather triumphantly.

Betty began talking to me quietly, fluently, with assured and intimate knowledge of our common experience and living. There was no "fishing" and no fumbling. That part of it became almost ridiculous, it was so easy for her where with usual "psychical research" it has been so difficult.

Here, in this first evening, she literally poured out a succession of these authentications. She mentioned not one, but dozens, of small events out of our past, of trivial facts in our mutual experience or surroundings, none of which could by any possibility be within Joan's knowledge. Many of them, indeed, were gone from my own memory, until Betty recalled them to me. And all of them — *except just one* — clean-cut, air-tight, without need of interpretation. A dyed-in-the-wool psychic researcher would have gone mad with joy over such a demonstration, which would have furnished him enough material to have lasted him for the next seven years!

Darby was taking the notes. He has not my verbatim "shorthand," and confined them mostly to what he considered significant in what Betty was saying, which was why his script missed the "evidential." It sounded unimportant to him. I myself was so amazed — and excited — that it did not occur to me to write anything down. So most of it was lost, as far as record goes. That does not matter. Betty's purpose was merely to authenticate for us herself — and incidentally her command of Joan — in order to bespeak our attention to what was to follow.

That for me — and for Darby when afterward I explained to him the appositeness of what had sounded to him like chit chat — was done so thoroughly that from that evening on we could not doubt that we were hearing from Betty; and that Betty had something to say. Not without accusing our own plain common sense.

It would be possible to gather some of these scattered bits together, and the reader is certainly entitled to something beyond my simple statement. But such a compilation would be fragmentary, and in addition would depend largely on my own assurance of its factual character. Therefore I will not make that attempt. But fortunately there were three other incidents of "evidential," quite as brilliant and as detailed, involving others outside our little group of three, which *did* get recorded. These I shall narrate — and that at last brings us back to Joan's outrageous purchase of the two Chinese boxes she did not want.

"Well!" Betty began with a chuckle,* "I did have a terrible time in town! No, not a terrible time — I had a lot of fun — but I had to work hard to get Joan to take the wrong bus so she would go to that store and see the truck with the gadget on it. I saw one in Chinatown † once, but it cost seventy-five dollars, and this one was so cheap. You'll have to lend me the money for it, Stewt. I wanted something that Millicent ‡ had had in mind for a long time; and I wanted it for the color and the birds; but Joan bought the wrong one, so I had to make her buy another. Tell Mill *it is for the color and the birds.* When we were little girls we used to be fond of watching certain birds.

"The boxes are in the game room, unpacked; and one of them, the yellow one, nobody wants. Joan had decided to send both back; and she was so amazed at her-

* It may be as well to state here that all speeches quoted from any Invisible are verbatim unless otherwise stated. I have a shorthand adequate for that purpose.

† In San Francisco.

‡ Betty's sister, who lives in a New York suburb.

self; and she didn't know what she was doing; and generally when she shops she knows what she is doing; and ever since she's been wondering why on earth she bought them, and what she was going to do with them.

"Tell Mill she will find the red one just as useful, to keep her furs in, as I found the tricky little leather dressing case that she gave me. Ask Joan if she will please give you four small gliders to put on the bottom. She has them in a small drawer. I think Joan is going to insist on — No, she isn't. [paying for them, perhaps?] The yellow one is to go back. The store got them from a Chinese ship in port, and bought the whole cargo, and that is why they were cheap. I wanted the *birds* for Mill; there were others with flowers, but I wanted the *birds*."

Now here was something! Three things we could verify at once, and did. The statement as to the reason for these boxes being on special sale was true. They were part of a cargo refused by the original importer and bought by this store to use as a "come-on" special: this fact, however, was already known to Joan. The reference to the furs might have significance in that I had recently given Millicent Betty's furs: a fact that was not known to Joan. The promise of the gliders we investigated at once. A search of the tool drawer, where such things would ordinarily be kept, disclosed none; but finally "in a small drawer" in the kitchen we turned up six of them. Two were large, and four were "small." But of course Joan's subconscious might have had recollection of them.

All interesting, but not conclusive. So at the earliest opportunity I went to see Millicent.

"Mill," said I, "what's your favorite color?"

"Well," she laughed, "you know I'm part Spanish, so I'll have to confess it's red."

"Any particular shade?"

She had a small box of Chinese lacquer, and instanced that. So far, exceedingly good.

"Have you had particularly in mind wanting anything like a Chinese camphorwood chest?"

"Yes," replied Millicent promptly. "When I was on the Coast with you in 1936 Betty and I saw one in Chinatown. I was crazy about it, but it was much too expensive. But later I thought it over, and I wrote her asking where I could get one — I must have written her three or four times, but somehow she never answered my question."

"Well, she's got it for you now," said I, and explained. "But there's something else. She said, 'Tell Mill it is for the color and the birds,' and she emphasized that, and added something about watching birds when you were little girls. Anything special about that? I suppose all children watch birds."

Millicent stared at me, for a moment unable to speak.

"Every spring," she told me solemnly at last, "every spring Betty and I used to climb up in the trees on our place, and sit very quiet for hours and hours to watch the birds build their nests! Why, I think that's wonderful!"

I agreed.

"Now, there's just one other point," said I. "How about the leather dressing case? Did you ever give her one that could be described as 'tricky'?"

"You must have seen it," was her reply. "It had a sort of double top, so you could get at the mirror and toilet articles without opening the suitcase part."

"Of course I've seen it," said I. "But I did not know you gave it to her."

I returned to the city. Barely had I entered my hotel room when the telephone rang. It was Millicent, very much excited.

"Did you notice what *kind* of birds they are — painted on the chest? They are *swallows!*"

"What of it?" I wanted to know.

"Why—why—" gasped Millicent, "it was swallows we used to watch building their nests. That's why we climbed the trees — to get level with the eaves!"

CHAPTER IV

"THIS IS YOUR HERITAGE"

1.

I HAVE said that, in view of Betty's "pervading-presence" demonstration, as it might be called, I was not eager for communication from her through a psychic "unless she had something to say." I meant that not only as far as personal messages to me were concerned, but in a broader sense and a wider application. For the world is full of books substantiating the existence of the unexplained, and I was no longer interested in generalities.

But that first evening with Darby and Joan convinced me, as already stated, that Betty did have something to say; something quite the opposite of generalities; something not only for those who, in the shock of personal loss, have struggled with the weariness of grief, but also something for those who, in the dismayed bewilderment of seemingly unwarranted failure, out of their despair ask that final, most disheartening of questions: "What's the use?"

And so, before I set down further evidence of Betty's authentication of herself, and of the individuality and continuity of that self, I think I should tell you *why* Betty had something to say; *why* — to quote her — "I am permitted to bring you this divulgence," at this particular time. And also to tell you something of its present aim and need.

"My very dear," Betty began one evening as if she were dictating a letter, "naturally what I have to say is directed first to you. But any truth that is of comfort and surety to one man may be of comfort and surety to other men. Always this has been so. Not that all can share your present experience — this sitting down, here in this pleasant room, and listening to my thoughts framed in my own words, though relayed to you by the voice of another woman. That experience is not for all, nor is it needed by all. What the all — all people — need is a new presentation of the truth in the light of their own times and the terms of their own knowledge; so that each may seek truth's comfort for himself, and find it — if he will.

"The world calls me — us here — dead. But sometimes people, unable to endure the thought of such a blanking out, speak of a loved one as having 'gone on.' That idea, *the act of going on*, is more correctly true. It is true that we are 'changed'; but so is man in his earth experience changed from a new-born child to adulthood. And not only is he changed physically, but his perceptions are changed, his power of assimilation, his control of himself and of the things of earth about him.

"It is so that I am changed — so all we 'dead' are changed; glorified with our own immortality. Even as you, too, will be glorified. We have indeed gone on beyond the comprehension of your present earth perceptions; but so is man beyond the comprehension — even the sight perception — of that new-born child. Of course it takes only a little while before a baby begins, as they say, 'to notice.' It is the same with you. You, the World — so small a child in Time's duration of the Universe — only notice us as yet. But just as the noticing of a child brings a feeling of personal comfort and stability to him, so would the world's acceptance of Immortality bring back stability and comfort to mankind. Individually and socially. Indeed, it is only so — only by a re-establishment of the old faith in the continuity, the worth-whileness, the purpose and responsibility of life — that people or nations can regain stability.

"Stability," she repeated. "*Stability* is what you have lost and are now seeking to regain. Not security. Security is material. Stability is spiritual. Stability is the soul, the character of peoples. Given that, man or nation makes its own security. But stability — real foundation-rock, unwavering stability — no man can have without *faith* in immortality. Why? Oh, my dear, my dear! Earth-life would have no point, would be too much to ask of man, without immortality!"

What was she driving at? For what does she hope? However difficult — or not — may be found the intellectual concepts as elaborated in later pages, of their emotional stimulus and purpose she leaves no slightest doubt.

2.

The old order of things has collapsed, says Betty. In some parts of the world, as in Europe, that collapse has been so complete that it seems everything of the old has been destroyed or lost. Elsewhere, as in our own country, much of the staunchness of the old order is still intact; but it is becoming increasingly obvious that even here readjustments are inevitable. The same elements that brought about the catastrophe in the Old World are at work in the New, and will proceed to the same conclusion if we continue fatuously traveling the same road.

What brought about this collapse?

"Loss of faith in the present fact of immortality," Betty states bluntly.

She does not mean, she carefully explained, a conscious attitude of agnosticism or denial. We may still profess belief in a vague and remote "heaven" to which eventually we shall go. But belief is not faith; and it is only *faith* — faith in the same sense that we accept the inevitability of death itself — that can transfer the field of our practical endeavor out of the present moment. When the present moment — the earth span of life — is all that concerns us, then the emphasis of all we think and all we do at once bases on materialism. We know that modern civilization has been drifting toward that point of view, whether we are frank enough to admit it or not. More and more we have been tending toward writing off everything but the gain of the day. We deny the claim of the future; we are increasingly indifferent to the coming generations. We are emphasizing *rights* rather than *obligations;* those obligations that a real faith in immortality must impose.

When humankind gets far enough away from the fact of immortality, said Betty impressively, it has to come back. Or perish. And the only way it can come back is to cease looking outside itself and search within.

"Furthermore," she told us, "any coming back always means a new pattern."

Yet if men redesign the pattern on materialistic lines alone, the same result must follow. The worth of the new pattern must depend on the basis of its establishment.

"That," says Betty, "is dependent on the free will of men. Your wills are free. This is your heritage and your glory."

Now to America, she insists, is entrusted the chance to

fix a new and better pattern. Why are we so entrusted? Why have we the job?

Because our nation's pattern of government was originally laid down closely in accord with a reality of consciousness which we call evolution. That is the structure of the universe; various *degrees* of development, high, low, and in between. Each must work freely in its own capacity toward the development of the whole. Leave out the word "freely" and you have totalitarianism. Put it in and you have democracy. In our beginnings we functioned pretty closely to that ideal. And still do; though we have backslid somewhat.

But democracy is not a form *of* government. It is a pattern *for* government. It is the union of all the parts in the common good of all, with — to repeat — complete opportunity for each individual to do that which he *can* do; but only to his capacity, though to his full capacity, and with no obligation to do more — or less!

"Neither the 'more' nor the 'less,'" said Betty, "may set the pace for all."

In this sense the democracy of our Republic was, and is, the nearest parallel, reflected in government, to the Reality of Consciousness. By which is meant the mode or law of the operation of Consciousness. And this is why, says Betty, the responsibility has fallen on us, the United States, for the set of the new pattern.

Now, she demands, how are we going to do it? Surely not on the old material basis that has collapsed in Europe; not on the basis of each day for itself and devil take tomorrow. Must we not dig down into the consciousness of men and lay bare the only rock strong enough to support the many-storied and varied superstructure that today's science has made ours?

"But what is that rock?" we demanded of Betty.

"Recognition of the creator as greater than the thing created," she answered promptly. "Acceptance of the Oneness of Consciousness as a whole. Realization that man's thoughts and activities are a real and vital part of the scheme of things, having their effect on the Whole as well as on himself. Not only here and now, in his own little segment of the universe, but on out in an eternal continuity. Immortality! Not as some vague and distant possibility! But you — here — now! This is the thing you must recapture as an immediate and working principle if the new pattern is not to crumble as has the old."

Such, Betty told us, is the purpose of her divulgence.

"I must make reasonable," said she, "the *hereness* of immortality. For you as well as me, and for me as well as you. Man has always had some conception of the *thereness* of immortality. And the thought was good — fertile in aspiration and inspiration, pregnant with comfort and content. But the new thought I would bring to you is better. For the *hereness* of immortality, once you understand it and accept it, will make what has seemed to you vague, entirely and triumphantly real."

I shall have more to say of this when the unfolding of her divulgence is finished.

CHAPTER V

THE CIVIL ENGINEER AND
THE BLUE SLIPPERS

1.

BETTY's sister, Millicent, had always accepted Betty's psychic work simply because she believed in Betty. But the acceptance had been more acknowledgment than belief. The Chinese box episode had startled her; but back in her mind, I suspect, lingered the thought that if all this were really so, in all its implication, she would before this, somehow, through someone, have had word from her husband, who had died suddenly several years ago. I must confess that I myself wondered a little why Betty said nothing of the one thing most important to Millicent.

"I was not ready," said Betty a week or so later. "I wanted to do it all in one fell swoop."

Then she began to "show Joan pictures," as we call that process. Joan is made to see things, which she describes. Only later do we know whether they mean anything or not. At the time they generally sound like a confused jumble to us, but I take everything down faithfully, for you never can tell! Betty "showed pictures" for about twenty minutes. Then Francis, Millicent's husband, dictated a short letter to her. This took about two minutes. It was an affectionate note, such as any husband might have written to any beloved wife. Without the authentication crowded into the previous twenty minutes it could have meant little or nothing.

Betty was fairly satisfied.

"Some is good, and some isn't," said she. "But some is. When pictures start — Joan being very susceptible to pictorial vision — it is hard to segregate her own memories from *our* impingement on her subconscious. That is why, in getting this, there will be some you may not understand."

In consequence of this cautious remark, when I took my notes to Millicent next day, I did so with no very keen anticipation of more than the usual proportion of "hits"; and hoped that enough would be recognizable to her to give her some measure of comfort and conviction. The result was amazing. I certainly should have been wholly satisfied with less.

"Now, the first thing Joan said," I told Millicent, reading from my notes, "was this: 'There is a man here. He has a watch chain across the front of his vest, and there's a sort of dingle-dangle thing on it. The watch ticks too loud, and it lies on a table by the side of the bed.' How about it? Of course he had a watch chain, and —"

But Millicent cut me short. She was staring at me and gasping a little.

"Why, Stewart! Why, Stewart!" was all she could say. After a moment she recovered herself and could explain. It seems that Francis was about the last man she knew to cling to an old-fashioned thick "turnip" watch, because it had belonged to his grandfather; that it had a chain so unusually long that, on his death, it was divided in three for the three boys and made for each of them a perfectly adequate chain; that a heavy seal — a "dingle-dangle" — depended from it. Furthermore, Francis tried to keep the watch on a table by the side of his bed, but abandoned that because its ticking kept him awake. It did, indeed, "tick too loud."

That short sentence had certainly proved full of meat. Presently we went on to the next.

"This is good enough, but by itself it does not mean much, I think," said I. "It simply reads: 'Boots he has: with his trousers tucked in.' Might be a sort of identification of Francis as a civil engineer."

"It means a lot more than that," Millicent assured me.

It seems that, when Francis was building the docks at Bordeaux, during the last war, he had bought a pair of French half-boots that had pleased him so much he actually used to bring them out to show dinner guests what proper engineer's foot-gear should be; and on the slightest excuse he would put them on and tuck his trousers in them to rake leaves or otherwise work around the place. That bit we agreed was rather splendid; for it was not only correct, but it meant so much more than I had guessed.

" 'Something about a surrogate court.' " I read the succeeding sentence of my record. That was a hit; for Francis had left an involved estate that had only recently been settled to the point of attention by the surrogate. However, I took up the next without expectation. " 'Oatmeal,' Joan said, 'something about eating oatmeal.' Of course there's something about eating oatmeal — in any family with children," I remarked, and was about to proceed. Millicent burst out laughing.

"Oh, that's *good!*" she cried. The children ate breakfast alone. Francis was a great stickler on oatmeal for the children — many fathers are. The children grumbled and balked on the subject of oatmeal — many children do. All but the youngest. His face, and his plate, were always bright. *But* — when housecleaning time came around, behind every picture on the wall were discovered great dabs of oatmeal!

Joan had next described — and illustrated — "someone who put on their nose-glasses this way." Before reading this I asked Millicent to put on her glasses. She duplicated Joan's performance. Subsequently I asked other members of the family to show me "how Millicent puts on her glasses," and received the same demonstration.

"'Don't forget the creek: mustn't forget that!'" I continued. I confess that looked to me like a clean miss. None of the various residences of the various members of the family were within miles of anything that could be described as a creek.

"Could I *ever* forget the creek!" cried Millicent fervently.

Francis, as has been mentioned, was a civil engineer, engaged in heavy construction — like the docks at Bordeaux and a good deal of New York's waterfront. His estate included a lot of heavy machinery, dredges, pile drivers, barges, and the like, which had worried Millicent for years. She was unable to get rid of them; she paid taxes and storage on them. And they had been kept all these years in an inlet of the Flushing marshes known by name as The Creek.

Now followed a number of small, less striking references which it would be tedious to analyze in detail. For instance, "A portrait. There's an old portrait." Now, every family has old portraits. But Millicent told me that a portrait of Francis' grandfather had somehow got separated and had gone to a collateral branch of the family, and that it was only after a long search and much trouble that he had managed to buy it back. Another was a simple insistence on the number seven. It seemed that

Francis died just seven years ago; a fact not recalled to my mind even by the mention of the number.

There were, however, two more statements that hit Millicent hard, bringing her both to laughter and to tears.

" 'Street car,' " I quoted Joan, " 'the episode that occurred on a street car. I think,' said she, 'the boots, and the watch and the portrait, and the creek and what happened on the street car are important.' "

Here is where Millicent laughed. In the old days of ferry boats, said she, Francis was accustomed to go to the city each day with a neighbor, whose temper was somewhat peppery at times. One day — on the street car — this neighbor was rudely jostled, and promptly broke a paper bag of apples over the offender's head. Result: a near riot, and a family warning when anger threatened — "remember the street car!"

The other statement: "This man says to tell Millicent, 'the child that never got born is here with me. Little girl.' "

A little girl had been born indeed, but never breathed.

"It was the only time in all his life I ever saw Francis cry," said Millicent.

I knew nothing whatever of this fact until I heard it then.

"Betty is laughing and nodding her head," Joan had concluded. I should think she well might. Joan knew nothing of Betty's sister: she did not even know Millicent's last name.

This looked to us like a pretty close hundred per cent, when we got together to analyze my report from Millicent.

Betty had shown — "on the screen" — and Joan had described twenty-three distinct pictures. Of these eleven were brilliantly striking; six were exact but of lesser importance; the other six were not recognized, but might have been apt; none could be categorically denied as certainly untrue. I think anybody familiar with the methods and difficulties of psychical research would have pardoned us elation over somewhat of a record in the way of "evidential." It must be reflected that none of these matters was in either Joan's or my subconscious mind. She was wholly unacquainted, either in person or by hearsay, with Millicent and her family: I had never known or heard of any of these particular things.

With this authentication for Millicent's conviction, the letter from Francis was then dictated. It began with the address "Old Lady" (which Joan unnecessarily assured us was a term of endearment!), which, said Millicent, was his common form of reference to her. And that might be considered as evidential number twenty-four.

Of only one did Millicent profess complete and blank ignorance. That was the description of a house. Joan had given it in detail. "A big house," she had said, "built when they had square towers, and full of great heavy furniture." She spent a lot of time on that house, mentioning the arrangement of its rooms, and the porches, and much of the furniture. A hat rack especially held her. "There's a joke about it," she had said. "Some children played around it." And a very important coal scuttle; and a lot more.

"It *may* be Francis' boyhood home," said Millicent, but doubtfully.

We let it go at that, but months later I had a chance to check with one of Francis' immediate family. That house was a clean miss. And — believe it or not — that fact pleased us! It had looked to be *all* good. Betty had said: "Some of it is good, but some isn't." And we needed a miss to verify Betty's remark.

2.

And now, before leaving this particular subject, I want to go back to that first night of Betty's verbal communication with me through Joan. It will be recalled that I said the evidential she piled up especially for me with such fluency and ease was clean-cut, air-tight and without need of interpretation — except *just one* item, "the blue slippers." That meant nothing to me.

It was an astounding record for a conversation lasting almost three hours. As I look back and remember the minutiae of it, the whole performance assumes ever greater and more significant proportions, for I do not believe any two carnate people could sit down together and reminisce for that length of time without one of them making a slip. And in this case I was a yes-man only. Betty necessarily led the conversation, and in every instance it was she who said, "Do you remember . . ." and supplied all details.

Her one miss, so far as I personally am concerned, was when she announced, "I never thanked you for bringing my blue slippers."

"What blue slippers? Where did I bring them?" I asked. "I don't remember."

"You will!" she replied confidently.

Nevertheless, I did not, and the slippers annoyed me, because I *had* remembered many things quite as inconsequential. Only recently, in California, was that reference tidied up.

Twice again, at intervals, she prodded me about the blue slippers. Still, all I could remember concerning the slippers was her own three references to them — each pointed enough to make me realize that in this instance my memory, or hers, had failed. I racked my brains trying to remember, for, with this solitary exception, Betty's record of evidential personal communication with me had been perfect. I did not want her achievement even so slightly spoiled! But I could not conjure up the haziest recollection. The slippers were out.

The last week in February, 1940, before starting the work of putting this book together, I cleaned up a number of matters entrusted to me by Betty. Among them was the typing and delivery of several letters she had dictated, through Joan, to various friends. One of the letters was to her favorite nurse who had accompanied her home from a hospital siege in 1937 and stayed several weeks in the house. Betty had nicknamed her Johnnie and the two women had become very good friends.

I left Johnnie's letter till the last. Betty had said when she dictated it, "Johnnie thought I was a nut. At first she thought I was crazy. I knew it all the time. I said to myself, 'Well, I'll show Johnnie!'"

I had not seen Johnnie for many months. Beyond Betty's comment that Johnnie had thought her "a nut" I had no idea what Johnnie's attitude might be toward psychic phenomena. I did know that her training and experience had, of necessity, given her a pragmatically scientific and probably thoroughly materialistic outlook. Her job is to fight disease and death. She does it magnificently, never wavering for an instant. But when death comes, so far as Johnnie's training is concerned, the job is done.

From the context of the letter I knew it would be either highly evidential or — probably — a complete dud. It was full of specific and intimate personal detail. And I had not forgotten the specific and detailed description of the "house with the square towers" presumably intended for Millicent that turned out to have no significance. This house and the blue slippers were, before my going to see Johnnie, the two outstanding marks against Betty's incredibly high batting average.

As I say, I did not know Johnnie's attitude toward psychic phenomena. Neither did I know if — broadminded though she might be about it — she knew anything of the technical difficulties of communication or the technique of sifting out "evidential." In other words, if there were inaccuracies in the letter, would she — as my experience has taught me most people of her highly specialized training do — ditch the *whole* incident and in the back of her head write down Betty even more definitely as "a nut." I mailed the message, however, but anticipated an impending visit from Johnnie with a good deal of diffidence, I must admit.

One of the things that bothered me was an emphatic statement by Betty: "The child will get well." What child? Johnnie is a surgical nurse and more or less specializes in adult patients; or such was my understanding when she was taking care of my wife.

However, "the child will get well" proved particularly and peculiarly evidential. In fact, a great part of the letter was evidential, as Johnnie, no matter what her personal attitude on psychic phenomena, was quick honestly to admit. Some she failed to recognize, but her sharp and ruthless analysis of the detail of the letter was to me exceedingly satisfactory. Far more satisfactory than any polite acceptance or evasion would have been. So I told her something of Betty's other communications and finally of the blue slippers as the one personal thing I could not identify.

"I can," said Johnnie promptly. "When Mrs. White was in the hospital in San Francisco she asked you to bring her a pair of slippers from Burlingame — from home. And I'll never forget how she laughed and laughed over the ones you brought. You picked out the fanciest high-heeled slippers she had, and what she wanted was bedroom slippers, not style. But I can't remember the color."

Later in talking with Reider, who does everything nobody else does in my household, I told him of having seen Johnnie and of the slipper incident as amusing, fortunately withholding the color angle. Reider has been in my employ for more than ten years. He has a memory for detail that never fails.

"Why, I remember that!" cried Reider. "You came home from the hospital with a list of things Mrs. White wanted. You got them together and I made them into a package for you. Among them were her blue slippers."

"*Blue?* Are you sure?" I wanted to shout, but refrained.

"Certainly I am sure," said Reider. "I rather wondered at the time what Mrs. White wanted with her blue slippers. It is too bad that you can't remember yourself, sir. But several times Mrs. White sent home from the hospital for things and I made them into bundles for you to take to her. I would hardly expect you to remember what was in the bundles, sir."

Hardly expect me to remember. . . .

I departed for my study in haste and pawed through the records to re-read Betty's three references to her blue slippers. And found that she had not wanted me to re-member! That she deliberately had chosen something she knew — or hoped — I would not remember!

"Too bad" that I couldn't remember? It was glorious that I hadn't—and still couldn't remember. With Johnnie and Reider to remember, those blue slippers are just about the best piece of "evidential" a man ever had.

CHAPTER VI

WE SET OUT

1.

IN WHAT follows Joan will be referred to at times as "the receiving station" or, more briefly, "the station." To avoid possible misunderstanding on the part of the reader, as well as to give a fuller comprehension of this term, it should be explained.

Back in 1916 when Joan — accidently, like Betty — discovered she was psychic, transmission of the Morse code by wireless signals had come into its own, but radio as we know it today, and its now familiar terminology, were still several years away. For the general public this long-distance projection of the human voice without wires through the mechanism of broadcasting "stations" and millions of "receiving" sets all came after 1920.

Yet even in 1916 Stephen was calling Joan a "receiving station." Occasionally, Darby tells me, he used the word "psychic" but never the more popular word "medium" — not once in all the hundreds of pages of notes comprising the Stephen records. From the published portion of these records, *Our Unseen Guest*, I quote:

"The process of communication," says Stephen, "is more like the transmission of a wireless message than anything else in your experience. Our term, receiving station, is very good, not because it is metaphorical, but because it is the exact opposite of metaphorical."

Betty, for the last twenty years of her earth life, had been a receiving station — a much more prolific station than Joan. For, after the rounding out of Stephen's philosophy, Joan had only at long intervals and for short periods invited communication. All her adult life she has been a busy woman, with a personally satisfying — and exacting — job to do. Not for seventeen years,* had she done any really sustained psychic work. I knew this. And after Betty's death Darby had written me that, though he had hoped to reach Betty through Joan, he had been unable to do so.

"We have so seldom tried for communication in recent. years," he explained. "Not that Stephen or Anne ever fail to appear when we do try. But they are old standbys. We have not been able to contact Betty. Joan says it must be because she herself is rusty."

Joan was not rusty. But I think Betty's failure to speak through her until I went East six months later inclined us to agree with Joan's suggestion that she *might* be rusty. I wanted to see Darby and Joan in any case, because, as I have explained, we are friends. But that first night in their home I really hoped we would not try to get in touch with Betty. Suppose we failed! Darby, whose experience and background have trained him in the habit of controlling troublesome situations, kept our after-dinner conversation going pleasantly enough about the novel I had come East to see made ready for the press. But he did not fool me; and Joan, quite unlike herself, was openly nervous. How deeply distrustful of her talent, how downright fearful she was of the possible disturbance failure might cause in my acceptance of Betty's voiceless but continued Presence, I had no conception for a week or more. Parenthetically, that particular fear was

---

* See Appendix of *The Betty Book*.

unwarranted. Nothing could disturb that Presence: it is too actual and vivid.

Joan confessed her anxieties days later and only after Betty had suddenly thrown an entirely new slant on the importance of evidence.

I have told how quickly and cleverly and abundantly Betty piled up proof of her identity that first night. Darby and I certainly needed no more "evidential." Nevertheless, from time to time, in our subsequent sessions, she would suddenly and unexpectedly slip in another bit. We told her, at last, not to bother.

"You don't understand," Betty explained. "We do not do it only for you, but also for the protection of the station. To assure her, in her subconscious, and afterwards when she sees the record, of her own integrity as a station, and that she is really giving the right message. Do you think that if Joan felt for one instant that this was not I talking, she would ever again go 'out' for me?"

2.

You will remember I said that in that initial evening Betty convinced me of two things: her identity, and that she had something to *tell*. The foregoing chapters are intended to cover the first. But before we go on to the second I want to say that I well know mere evidence is little good except to those at whom it is personally directed. Curious, but true!

We accept, as part of our mental equipment, "facts" of which we know nothing whatever, merely on the testimony of some physicist, or astronomer, or medico, or traveler, or whatnot, as to what he claims he has seen. We haven't seen them, but we believe them. Yet we — as a race — remain unmoved by equally specific and supported testimony, as to what they claim they have seen, of such men as Sir William Crookes, Flammarion, Sir Oliver Lodge, Richet, down to the bewildered — but stubbornly honest — chiefs of police so often lugged into research of psychic phenomena on the naive assumption that they must be particularly qualified to detect fraud. We haven't seen; so we don't believe. Same *kind* of testimony, by same type of witnesses. If we simply *must* explain to ourselves, we say they've gone a little dotty, and let it go at that!

Probably that is as it should be. This type of evidence may be intended only for the person to whom it is directly addressed. It may be the job of each to search out his own experience; or have it seek him out when he is ready for it. The only real and satisfactory "evidential," in the long run, is not the testimony of phenomena, but of ideas. Darby summed that up well in the last paragraph of *Our Unseen Guest*.

"We believe," he writes, "Stephen is real, not because of the tests, convincing as they have been; for these, it is conceivable, might be explained away. That the terms of his philosophy should have come to us as though out of the air, with us ignorant of their meaning until Stephen elaborated them into a connected and dignified metaphysical system, seems a test unlikely — as far as we are concerned—to be explained away. Yet granted it were — still would Joan and I be compelled to accept the reasonableness of Stephen's message. And that the philosophy should be reasonable and the phenomenon a deception is a contradiction which, to use Stephen's words,

Joan's mind and mine are not 'nimble enough' to entertain."

With that I agree heartily. Your own persuasion should await the completion of what Betty had to say. The "evidential" of the preceding chapters was not narrated to convince you: merely to show you the manner by which we personally were convinced. Now, in order to show how Betty managed to persuade us that she had indeed something to say, it might be well to set down the high lights of the first few evenings.

After Joan had gone in trance that first night, a long pause ensued. Then a whisper: "Yes, yes." Suddenly the voice came through clearly.

"Where shall I begin?" it said. "You see, Stewt,* Joan's all clogged up with emotion, and I can't . . . She wants to. She wants to let me have her mind to use for you. I think the best thing is just to begin the job, and that will quiet her down and give me a better chance.

"You see, the thing I have to do now is what I did before, only from the other end. I have to come back and tell you *how* I come back. That's my job: that's what I have to do."

The facility abruptly failed. In such cases a question often helps. An earlier "message," purported to have come from Betty to a friend, and relayed to me, was that she was "working on the subject of pain, its nature and the technique of handling it." I asked about that, merely to get things going again. It worked.

"That is a very definite part of what I am doing," she resumed. "We are all of us working so hard on people

* In a manner of speaking, this was the first bit of "evidential," though it was not particularly important. Only Betty had ever called me that; and — as far as we know — Joan had never heard it.

who are coming over suddenly now. [This refers to the fighting in Poland. S E W] Our friend the Doctor is helping on that. He and I are working together. It is all confused here now: so many coming suddenly, and they don't know what has happened to them. You see, to people like you, and me when I left you, who know the facts of the very narrow no-man's land between what you call life and what I now call life — well, we can aid those who come out to help us in going over, and meet them all clean and glorious and sure. Always those who go naturally are met and told what the change is, so that there is no disconcertion on their part. But those like you and me, we can help of our own volition and knowledge. We are not only spared the surprise of finding ourselves suddenly in another sphere, but we ourselves can wipe out the tensions of our memories."

Her reference to working with "so many people coming suddenly now . . . not knowing what has happened to them," while those "who go naturally are always met and told," is an old story. Most of the books on psychic experience, especially those published during or immediately following the 1914-1918 World War, carried this same statement, endorsing the age-old plea of the Litany: "from battle. . .and sudden death, Good Lord, deliver us."

Betty's new and reassuring thought was how we — "people like us who know the facts of the very narrow no-man's land" — can meet death, sudden or natural; how we can rejoin our friends on the other side "all clean and glorious and sure" and "wipe out the tensions of our memories."

This last seemed important to us; and very comforting. It struck Darby as especially so, and he made a contribution.

"A long time ago," said Darby, "soon after a medical friend of mine died, I was talking, through Joan, with him about his own passing. And among other things he said this:

" 'Birth is the mystery, not death. And did you ever stop to think that if a child about to be born could be awarely conscious, how confused it would be, and how afraid of the strange new world it had to face?' How about it, Betty?"

"Your friend was right," she replied. "Of course death is much simpler than birth; it is merely a continuation. Earth is the *borning place* for the purpose of individualization. That is one of the things I am to tell you about later."

Nor could we persuade her at this time to explain further.

"No," she said firmly. "I could not make you understand yet. What I am being permitted to tell you has a pattern -- a well-thought-out, step-by-step pattern. It will be easier for all of us, if you do not disturb the pattern."

I asked another random question, with the same object in view: to keep things going.

"Do you see and feel the physical sensations of my world that I see and feel?" I enquired. "If so, do you get them through me? Or on your own?"

"I have all the senses you have, only more," she answered.

"Then," I persisted, "you can actually share a physical sensation with me, as smelling a flower, or seeing a landscape?"

"Of course. And I've done it. All that you have I take, and I want it. And I can induce a sensation in you.

"But our next job together," she continued, " is philosophy, though my study of pain is important. You see our last book* tells about how I went 'out,' how I came into contact while I was still living on your side, how anyone can teach himself to come in contact, to some extent at least, with this side. Now I must evolve a method for telling how we *come back,* how I do it, so that you can receive more easily. You have learned how to project your consciousness into my present state of existence and draw sustenance from it; but you do not know how to permit us, on this side, to project ourselves back to you. I did the one thing there; now I must do this here.

"If Joan knew just how to let me come, it would be perfect. We will try to make progress as fast as we can. I want you to be with me; I want to — Oh darn!" she interrupted herself as the station fumbled. "If Joan and I can only work together until I can rub out the wrinkles in her brain — it's all here to be told. It requires a keyed-upness from the spiritual side; a calmness from the physical. You have to be spiritually alert, physically passive. But that alertness is peculiar. If you are *too* spiritually alert you get keyed up to the point where you are not dominated. It is under high tension that visions are seen — Angels of Mons, and so on. But what I am talking about is the day-by-day means of natural normal communication with me, and me with you."

That certainly sounded interesting enough, aside from all the personal and the evidential, from which I extract these excerpts. At the next opportunity I reverted to her statement as to her senses.

"You said, or implied, that you received sensations

* *Across the Unknown.*

from our physical world. Do you get them actually through the contacts with it of your present body — what we used to call the beta body* — or do you get the *idea* of contact first? Do I make myself clear?"

"Clear as mud," laughed Betty. "But I'll tell you how it is, I do touch you, and sometimes you feel me, depending on whether your sense is keyed to it. *My touch of you to me is just as real as ever.* We *are* real. We are entities. I am."

"In psychic literature," suggested Darby, "we are always reading about the 'density' of earth conditions that it is necessary for the discarnate to penetrate for the purposes of communication, and we get the idea somehow that you do so with difficulty, something like a man under water. Doesn't that affect your other contacts with our world —"

"The density is not for us," she interrupted. "It's the density for you. We can see you. There is an earth density that is factual that you can penetrate only under certain circumstances — emotion, shock, trance, and so on; and then there is a spiritual density created by the minds of people."

"Then your own faculties are not dulled by it?" I pressed the point.

"No. Take a radio: the announcer is in full possession of his faculties, he is not dulled or fuzzy. But there may be static to spoil reception. The limitations of relationships between the two worlds are for the most part limited only in your world. Your world and mine are the same, only you are not conscious of mine. I see both."

* See *The Betty Book.*

CHAPTER VII

ONLY ONE UNIVERSE

1.

"LISTEN!" Betty paused. For a breath there was utter silence in the room. Then — "Listen," she said again. *"There is only one universe."*

Darby's eyes, lifting from the notes he was taking, met mine. Here, indeed, was a new concept if Betty meant her statement to include herself as well as us.

Granted a Hereafter as a necessary accompaniment of immortality, where was its *place?* Most moderns, I think, have discounted the pre-medieval imagery of a Heaven set above the clouds with golden streets and golden harps in the hands of gold-crowned angels. Yet my own ideas on the subject, I suddenly discovered, were pretty nebulous. Betty existed. I had no slightest doubt, emotional or intellectual, as to that. She had come back to me on the hillside not thirty minutes after she had died, flooding me with her presence and personality. Since that night she had done the same thing repeatedly; again and again and again. Now, speaking through a receiving station, she had come back to identify herself by means of specific statement of veridical facts.

She had *come back*. For twenty years her Invisibles and mine had been coming back; but — coming *back* implies "from." From what? A mode or state of being? Or from some *place*, some *where?*

Darby voiced my confused bewilderment.

"Don't get that," he said shortly. "What's the implication, only one universe? Are our universe and yours one and the same? Do you mean what you say literally?"

"Literally," she replied. "This divulgence is an effort to get at the relationship of our two worlds. The immortality theme has been developed; you believe in immortality. Until actual laboratory work is ready, you have to go on laying the foundations. For instance, you have to have a goal and a premise to work from. If I can only tell you how we come back; chart some kind of a course to be followed later scientifically. I want to get over to you in terms of mechanics the possibility of the two worlds being the same. There is only one universe."

"Possibly two viewpoints of it?" suggested Darby.

"Many," she admitted. "But the only viewpoint we are interested in now is yours and ours. Only one universe: two viewpoints is just *your* perception. I want to make you understand, first, the reality of my existing in the universe of which you are not wholly conscious. I want you to understand, secondly, the *possibility* of my existing in a universe of which you are fully conscious. And the third job is the *actuality*. I want to make you understand that I *do* exist, and in a one-and-only universe, wherein you too live, but amid the world's obstacles. What I am really trying to say is that I live in the universe you don't see, and also in the one you do see. Therefore, I live in the *whole* universe."

"And as a corollary, to show that a great many things supposed to be lost by separation are not really lost?" I suggested.

"The only things that are lost are those apperceptions controlled by your senses — and not those entirely.

"One of the things that makes it seem to you, in your

existence, that my universe is not your universe is Frequency.* Let us examine the subject of frequency.

"I called frequency to Joan's attention when she was mending the electric fan. She could hear the hum. She could look through the fan and see the door case back of it. The fan was running so fast that so far as her vision was concerned it had lost its solidity. My co-existence with you is analogous. If the frequency were different for your human focus, you could see me. As it is, you look through me. I am not there.

"Now suppose you cast your mind back to my efforts, when I was with you, to project my consciousnesses beyond my then universe. What I was doing was to project my consciousness beyond my then limitations. The limitations of human existence vary according to the individual. The mode of existence of certain individuals is farther out into the whole. Grant that, and you immediately grant that you have a shifting line, an unfixed horizon, even in your own universe."

I asked some question, irrelevant, unimportant, unrecorded and forgotten.

"Again that is beyond the point I am trying to make," said Betty reprovingly. "I insist that you stay for the moment in your own natural habitat, and grant, in it, a shifting horizon. It is already malleable in your life. I am speaking of the shifting line of your existing universe for the individual. You live in that universe. You work in it. How different do you suppose that universe is to you than it is to a child? The application is that there is no division — neither for you nor for me. If you can dis-

* "Frequency" as Betty used it had a definite technical meaning which will in due course appear. In this connection, however, the context makes it sufficiently clear.

cover the frequency, you can reveal my universe. That would not mean that you could inhabit my universe. It would only mean that you would know that *I* am inhabiting it."

Something like looking at fish in an aquarium, one of us suggested half humorously; you can see them, but you can't live with them. Betty was inclined to accept this.

"Let's get back to the child," said she. "You know how a child develops its five senses. Touch is the first; hearing is the next, and so on. Now *there* is a shifting universe."

"You said your frequency is different from ours," I observed. "Do you have to leave your natural frequency to come in touch with our physical world?"

"We do not have to," was her unexpected reply; "no especial effort. The only change of frequency required of us is in order to apprehend more fully our own new existence."

2.

All this was, naturally, of extraordinary interest to us, and opened up many fresh avenues of thought.

We recognized the importance of the concepts coming from Betty — Betty who had authenticated herself beyond question. Betty had got us that far. But our acceptance of her universe and ours as one, was something else again. With the body of the world's opinion, as expressed in religion, literature and art — to say nothing of science — against us in this matter, it was difficult for Darby or me to assimilate Betty's idea of her one and only universe.

We sweat over it. We argued it between ourselves and

with Betty. It stayed over our heads for several evenings. And then finally we got it. Betty herself had given us the key for logical understanding, but we had not recognized it. We had failed as "conceiving stations." And here, by the way, is a term much used by all our Invisibles.

As Betty explained it, a conceiving station has two functions.

"I know what I want to get over," said she, "and I express it. But how can I tell how much I have conveyed, unless I get a reflection back from your minds? What can I read of your comprehension from blank silence?"

The second function goes a little further. The conceiving station must not only comprehend what is said, but he must on his own hook develop implications as they occur to his habit of mind, and report them back and discuss them. Many times these contributions are negatived or drastically modified by the communicator; in which case they are valuable as clearing misconception. More often, through restating Betty's concept in other terms, they indicated full comprehension. Rarely — but often enough to gratify — we actually carried to conclusion premises she had started. Then Betty was jubilant, as over the brightness of a precocious child.

Therefore a conceiving station, unlike a receiving station, must know his subject, or at least he must be able to learn it. First or last, he must comprehend the meaning of the material coming through. Unless there is an alert and adequate conceiving station, the value and importance of what comes through the receiving station is generally lost.

"Photography," Betty had said in the midst of one of our boggings-down, "you ought to understand the oneness of your universe and mine through photography ..."

Joan likes to hear the records read after each session. As she says, it's all *she* gets out of our parties! On such an occasion the three of us were discussing the evening's work. It had been very full of meat. Betty, not impatient but persistent, was hammering bigger and better ideas at us constantly. And our failure to comprehend her *only one universe* was holding everything back.

"Stewart," asked Joan suddenly, "what was it Betty said the other night about photography? Could the analogy be there?"

I don't know whether the great illumination burst over Darby or me first. But out of our ensuing debate was evolved this:

Take a black and white photograph — it registers a reality. Take a color photograph — and it registers exactly the same reality, *but* — a reality beyond that depicted by the black and white.

The illustration proves nothing, of course. Nevertheless it helped us to understand how there might be two different appearances of one and the very same thing. The color picture is only an extension — a more detailed and accurate registration — of the identical scene originally photographed in black and white.

Assuming that we here normally live in the black and white universe, it is now entirely *possible* (Betty's word and emphasis) for us to imagine a "color" universe in which she might live. So there you have apparently two universes; one black and white, one in color, but nevertheless the same.

"So analyze them as you will," said Betty, "they are only two appearances or aspects of the same thing. There is only one universe."

3.

It soon became evident, however, that her aim, and the aim of those with whom she was working, was even more ambitious.

"Now, Stewt," said Betty one evening, "you remember when my consciousness was voluntarily projected into this unobstructed universe,* I brought back to you examples and imagery to explain phases of living. I was given here a pattern for earth-life development. Now my job is to bring back to you — and I mean *bring* — a picture of the existence in which I now have my being.

"All the concepts that I have been assigned to bring to you," she repeated, "must be based on the fact that *there is only one Universe*. The next step is your recognition of the shifting, even in your consciousness, of the dividing line between the obstructed and the unobstructed universes. Next is your realization, of what your scientists have admitted, that there exists — in the only-one-universe of which you are part — much that your senses cannot detect, but which you have proved to exist by means of instruments invented by man. This unobstructed universe of mine is part of your universe, just as your obstructed universe is part of mine."

"We must," she insisted, at a later session, "say, over and over, *there is only one Universe*. That is the fundamental premise. We have established the reality of consciousness, and the continuity of the individual division of consciousness. That was done long ago. Now, and more than ever, for a laboratory starting point, a pre-

---

* She means her work as explained in *The Betty Book* and *Across the Unknown*.

mise, a goal to be proved, we must rationalize for a reasonable mind the second great reality, that of the *only one Universe. The great difference between you and me is in our awareness-mechanism;* and even that awareness-mechanism is *fundamentally* the same: the difference is not so great."

"Awareness-mechanism" is a term much used by our Invisibles when Betty was here, working with them. Later, through Joan, Betty made out a glossary of terms which she wished for complete accuracy in this present divulgence. "Awareness-mechanism," she defined, "is that equipment of self-aware consciousness whereby the individual perceives that which is objective to him."

In view of her statement that she was to "bring a picture" of her state of being, I was a little curious as to why her Invisibles in all her twenty years' work while she was here had always so steadfastly refused to tell anything about the conditions of life there; and, furthermore, had never permitted Betty to attempt any descriptions of her exploration. How does that come, I now asked her.

"Two reasons," said she. "First, you were not ready to receive explanation. Second, there was never before just this combination. I mean a hookup like Joan and me. You see, I put in many years of projecting my earth consciousness into the universe as a whole. Most of my understanding that I brought back was in the terminology of earth symbols. I did not then know how *factual* that terminology was; how good it was for one side as for the other."

"I want to make this as all-inclusive and simple as possible," she told us on still another occasion. "My work has always been an explanation of reality. It is now. But the purpose of this further exploration of reality is not to broaden communication between the obstructed and the unobstructed universes. It is not to make the picture of my existence so attractive as to create in earth consciousness a longing to come here. Each individual is put into the world to do a job; and he comes here best and happiest only when it is completed; after he has gathered to himself as nearly as possible his requisite of work and experience. The purpose of the present divulgence is to restore in earth consciousness the necessity of individual effort, and the assurance that the effort will not be wasted. The only assurance of this is a return to the belief in immortality.

"A second purpose is to instill into earth consciousness the oneness of the whole. *This broadens your ethics and restricts your morals.* Both have been too loose for the comfortable living of mankind. Incidentally, one of the causes for the instability you note in peoples, individuals, society, thought, art, is the ultra and sudden ease of communication in time and in space. The use of radio, the automobile and the airplane is not stabilized. They have been too rapidly developed and perfected for the assimilation of society in general.

"Knowing these things even better than you, it could not, therefore, be our purpose to do more at this time than reestablish on the basis of your present knowledge — and the needs of your present knowledge — the faith in the validity of self that is tottering. So much for your general reader.

"For the special reader, your scientist in his research laboratory, we do hope to promulgate ideas upon which he can build toward us an actuality of truth. That does not mean that the man in the street, going about his business, could be in constant communication with us, either see or hear us. It is the acceptance of reality that we seek for the sake of the return of the individual's self-respect.

"It is only through the application of the reality of law, the acceptance of responsibility by the higher quality, the recognition of the need of the lower qualities for aid in their individual fulfillment of their work and obligations, that the world can settle into a true evolutionary process. It is important not only for you, but for us, that this occur."

I hope the reader must agree with us that as a prospectus for exploration all this was sufficiently attractive: that Betty had, indeed, something to say.

CHAPTER VIII

WE WORKED OVERTIME

1.

ON THE strength of all this I modified my plans. As many of my week-ends as I had not previously engaged, I spent with Darby and Joan. Occasionally I managed an overnight in the week itself. Finally, I extended my stay East to its last possible limit in order to visit them. During those last days we worked every evening, and on Saturdays and Sundays we could manage two and sometimes three periods. In this manner, all told, we finished off with exactly forty work sessions.

We worked hard; no question of that. Betty had new and big concepts to get over: and she had not only to state them, but to make us comprehend them. To accomplish this she encouraged talk, argument, and contribution on the part of Darby and me — the "conceiving stations." Darby did much more than could I. There were moments when the job of getting down verbatim some pretty rapid talk, and at the same time endeavoring to absorb enough meaning to evolve some slight contributing intelligence of my own, made me feel as though I were trying to take in the whole of a three-ring circus. Some of our offerings proved helpful: many of our most gorgeous deductions and theories, that looked perfectly all right to us, Betty turned down flat — and continued calmly along the line on which she had started. Reading the records later, as a whole, I can see how ludicrous it was. She gave us scope to frisk all over the intellectual landscape, but herself proceeded straight and undeviating toward her objective. Or, to change the figure, she played us as a fisherman plays a trout: gave us plenty of line, but reeled us in at last to where she wanted us. A good method. It cleared our minds of what isn't so!

Usually each session lasted from two to two and a half hours. At the close of each, Betty — oh very politely! — dismissed Darby from the room. "You see," she explained quaintly. "I must change myself back, for Stewt, from a schoolma'am into a gal." Then for ten minutes or so she would talk to me of personal things. So intimate to ourselves, at times, was some of this that at first I could not quite avoid a slight uneasiness.

"I know it seems strange to you to be talking this way with this woman present," said Betty. "But she is not present. She is a thousand miles away! She goes so willingly and sweetly," added Betty appreciatively.

These little private talks — if I had stopped to think of them that way — fairly bristled with the most brilliant "evidential." But I did not wish to think of them that way. They were just talks with Betty, about our own affairs.

2.

I have used the term "what Betty had to say," merely because it was she who actually said it. She did not pretend — indeed she specifically disclaimed — that this was all her own effort. She was always referring to others with her, who were directing and advising as to the course of the discussions.

"I don't know; I'll ask," she would say when we asked something outside her own knowledge. "Those I am working with suggest —" she would preface some advice. And occasionally, when she got into difficulties, or perhaps by way of epitome, one or another of these collaborators — or directors — would speak in his own person. But briefly. There was "Anne." for example. Anne is a personality who, along with Stephen, immediately began communicating through Joan once the latter had discovered her psychic powers. She was a Scotswoman of, probably, about the sixteenth century. Her broad dialect is archaic, interspersed upon occasion with pure Gaelic, and, until one's ear becomes accustomed to it, far from easy to follow or understand. Anne, or "the Lady Anne" as other Invisibles usually refer to her, did not appear in *Our Unseen Guest*, though she had much to do with that book's making. But because she is so beloved by Betty, and indeed by all of us who know her — on this side as well as there — Anne is to be included in these pages.

"The Lady Anne is a very great personage," Betty assured us. "I don't suppose you people really appreciate — I didn't — what an honor it is to have an individual like Anne take so much trouble. And she *is* so funny!"

Anne's wit is brilliant; her tolerance and wisdom profound with the simplicity of broad and unemotional thinking. Nevertheless I shall not attempt to reproduce here either her repartee or dialect.

"Anne knows much more than I do," Betty told us, "but I was selected because Joan and I were nearly of the same frequency while I was there; because I have so recently come over, and therefore am in closer touch with you and your ways of thinking; and, finally, because I worked so hard at it while I was there, that I developed certain qualifications.

3.

"The only difference, really, between our worlds is a difference of frequency," Betty continued.

The gap between has never, as yet, been *mechanically* bridged. That is to say, the highest frequency we have mechanically produced or isolated is lower than the lowest frequency of Betty's state of being.

"You see," said Betty, "when I was there with you, I was very close in degree to Joan. I am stepped up now higher than she."

In order to communicate through Joan, explained Betty, she must first of all close this discrepancy; "step up" Joan's frequency to a meeting point with her own, so to speak. That was roughly it, but the statement is not exact. Nor was it made exact; but a glimpse was afforded by the illustration of striking a note on a piano and getting vibrations on all the other octaves of that same note.

"The only reason," said Betty, "you cannot exist and operate in the *entire* universe, as I do — for I operate in your universe as well as in mine — is because you are not able to step up your frequency. That is the basis of Joan's talent; she can, upon occasion, step up her frequency. But it is not a constant with her, which is why she isn't living with me here now.

"And further," Betty amplified, "Joan can also permit me to help step up her frequency." There seemed to be considerable technique to that.

"A station's ability to release subconsciousness and be stepped up in frequency *is* a talent," she repeated. "It's a part of that person's make-up, like any talent. You all have it to a degree, the simplicities of it. Everybody is more or less 'psychic.' Some know it; some don't. Darby is a good conceiving station, Stewt is a combination. Joan is a super receiving station. During communication I use the released subconscious of the station, and its storehouse to produce my message. It's a talent on my side, too. In a way we have 'mediums' here. Certain of us can communicate with more facility. I have to contend with the frequency of Joan's physical body, just as she does to communicate with me. That is a resistance. In many cases the deflection is so great you get no communication at all."

All this was really aside from the line of the philosophy Betty was then trying to get into our heads. Nevertheless it interested us enormously. We were curious as to what made the wheels go round. We often wanted to know things that had little to do with the presentation of the argument, and generally were squashed by the simple statement, "That is aside from the point I am trying to make" — expressed with the finality of Queen Victoria's "We are not amused." But this question of the technique of communication was an exception. Betty was willing to touch on it, from time to time. Perhaps she was indulging the children. Perhaps she felt its understanding would add to the reality of the situation. I do not know.

"You said a while back that you 'used the released subconscious of the station and its storehouse,'" I reminded her one evening. "Of course we have known that you people over there pick a station for its vocabulary. Do you also pick a station for its content of knowledge of a subject?"

"Rather for its *potentiality* of knowledge," she amended. "Joan has no metaphysics, but it was possible for Stephen to give his philosophy through her because the potentiality was in her mind. So I do not think we shall have much difficulty in getting the present divulgence through her. Of course, there is here a profound and sort of consecrated eagerness to receive. Every time I come I realize how much she wants to open her mind to the use we want to make of it."

"Now as to this attuning of your frequency and hers, one to the other. Do you tune hers up and yours down?" I asked. "And when you meet us, as you say you do, do you tune us up and yourself down?"

"I do not tune down my individual frequency to meet you," she replied with dignity. "I do stimulate yours, and I deliberately use a complementary frequency on this side to meet it. It happens that my frequency and yours and Darby's and Joan's are very close. But Anne's frequency is away beyond mine. I am telling you how she does it."

"What is this complementary frequency?" I asked.

"It is *the frequency on my side that is exactly equal to your own on your side*. It is lower than mine. But there is a degree here that is an exact complement of Joan's, but it is lower than I am now. I have to be able to manipulate that frequency in order to complement her.

"Suppose," said Betty, surrendering at last to our persistence, "we first take up the procedure from your end. Now, here is Joan, with a talent for receiving impressions outside the ordinary world impingements. She goes about her business all day, having her share of hunches, but no more than the average person. Then we four get together.

"Now, one of the reasons Joan is such a good station

is because she can be turned on and off by somebody else. In her case, by Darby's touch on her wrist."

Something of the sort seems to be the case with professional mediums — I epitomize Betty's statement here: they have their "signals" for entering the peculiar state of communication. Some have a crystal ball, or tea leaves, or playing cards, or the singing of hymns — there are dozens of devices. The ancient soothsayers used the entrails of sacrifice.

"Nevertheless" — I resume the verbatim report of what Betty said — "in none of their cases is there that little peculiar device, like clicking on and off a radio, that we have here. When Darby touches her wrist, that is merely a signal — a command-impulse from him for her to release her subconscious — that I comprehend in response.

"Now suppose we describe that subconscious as a magnetic field of a certain degree of attraction. If we were dealing with pure physics, you would at once recognize that a like field could send to it or receive from it any impulse.

"Now, operation of the field on my side is just as much a gift as is the opening of the field on your side. Nevertheless, even failing that operation, *impressions* do get through, but neither clearly nor correctly."

"And that presupposes also the possibility of leaks through from other sources," suggested Darby.

"Yes. We have here a magnetic field. And there are other magnetic fields of approximately the same tuning. That is why, in the middle of a perfectly evidential and correct message, you will get words we, or the station, have not been able to edit out. As we learn better to control the field, and as the station learns better to edit, you get less and less of that.

"When Joan is in this communicating state — that is, while her magnetic field is opened — anything you say registers, and because she knows it at the time, she is able to edit. Nevertheless her memory is blocked off. Now, when *I* get in the communicating state, through her — when I begin to work my complement field here — I am in a like state. That is, not *precisely* like, but comparable. And I've put myself so in tune with *her* senses that I get back a most pleasurable reaction to them. That is why I like to hear you address me audibly, though it is true I can pick up from the entire field, on which you two [Darby and S E W] impinge."

That is, she could "read" our thoughts and mental questions.

"Now we're on the subject," said I, "how about this mind-reading business? Suppose I am making a mental comment to you. How literally do you take that from my mind? Exactly, or only in gist?"

"I get more than the gist of your comment. I get your exact words when there is a *direct* communion between you and me. When there is a station, I would not only have to get your words myself, but in most cases I would have to get enough of the sense of your question into the station's mind to be able to answer it through her."

"It has been stated, quite often, that in your world you communicate with one another mentally, what you might call telepathically," I continued. "Is that true? It doesn't sound very sociable."

"We have voices. We can communicate with each other mentally, but we use words over here simply because it's easier. There is a little more technique to getting it out of the mind. Just as there is to getting it out of your mind, to carrying on a mental talk with you. And of course my awareness-mechanism has to be more acute in getting what you think than when I converse with another individual in my state."

There is, she explained, a "communication band" of frequency, common to all.

"It isn't important," said I, "but there's a current idea in occult circles that every time we think of you people, you are aware of it and have to respond —"

"I should say not!" Betty's scorn was vast. "If you thought you really had something to say, of course we would come," she relented.

"Now," she finished off that aspect of the subject, "I want to call your attention to one fact. In this type of communication we are using now, you have never had to contend with a lower degree." *

"Am I to understand that the control of this station by a lower degree than the station is practically impossible?" I wanted to get this clear.

"Yes, it is. Let's go into it more deeply. Just how much effect on your actual mentality, your think tank, not your emotions, would the meanderings of a child have in influencing judgment? Little, or none. It's exactly like that."

It is true that all this series of dissertations proved astoundingly free from what we call "coloring" — the interposition of the station's own subconscious; and of what we call "interference" — presumably from outside entities. We remarked on that one day.

"Oh, I can handle this woman," said Betty, almost smugly.

---

* Of outside interference.

I think she must rather have hoped that all this would settle our minds so we could get on with the main job. And, after all, our minds had to be settled. It is part of how we worked, and that is one reason why I include it in this chapter. Another reason is that I think it interesting.

"Now look here," I challenged, "you've got me scared. If you people can enter our minds at will, pretty soon I'm going to be afraid to think. And you say you can go anywhere in our world 'because to you it is not an obstruction.' Where's our common ordinary privacy? Irvin Cobb's goldfish in a bowl has nothing on us."

"Certain things you call traits of character and convention have a different meaning here than there. They are enormously intensified. Such things as honor, honesty, self respect, and the like," said Betty.

"Does that intensification impose on you an actual inability to intrude, as a locked door with us?" I wanted to know. "Or is it merely voluntary?"

"There are certain things you could not do — that you need no conscious inhibition to keep from doing. You never would think of them. Murder, for example. Then there are, in addition, conventions that perhaps you have consciously to think about. You might break a convention, and then you'd be sorry. Such things do go farther on our plane. They are all of them protective."

"How about lower degrees without the full sense of honor, privacy, and so forth, of the higher degrees? I instance not reading a man's diary. True of us; but not perhaps of the typical landlady of fiction."

"One of the difficulties on earth is that you have idealized truth out of your social set-up. Yet you have your prisons. The reason you have so many of them is because you have permitted the lower degrees to run amok," she replied.

"How do you keep them from running amok over there?" asked Darby.

"In the first place," said Betty, "laws are obeyed here. The recognition of law is imperative. Law is a *thing* here. It operates. And here we all understand that if we run up against a law, we bump. The breaking of a law here has a different reaction on the individual consciousness than does the breaking there. And it's not done."

"These lower degrees are then *unable*, by their nature, to invade privacy?" was my question.

"It is the very nature of things that makes them unable."

CHAPTER IX

WE MAKE THE GLOSSARY

BETTY early began to have trouble with terminology. The ideas she wanted to convey were exact; and our habit is to use words inexactly. Her ideas were new; and they deserved new terms. However, at first she used those with which we were familiar, and eased us out of them only when by their means she had penetrated our density.

As an example, for some time she distinguished her universe and ours as unlimited and limited. "It is all one universe," she insisted, "but yours is limited."

That did all right for the first rough exposition. "But *we are not* without limitations," she later reflected. "They are not limitations of your kind of matter, but . . ."

Then for a while she switched to "restricted" and "unrestricted"; but this would not do: she admitted she *did* have the restrictions of her state of being. Finally she settled down to "obstructed" and "unobstructed"; and was satisfied. So was Anne.

"And," the latter pointed out, "you will remember that at the very first Betty said there is the *obstructed* and *unobstructed* universe." This was true — as a phrase — but we had forgotten it.

We had the same difficulty with the word "constant." It took us some time to learn, by the context of the record, that Betty used it in the sense of "constantly accompanying," as an integral necessity of being. But its stricter connotation is mathematical. It would mean "fixed" to most people, and that was not what Betty wanted at all. "Substantial" — standing under — had too many connotations: "Co-efficient" — analyzed down to its derivatives — was good enough; but no reader would stop to analyze. He would simply take its mathematical significance, and let it go at that. So we had to search still further.

And in another connotation Betty used "constant" for a while in such phrases as "constant time," "constant space." On Darby's suggestion we substituted "absolute." That was a comfortable enough fit for the foundation ideas. But later it could not contain them. Betty became more and more dissatisfied, as did Darby.

"We have to ditch the word 'absolute'," said she at last. "'Absolute' connotes static; and ours is not a static world; it is in evolution. We have had to use terms at first that were *absolutely* gray-headed. That is why we had to get the word 'orthos.' "

That was a brand-new word Betty had managed to coin some days before, and had defined for us, after a fashion, but whose real intended use Darby had "conceived" only now. We had been fumbling, with much give and take of discussion for her conception of "constant time," or "absolute time," and finally in despair fell back on "third time" — the other two being ordinary sidereal or clock time, based on astronomical movements, and psychological time.*

" 'The Greeks have a word for it!' " quoted Betty.

At the moment we thought that a flippancy, nor did we change our opinion when, later, she repeated.

"You remember last week I told you 'The Greeks have a word for it,' " she insisted. "Strip down — as you stripped down your word 'essence' — *esse*, to be. The Greeks *had* a word for it."

* The argument will be developed in its proper place later.

She tried to tell Joan, and have Joan repeat it to us — a method sometimes effective when there is verbal difficulty. Joan produced *eros*, and in her capacity as a receiving station stuck to it in face of derisive hoots from both the conceiving stations. This, we protested, was no love story; nor one of those love-light-and-sweetness cults! Or was it? No, it wasn't.

For the time being Betty gave it up and went on using "constant" and "absolute," but always with dissatisfaction. Finally she got it over, through Joan, in automatic writing; a method Joan very rarely employs, and at which she is not particularly good. It was *orthos*;* a word which, audibly, sounds sufficiently like *eros* to one who, like Joan, knows no Greek.

Like all new words, it had to have not only meaning, but connotation poured into it before it could become medium of exchange. That came later for us, and will for the reader come later in this book. But it soon became sufficiently obvious, as our especial terminology accumulated, that we would have to go in for definitions.†

And that, for Darby and me — the conceiving stations — turned out to be genuine labor. Betty seemed to think, and probably justly, that it would be good for our understanding if she let us do the defining. She reserved the right of veto — and exercised it. And let us try and try again, with an occasional kind hint or suggestion — seldom more than that — until we had hammered out something satisfactory. It was really funny. We had so many bright ideas, and were so enormously pleased with ourselves, and were so flatly sat upon! Definitions of

* Greek — straight, true. As orthodox, orthochromatic, orthopedic, etc.
† See Glossary at end of book.

half a dozen terms would leave us, and the evening, exhausted.

"Now formulate and define orthos," Betty challenged us.

Before we begin, I beseech the reader not to try to make head or tail of this now. It will be discussed — and I hope clarified — in Part II. I quote here, only as amusing, an example of what we were up against in making these definitions.

"Well," fumbled Darby, "you have said that orthos is 'the elemental reality'; 'it is not synonymous with consciousness'; 'it does not include the obstructed universe aspect.' 'Orthos is the elemental reality of the unobstructed universe' — but really consciousness is the elemental. By its derivation, 'orthos' is 'the true.' If space and time and motion are, as you have implied, appearances set up in the obstructed universe, then orthos is that of which they are the appearance."

"Orthos — from the Greek for true — is the ultimate from which all appearances of the universe emanate," contributed Betty.

"Is it fair to say that orthos is the unobstructed universe, the frame, the concept of the unobstructed universe?" asked Darby.

"It would be fair enough," conceded Betty. "Orthos is the unobstructed aspect of the entire universe."

"Then," said Darby, "I'd say that orthos is the field of operation of consciousness and its co-existent essences in the absolute."

"But," objected Betty, "why did we coin the word 'orthos'? Wasn't it to get rid of the word 'absolute'?"

"Orthos is the field of operation of consciousness and

its co-existent essences in its unobstructed aspects," was my try at it.

Betty ignored this one.

"One of the subjects we want to talk about is the fourth dimension — the possibility of it, not its reality; you can't get the reality," said she.

"But," objected Darby, "you have said that orthos is in trilogy.* Add a fourth? Unless it is consciousness itself." Darby was doubtful. So was I.

"Well, if you add any fourth dimension tonight, *I'll* lose consciousness," I observed.

This joke was not appreciated. We returned to the job. After much anguish we evolved this:

"Orthos: the operation of consciousness through co-existent essences in its unobstructed aspect."

Betty passed this. "The next is 'orthic,'" she said.

"'Adjective: pertaining to orthos,'" I proffered glibly.

"Congratulations! A perfect definition, and right the very first time," said Betty ironically.

In this manner, was our glossary compiled.

---

* A trilogy of Time, Space and Motion. See discussion in Part II.

PART II

CHAPTER X

CONSCIOUSNESS, THE ONLY REALITY

1.

ALMOST a quarter of a century ago Stephen, through the same station Betty is now using, developed an original philosophy which many people, among them I, have felt made rational — or at least more rational — the continuation of the individual after death.

Early in Betty's divulgence I realized, as did Darby, that her own work of the past twenty years, as recorded in *The Betty Book* and *Across the Unknown*, and that of Margaret Cameron as detailed in *The Seven Purposes,** as well as the philosophy of Stephen of *Our Unseen Guest*, were of the same piece as her present effort — perhaps a groundwork and preparation for her present effort. Indeed, it was Betty herself who later suggested that her current thesis, while inclusive of the pragmatic and ethical teachings of *The Seven Purposes*, was so definitely a metaphysical extension of the Stephen philosophy as to make a résumé of his earlier thought imperative for the present reader's best understanding.

"It is felt here," said she, "by intelligences who, when operating in the obstructed universe, had much to do with stimulating public thinking, that this particular book on which we are working should pretty much encompass the whole teaching. We must get from Darby and Joan permission to restate the substance of their publication, and build this presentation on a combination of what

* See Appendix II — *The Seven Purposes.*

Joan received and what I received, as a foundation to what Joan and I are now doing together."

Therefore, at Betty's behest I epitomize briefly Stephen's concept, which rested on the following:

There is but one reality. It is all-inclusive, but in degrees. Its highest expression on earth is consciousness, the self-aware I-Am of man. Consciousness, in degrees, is the one and only reality.

This is not a statement of subjective idealism. It is as far from that as from materialism. For as Stephen phrased it:

"Your men of books and laboratories...all seek to find a fundamental in their favorite attribute of reality. The idealist has made mind supreme...the materialist has made matter supreme. The truth is that both mind and matter are...attributes of one that is greater than either."

To that "greater than either" he gave the name of its highest expression — Consciousness.

Betty developed this thought for a visitor unskilled in metaphysics.

"What is *your* reality?" she asked. "What do you *know*, beyond question? Take this room. Are you *sure* these walls are green? Maybe your eyes trick you. Maybe these walls *are* gray — just as one of your friends has always insisted! Take the salt in the soup last night. Maybe there *wasn't* too much — nobody else thought so — maybe your taste tricked you! Take all of your sense-perceptions — any of them can trick you! So what do you know? Just one thing. You know that you *are*. That is your reality — — consciousness. Consciousness is the one and only reality."

"You know the people you love," the visitor objected doubtfully.

"How do you know them? What do you know of *their*

I-Am? Of course you know that they are entities in your obstructed universe. But the only thing of which you are absolutely sure, what you know in any specific dot of time and space, is I-Am. Everything else you know is in *relation* to your I-Am.

"Consciousness," said Betty, hammering home Stephen's basic concept, "is the only reality."

2.

Next, the Stephen philosophy undertook a *qualitative* and *quantitative* analysis of consciousness — exactly as a chemist might undertake a qualitative and quantitative analysis of elements and compounds — showing that here on earth evolution advances from a *quantitative* aspect only. In other words, so far as earth evolution can be noted and measured by science, a set pattern is followed; we get higher and higher developments of the earth species, but in any observable span of centuries no *new* species occur, no new genera. One can breed better dogs, bigger or smaller dogs, curlier or smoother dogs; but always they are dogs. Yet science also knows that in the various ages of the earth's history new genera *have* appeared. Man, for instance, the *genus homo*.

Where from? Monkeys? Or a common ancestor of man *and* monkeys? That is one theory of evolution. But even to the most convinced Modernist — the believer in evolution as opposed to the rapidly decreasing group of Fundamentalists who dispute evolution — the suggestion of an ape ancestry just won't click. Somewhere along the line there's a missing fact as well as a "missing link"! However, back in 1916 Stephen had said:

"Your science knows but *half* of evolution."

Granting the truth of evolution's quantitative development here on earth, what about evolution's *qualitative* development — those periodical appearances in this world of new genera and new species, or even of new varieties in those species so radically different as to cause science, unable to account for their source, to call them "mutations"?

Postulating earth-life as quantitative evolution, Stephen proclaimed the other "half of evolution" to be qualitative. Thus he established for Consciousness — the one and only reality — two planes or, better perhaps, two modes; *quantitative evolution*, or life here as we know it, and *qualitative evolution*, or life there as he knows it after what we call death. His plane, or mode, of consciousness, he said, is qualitatively free; quite as our earth plane, or mode, of consciousness is quantitatively free or, at most, subject only to such limitations as result from the fixed quality of individuals and species.

On the basis of evolution, then, and evolution's own need to account for its mutations, the Stephen philosophy asserts a qualitative plane or mode of existence as an inevitable necessity for the development of these mutations.

Again:

1. Evolution was accepted by Stephen as a fact or law:
2. The whole of consciousness, the fundamental reality, is in evolution:
3. The earth manifestations of consciousness are in evolution quantitatively only:
4. It follows that the *qualitative* aspect of consciousness can be in evolution only on *its* own plane — a someplace beyond earth-life.

And in this "someplace," said Stephen, exists all consciousness not observable at any given period on earth, since no particle of consciousness can be lost.

He further asserted that the fact that qualitative consciousness is limited in its evolution to its own plane accounts for the *fixed* quality of the earth species — man as man, tree as tree, gold as gold, electricity as electricity.

But we must not forget that Consciousness is the fundamental — the one common reality, despite all manifestations and attributes.

"The consciousness of the weed is no different in kind from that which manifests itself as an electrical current, and the consciousness manifested by the electrical current is no different in kind from that which manifests itself as what you call inanimate, inorganic matter. Consciousness is. It is the one and only reality, alike always in kind, though its degrees are many," stated Stephen.

In fact, there are degrees within degrees. To illustrate:

Man is born into this quantitative world out of the man-degree of quality, not the tree-degree, nor the dog-degree, nor the electrical-energy-degree, nor any of the other manifold degrees, but out of his own human-degree. Nevertheless, though the individual man is born man, his capacity as an individual varies greatly from that of his fellows. In the man-degree of quality itself there is a procession of what we might call sub-degrees, accounting for individual differences.

So man, like any individualized bit of consciousness, comes into this quantitative world with a fixed degree of quality. He is born man, and he can't change that; but he is also born with a degree of quality individual to himself. This, too, he can never change — his capacity for doing, for understanding, for becoming. But he can fulfill that capacity; he can win for his individual consciousness a degree of quantitative development proportionate to his quality.

There is nothing complicated about this thought. We know it already. Nobody would contend for a moment that Tony in the ditch and Einstein in the laboratory are of the same degree of quality. So when a man is born, he is a *man* because he is born from the human quality of consciousness; but he is born his *kind* of a man because he comes from his own particular sub-degree within that quality, bringing with him not only an unalterable humanness but a fixed individual capacity. So what can he do? Obviously, he can develop quantitatively. He can fill his capacity, — or come as near filling it, or as far from filling it — as his free will chooses. In any event, he does so by doing his job, undergoing experience, and assimilating that experience. In other words, by living earth life. The manner in which he lives it determines how high a mark in his capacity he makes. And, incidentally, in any human being there is more capacity than his best efforts are likely to fill. He won't spill over!

3.

This, in distinction to quality of consciousness, Stephen called "accumulation of quantity of consciousness." That, of course, is terminology; and, like all terminology, must be broken in before it becomes an easy fit for the mind.

Stephen broke it in by the use of simple illustrations:

"Take a common field daisy," said he. "It will, in its earthly character, always be a daisy, though by cultivation it may be made a thing of many petals, of intricate life. So it is with the individual."

Tony in the ditch can go to night school, and support his crippled parents, and get to be quite a man; or he can stay in the ditch and arrive at old age pretty much the same Tony. Not quite. There is no one but accumulates some quantity. Both a Tony and an Einstein, each according to his quality, can, and do, grow here on earth intellectually, morally and socially. Each builds what we call character. And we know that the extent of that building depends upon the personal initiative of each, on his individual free will.

For this quality-quantity thought concerning man is as old as the ages. Remember the "Parable of the Talents?" How to one man had been given five, and to another two, and to a third one? And how the five-talent man accumulated another five, and the two-talent man another two, while the one-talent man — burying his in the ground — did not even try? And the Master commended the first two "servants" in the same words, equally, though the five-talent man had returned with ten talents and the two-talent man with but four. Only the one-talent man did the Master rebuke, because he had not even tried. Each of the first two had made the most of his individual capacity; each of them had fulfilled his own degree of quality quantitatively.

4.

And now to this bare outline of Stephen's teaching must be added two more major ideas, both stated by him but left, apparently, for development by Betty these many years later. The first:

"Form is an attribute of consciousness... all manifestations of consciousness have form... in qualitative evolution as well as quantitative evolution" — in the unobstructed as well as in the obstructed universe.

This is a comfortable thought because here on the quantitative plane we are so used to form. All that we see or perceive has form; all that we cannot see, but nonetheless have learned to measure or use, has form. We ourselves have form; an electrical impulse has form. We cannot see qualitative (unobstructed universe) form — but neither can we see *all* quantitative (earth, obstructed universe) forms — air, for instance. However, Betty will tell us more about that.

The second proposition to be noted now is what Stephen called Parallel Law.

"There are two great glimpses," said Stephen. "Evolution is one of these. With this truth your world already is familiar.... In inorganic matter, evolution finds one expression; in the reproductive process of life, another; in the intellectual and moral phases of human endeavor, still another.... But always it is the same law, its varying manifestations parallel each other. Now here where I am there are laws, just as natural as yours... which parallel the laws, evolution included, of the earth-plane."

"Do you mean," Darby asked (back in 1916), "that spiritual law is simply a more complex expression of material law, and that the law of your plane is but a parallel of the natural or earth-plane law?"

"Parallelism, so defined," Stephen replied, "is the second of the two great glimpses, the greatest really of all glimpses. If earth scientists will... interpret psychological laws on the basis of so-called material laws, they will lift the assurance of the existence of my plane out of the field of mystic belief into that of reasonable fact."

And there, for the time being, Stephen left Parallelism, despite his having called it "the greatest really of all glimpses." Perhaps it was left for Betty's more precise development.

One more of Stephen's terms seems pertinent — pluralistic monism. It's a serviceable handle for thinking, though just another way of saying "many in one" or, for that matter, "e pluribus unum." The United States, for example, is one nation, manifested, however, in forty-eight states. The oneness of consciousness is a fundamental of the Stephen philosophy, but just as fundamental is his insistence that consciousness, being in evolution, manifests itself in degrees and in individualizations within those degrees. Thus it is on earth, and thus it is, said Stephen, throughout all of consciousness, qualitative as well as quantitative. Hence pluralistic monism.

"A reasonable peg, in the light of your own knowledge," said he, "on which to hang your faith" * — faith in immortality.

But between the immortality of his qualitative-plane in some afterlife and the mortality of our quantitative-plane in this life Stephen left a wall; a wall between *two* planes — one *here*, the other *there*.

Now, twenty-four years later, Betty, having died, "comes back" through the same station to proclaim that *"there is only one universe."* Her job, we were given to understand that first evening she spoke to me through Joan, was to try to break a hole in Stephen's wall.

* All quotations of Stephen are from *Our Unseen Guest*, published by Harper & Brothers, February, 1920.

CHAPTER XI

FOUNDATION STONES

1.

"Consciousness," said Betty, "is the starting point for everything." A familiar statement to us; yet of such importance that she thought it worth returning to so often that we began to make jokes about it.

"Consciousness —" she began one evening.

"— is the one and only reality," Darby and I supplied in chorus.

"— as I have told you over —" she continued unperturbed.

"— and over, and over, and over, and over," we finished for her.

Nevertheless she was not deterred from saying it again.

That is true in the cosmological aspect; in other words, consciousness is the everything. Beyond consciousness is nothing. Back to consciousness all manifestation can be traced. On the acceptance of this concept will depend the later development of Betty's argument.

It is also true as to us individually. We do not need much reflection to see that this is so. Betty made that clear in her little homily to our visitor unversed in philosophical enquiry. With us she established it as basic concept Number One.

Consciousness is the one and only reality.

2.

Then she beat over again the ground she had covered

in introducing us to her own first new concept: that there is only one universe.

"All the new concepts that I have been assigned to bring to you," she insisted, "must be based on the fact that *there is only one universe.*"

As a premise to start from, we had to accept more or less uncritically her initial assertions concerning the obstructed and unobstructed aspects of this universe. She said that we lived in the obstructed, she in the unobstructed phase. She pointed out that we are obstructed by matter — "you bump," as she put it, up against a stone wall; it obstructs you and you have to climb over it or go around it. You bump up against space — linear distance obstructs you and you have to employ some means to get from place to place. You bump up against time; you say, "I haven't time to do" thus or so, and you mean that the fixed duration of an hour or a day or a year is obstructing you. You bump up against motion; some rate of speed, slow or fast, is continually obstructing you. You bump up against thought, people's ideas; every day they are hindering, limiting, obstructing you. We could cite examples indefinitely. There is no question but that we live and operate in an *obstructed* universe.

"Even so," Betty said, "you have an actual, present perception of my unobstructed universe. You will be amazed to find how much of *my* universe is in your present knowledge."

This, of course, was really her basic thesis: that there is an unobstructed universe, and that it interfuses with our own; that, furthermore, even our obstructed aspect is obstructed only to us, and not to her. So really her major arguments in proof belong with such extended discussions as we shall encounter in her detailed analyses of time, space, motion, matter, and so on. But from the beginning she did take time to point out to us that right in the midst of our obvious obstructions are many things we know about, or take the word of specialized science concerning, which to us as human beings are not obstructions.

"You know," said she, "that all about you, all the time, are colors, sounds, energies — even infinitesimal floating particles of organic as well as inorganic matter that you never perceive; of which you go about your day wholly unconscious. When you stop to think, you acknowledge the fact of a radio wave — and you might have walked through one. But it did not obstruct you. So for you it just wasn't there. If you will only *think*, you will find that already you know quite a lot about an unobstructed universe. At least you know that there is a whole physical world, or field, of measurable and usable actuality which causes you no inconvenience and of which you are not normally aware. Even with you now there is an unobstructed universe beyond your ordinary obstructed universe, and with it you deal every minute of your days."

And so we drop in place her second foundation stone.

There is only one universe. One universe, of which there is an unobstructed as well as an obstructed phase. And as a corollary: *unknowing, we already, to some extent, inhabit the unobstructed aspect.*

3.

The next basic concept is what, for convenience at first, Betty called parallel law.

You will remember that in the foregoing review of *Our Unseen Guest* Stephen was quoted as saying that Evolution and Parallel Law were the "two great glimpses," and that parallel law, or parallelism, was "really the greatest of all glimpses." Nevertheless, Stephen went no further than to assert that all known earth laws are paralleled on the invisible plane. Betty approached her own development of this idea with caution.

"My words are heavy: I have to weigh them," said she. Then, after a pause, apparently for consideration, she began:

"The law of parallels, which Stephen promulgated, is more concrete than at that time it was possible for either the receiving station or the conceiving station to embrace mentally. You have no familiar attribute in the obstructed universe, that is not paralleled with a coinciding, operating attribute and law in the unobstructed universe. That is important. Now let's *chew* on that."

We chewed on it, to some purpose evidently, for some days later she returned to the subject — with much diminished heaviness!

"The deeper we get into the thing," said she, "the simpler it becomes, because, as I told you, there is only one law. All you need do is to take your limited law and project it out into an unlimited operation. What understanding of limited law I brought with me has made it possible for me quickly to adjust myself and project myself into understanding of, and cooperation with, the unlimited aspect of the same law. You must stress *parallelism*. Reach out along the limited laws you best understand, to meet me.

"What you call natural law is just a reflection, so to speak, of the orthic law governing my unobstructed universe. There is only one universe, one reality. The only-one-universe is pluralistic, as consciousness, the fundamental reality, is pluralistic. My aspect of the universe is unobstructed. Your aspect of the universe is obstructed. But there is no condition or fact that we have here that is not at least foreshadowed in your world.

"Now your laboratories are constantly discovering new manifestations, new laws. Every one of those laws has a parallel here, and every one is useful to you and to us. All the laws and manifestations discovered on your side are operating on our side. And on our side are many laws and manifestations you have not discovered and do not sense. Years hence all this will be told again in the terminology of our laws yet to be discovered by you.

"But" — and here was the important point — "it is not a case of actual *parallelism* at all. It is actually an *extension* in operation of the same law, that's all. If we are going to use the word 'parallel', we must make it clear that it is not a case of two different laws. Of course there are laws operating here that you have not discovered. When they are all discovered, it will indeed be one universe. *I* can't tell you about them, for there are no words yet. The reason Stephen used the word 'parallel' was because the entire universe is, as far as you are concerned, divided into the obstructed, or your world, and — in your hopes at least — the unobstructed, or my world. For him to have said that there is only one law that extends through the entire universe would have been incomprehensible. The thing I want to make perfectly clear to you is that every law in the universe, that you comprehend or that you do not comprehend, whether it operates within or without your apprehension, extends through the *entirety* of the universe. There is no law here that is not potentially discoverable in your world, though of course there are many not yet discovered."

The same law works in both aspects of the universe.

4.

The thing she wanted to get to us next was that consciousness, individualizing itself, dividing into the countless entity manifestations that make up the entire universe, operates in trilogy — in threes. In that no occult significance of numerology was intended. It was merely another way of saying that the universe is three-dimensional; though ordinarily the term means to us only length, breadth and thickness. Betty needed to extend the field covered by that term.

As often happened, she sprung the idea on us suddenly, and then, little by little, here and there, in the course of many sessions, gave it contour.

"First, I want to establish the word 'constant' as defining an ever-present and inclusive aspect," she began.

We immediately objected. "Constant," we reminded her, has been given an inflexible mathematical meaning by the physicists.

"It means fixed, unchanging, invariable in intregal calculus and such," explained Darby.

"I am not familiar with intregal calculus," replied Betty rather scornfully. "Neither is Joan. But there are those here who tell me that you are right. What I am familiar with is the everyday use of the word — the vernacular use. When I said to anybody, 'It rained constantly for two days,' I meant that it rained without interruption for two days; and I was so understood. I have to use words — Joan's words. The noun 'constant' means to her what the adjective means in her everyday speech — ever-present without being fixed. It could drizzle or pour for two days, and yet constantly rain. Ever-present, but not fixed. In no sense fixed."

She was emphatic about the meaning not being fixed. So after much discussion we added "co-existent" to our growing terminology. It was a word, we found, that Betty herself had used back in our fourth session. And the record reads, "Note the new terminology I am using." This sentence was thrown into a long paragraph of dictation as a parenthetical phrase. We had not noted it; a failure that had caused us endless mental gyrations. But we had caught it in time. Betty's "three-dimensional" universe is far from fixed. It is most emphatically in evolution. But it is co-existent with Consciousness.

"Now if you have that meaning in mind," she continued, "I will discuss with you the co-existent trilogies of your obstructed universe. You have, for instance, solids, liquids, gases: earth, air, water." She rattled off at least a dozen more, merely to illustrate, as a sort of "come-on," but too rapidly for my "shorthand." "In the trilogy of space you have reduced it to the prepositions — *from, at, to*. Time is yesterday, today, tomorrow. All through your three-dimensional universe runs trilogy, scientifically, materially, psychologically, even mystically. There are the three Graces, three Fates. It took the great psychic, Christ, to propound the thought: 'Father, Son, and Holy Ghost; these three are one.' In any case, the trilogies of length, breadth and thickness and of yesterday, today and tomorrow are ever-present co-existents of your obstructed universe."

The obstructed universe — our physical universe — operates in trilogies.

5.

The immediate application she desired to make of this concept was:

The obstructed universe — our physical universe — operates in trilogies. But — *so does the unobstructed universe. So does consciousness itself.*

And for this basic operation or accompaniment of consciousness in her unobstructed universe, Betty, out of the thin air, coined the term *trilogia*, to differentiate from the trilogies of our three-dimensional earth experience.

"You have your trilogies in your everyday life. Better call the *eternal* verities of consciousness 'trilogia' instead of 'trilogy,' " she ruled.

Soon she was putting new content even into our everyday word "trilogy"; while her own new term "trilogia" became fraught with very special meaning. To illustrate:

Consciousness as we know it in the obstructed universe operates through that trilogy which we accept as Time, Space and Motion.

Consciousness as Betty knows it in the unobstructed universe operates through the *trilogia* which consists of the *essences* of Time, Space and Motion; these essences are Receptivity, Conductivity and Frequency, respectively.

From the nature of these essences, and from the interaction thereof, comes all of what we know — and do not know — of the universe. To understand that process, however, we have to get a notion of what they are in *orthos*, and not of what they are as we ourselves experience them. Remember that orthos is "the operation of consciousness in its unobstructed aspects." In other words, we must attempt to understand Betty's time, space and motion; and build from there.

CHAPTER XII

ORTHOS and the ESSENCES

To approximate comprehension of Betty's time, space and motion — or our own, for that matter, if her divulgence be true — we must acquire some mental picture or acceptance of *orthos*.

This is not easy. It was particularly hard for Darby and me, because both of us were still pretty well mired in Newtonian physics. Furthermore, despite Betty's, as well as Stephen's, repeated assertions concerning evolution as a fact rather than a theory, there remained in our mental background an established *something* that was absolute and therefore *unchanging* and *unchangeable*.

But as Betty led us further and further toward her unobstructed universe we realized that her statements — from which we could not move her by a whole battery of arguments — implied the opposite of what our world's intellectuals have been accepting as the most logical reasoning, from the pre-Christian days of Plato down to the materialism of the exact mechanics of our own twentieth century. We had been taught to think in terms of *absolutes*, real ones; and here was Betty knocking philosophy's favorite measuring stick out of our hands. Consciousness, the reality of the entire universe, is in evolution; what is in evolution can *not* be an "absolute." And that, staunchly maintained Betty, was that. Dogmatic, unshakeable, flat!

Not that she rejected a Supreme Degree of Consciousness. She merely pushed it back, out of the finite, into the infinite. Infinity we do not, cannot, understand, for the supreme degree is beyond our comprehension.

In attempting a discussion of this, while Betty was still here, the Invisibles had told us that we must keep steadily in mind the realization that the supreme degree is beyond earth understanding actually, and that, while we here are privileged to examine all consciousness for the simple reason that we ourselves are individual bits of consciousness, and therefore within us is the *potential* capacity of understanding, we must do so from the finite aspect.

In this concept rests the thought that reconciles completely Betty's attitude, as outlined above, with her naturally profound religious faith.

Within this frame of the finite, then, she had set up time, space and motion as the great earth trilogy. That we do operate in this trilogy is self-evident, once that fact is called to the attention. There is nothing else in which we of earth *can* operate.

Next she proceeded to project these three familiars of our universe into *her* universe, by "stripping down," as she called it, our accepted *characteristics* of each and thus arriving at their essential properties. It is with these essentials, she told us, that her unobstructed universe deals. And here is where her term "essence" came in; "stripped down" to the meaning of its Latin stem *esse* — to be.

These *essences*, the great trilogia of her unobstructed universe, correspond to the co-existent trilogy (time, space and motion) of our obstructed universe. Each of these essences will be explained separately in a chapter all its own. Nonetheless, and though they were defined in the preceding chapter, they must be restated here as the basic conception of orthos — restated even as Betty restated them "over and over" for the labored understanding of Darby and me.

1. The essence of Time is Receptivity.
2. The essence of Space is Conductivity.
3. The essence of Motion is Frequency.
4. The co-existent trilogy of the obstructed universe (Earth) is Time, Space and Motion.
5. The co-existent trilogia of the unobstructed universe (Betty's) is Receptivity, Conductivity and Frequency.

Those five statements are of the greatest importance — and to be remembered.

For a long while — it seemed long in our struggle to encompass her ideas, though, as I have said, actually she put over her entire concept in but forty sessions — Betty allowed our three-cornered discussion of receptivity, conductivity and frequency to advance not only on the supposition of their being the *essences* of time, space and motion; we were also allowed to consider them the "absolutes" of time, space and motion. As she said afterwards it was the only way she could get *her* wedge into our brains! Something like the theory of giving a fellow enough rope...!

Anyway, one night in the midst of a rapid and succinct discussion Darby suddenly right-about-faced.

"I don't like the word 'absolute,'" he announced. "It's too static."

Then came one of those abrupt, meaningful pauses — the station seeming to be held in a sort of suspended animation — that we have come to recognize as heralding something of special significance. We waited. The station remained immobile. To this assertion of Darby's, Betty apparently had no response. Certainly her silence did nothing to help him out. So we waited some more.

"Say," he ejaculated at last. "Why can't we use the word 'orthic' instead of 'absolute'?"

Whereupon Betty went off into a series of triumphant chuckles. It was Betty's own satisfied — and satisfying — laughter, not Joan's.

"Good! Good!" she cried. "You've got it yourselves now! That is *why* we had to manufacture the word 'orthos.' We *had* to ditch the word 'absolute.' Absolute does connote static, and mine is not a static world. It is in evolution."

Of course we had been told that "over and over and over." Nevertheless...

"I suppose," said Darby to me, "we should try to conceive Betty's unobstructed universe, *not* in terms of our time, space and motion, but in terms of receptivity, conductivity and frequency. That is *her* approach to time, space and motion."

"Approach to nothing!" Betty came back at him before I could answer in the midst of my mad "shorthand" scramble to get everything down. "Time, space and motion are the *result;* they are *appearances*, if you wish, in your obstructed universe of receptivity, conductivity and frequency as they truly operate in orthos. You remember how we gave you the word 'orthos' because in the original Greek it means *true*. It is only a word, of course. But it means — really — the condition or state of qualitative consciousness in my unobstructed universe, just as sidereal means the condition or state of quantitative consciousness in your obstructed universe. Don't forget: orthos means *true*. All this while we have had to argue from your perceptions of time, space and motion *toward* the true. That is all right. But to get it clear, so that you fully understand, it also should be argued *from* the true — orthos — toward *your* perceptions of the true."

We let this soak in for a moment or two in silence. Then —

"Maybe we ought to try for a sort of mental picture of orthos," I ventured.

"Maybe you had," acquiesced Betty dryly.

And so we started at it all over again; but this time from her top down instead of from our bottom up. I can be no clearer than to repeat the give and take of our questions.

DARBY: Just what is meant by your Greek word, *orthos?* Do you thereby express the complex of the so-called trilogia, covering all its co-existents from all aspects?

BETTY: Yes. Orthos is the true, the correct and the inclusive.

DARBY: It seems to me we must use it with one content. Does orthos cover the complex of the essence of space, the essence of time, the essence of motion?

BETTY: Yes.

DARBY: Does it also cover our obstructed universe aspect of the three?

BETTY: No.

DARBY: It is not synonymous with consciousness?

BETTY: No.

DARBY: It is then a word coined to cover the reality, as seen from the unobstructed universe, of time, space and motion?

BETTY: It covers the constituents of consciousness.

DARBY: By it we mean the complex of all the three constituents — the trilogia — of the unobstructed universe?

BETTY: It exists in the unobstructed universe, not in the obstructed universe. Orthos is the true, correct condition of my unobstructed universe: the one standard thing, the norm, of which all else is but a reflection. This does not mean that orthos is other than in evolution. It is in evolution. That which is true and correct as a norm can grow. But it can *only* grow correctly, undeviatingly, true to itself. Also orthos is a fundamental reality, while matter and force and all the things you play with in your chemical and physical world are the results only of various juxtapositions of the co-existents.

The last sentence of Betty's seemed to bring orthos right down to our obstructed universe. But this she would not allow. Nor were we to think of orthos as "heaven," though the old idea of fulfillment and unspoiledness as a *condition* of heaven, she assured us, is a "great glimpse." Glimpse was a favorite word of Stephen's and he used it in our everyday meaning of seeing or understanding a portion or part of a thing or a fact without encompassing its complete truth or whole. So I think we might go this far — the *conditions* of orthos and "heaven" are the same: unspoiled, undeviating as to observance of law, correct and true.

Betty was satisfied that we had the idea at last. It seemed simple enough then, and we were inclined to be apologetic for having been so slow. But this, too, she would not allow.

"Everybody has to go over and over a path to make a beaten track," she assured us. "What we are after is the beaten track, the visible trail that neither the rain nor the wind nor the growth of nature can obliterate. The only actual beaten tracks in the obstructed universe are conceptive ideas. These we are now creating. Good night."

Conceptive? Was there such a word? There was not. But on looking up the noun from which it must be stemmed I found other unusual adjectives, such as conceptional, coined by no less great contributors to thought than our own William James and George Frederick Stout of England. They, too, evidently felt the need of new words to express new ideas.

CHAPTER XIII

TIME

1.

"Now I think we should begin to clarify the subject of Time," began Betty. "There are three kinds of time: sidereal or clock time; psychological time; and then a third or orthic time, which we are to discuss. Sidereal time is a fixture of your universe; it depends on movements of planets, and is measured by calendars and clocks. Psychological time is more flexible. It is your inner sense of time. You, for yourself, can more or less control your sense of sidereal time by your psychological time. If you are happy, and busy, an hour is short: if you are cold and uncomfortable, an hour is long."

But, *if we will*, she went on to point out, we can often take any given hour and *make* it long or short. We can fill it with distraction, interest or amusement; or we can just sit still and be bored. In that fashion we do control sidereal time by means of psychological time. But the control, we must admit, is fragmentary and partial.

"In our universe we can — partly — control psychological time," acknowledged Darby, "but that does not actually change sidereal time."

"No," agreed Betty. "What I said was that in the obstructed universe the individual, by means of his psychological time, can control his *sense* of limited periods of sidereal time."

"That's all right," Darby pursued his point, "but he doesn't control sidereal movements, or the clock. He merely gives content to time."

"He is controlling the *kind* of time in which he exists," said Betty. "*Your psychological time is really the time in which you live.*"

This, on reflection, we had to concede is profoundly true. Our lives are not, in retrospect, measured by years, but by the content of those years.

2.

We in our obstructed universe have sidereal time and psychological time. Sidereal time is our measuring stick or constant — mathematical constant, that is; and, as far as we are concerned, we may be said to control it — partially — by psychological time.

"Now," said Betty, "I have in my unobstructed universe orthic time and psychological time. And I control orthic time in a similar manner, by means of psychological time. Only there is this difference: Your command of psychological time is only partial, as you will admit; mine is more nearly complete. In other words, I am freed from sidereal time; *and* I am not dominated by psychological time, but employ it in controlling the time of my own state of being.

"In your use and my use of psychological time there is a parallel. That is what I mean when I say that our psychological time we take with us, and we use it to control our orthic time.

"Orthic time is the reality. Sidereal time, which is a reality to you, is only an attribute of matter: it is an obstruction.

"One thing more — psychological time, by which the other two are modified, is the only variable for me just as it is for you. Both sidereal time and orthic time are 'constants,' in that they do serve as a basis of comparison as well as of mathematical calculation. Both are in evolution; but their evolutional process no more disturbs either your — or my — use of them as a norm than the movement of the earth upon its axis round the sun disturbs your physical equilibrium. In other words, sidereal time is 'constant' enough to serve your present individual awareness mechanism and the present evolutional status of the obstructed universe — a norm enough 'fixed' by the ordered movements of the heavenly bodies to serve your mathematical purposes. In the same way, orthic time is a fundamental co-existent of my state of Being. These facts — and especially the nature of orthic time — account for certain discrepancies and deviations that your laboratory workers find in their scientific research and which, so far, they have not been able to explain."

There followed a quick interchange between Betty and Darby.

"Please note that I am using the word 'constant' in the mathematical sense," he said. "In that sense sidereal time may be said to be a constant. Is orthic time, fully encompassed, also a constant?"

BETTY: That is true for the Supreme, in infinity. And sidereal time for you is an infinite constant — a concept — but that's all. It works as far out in your time as you can go, but —

DARBY: Yes, but our sidereal time is also a stabilizer for our psychological time. What I want to know is whether you — not the Supreme, but you — have a similar stabilizer.

BETTY: Orthic time is a stabilizer for us, of course. But your sidereal time is only a constant in the universal sense. Mathematically, you can work it out that way; but you don't ordinarily do so.

DARBY: Then your orthic time is a mathematical constant in a corresponding universal, that is, impersonal, sense? Without such a constant, subjective experience on your side would be a madhouse.

BETTY: *Certainly!* There would be no common denominator.

The importance of this exchange seemed to lie in this: that, as sidereal time is a universal constant at our option, and not by our habit, so orthic time is a mathematical constant to Betty at her option, and not necessarily by her habit. In other words, in asserting the constant character of orthic time we must also realize how ephemeral in our own mode of thought is the constant of sidereal time. Also of importance is Betty's statement that we can apply the constant of sidereal time only as "far out as we can go." Beyond our reach it becomes only a mathematical concept, not to be verified by cases.

3.

Now the thing that enables us to manipulate our psychological time, Betty insisted, is the fact that we have actually an inner awareness of orthic, fundamental time, in *our* state of being in the obstructed universe, though we do not recognize it as such.

"Indeed," she asserted, "contrary to your accepted conception, orthic time is better understood by you in your obstructed universe than any other of the universal laws that control the entire universe. What I mean to say is, that this time in which I exist, is not only shared by you, but can be conceived by you from your own experience — I was going to say fringes of experience. I told you that your psychological time is really the time in which you live. The time that is most ingrained, however, is orthic time. That is the time we have here."

That was a pretty bold statement. We protested that we understood nothing whatever about orthic time, except its name, which as yet was meaningless to us. Betty replied that she did not expect us to understand it; but that she did want us to recognize the *feel* of it — of time, just time, divorced of sidereal aspects.

"A child knows nothing of clocks. Nevertheless he has a sense of time. You are *trained* to sidereal time," said she. "As a child is born into the world, it brings with it the acceptance of time — just time. Certainly it has no conception of a longer or shorter period of sidereal time, while psychological time is still but one of its potentialities as a human entity. This initial knowledge — instinct, if you like — is of *my* time. Orthic time. Even an idiot, deprived of controlled mental activity, has a realization of orthic time. He knows he exists — in time. It is purely instinctive, because it's a co-existent of Being. It *is* Being; an ever-present time; without beginning and without end. Of course it is a difficult concept to your modern thought because the reality has been lost through your personal experience; just as, before you, it had been lost through the racial experience which is your earth inheritance.

"That is the price of civilization. Man has educated

himself out of inherent wisdom — 'eaten of the tree of knowledge' — and now by the sweat of his intellectual brow he must search out the truth for himself again. And being, you remember, 'only a little lower than the angels,' man will find the truth, since truth is here *to* find in my unobstructed universe; in orthos.

"But," she returned to her line of argument, "you have another aid in your understanding of orthic time, and that is sleep. Things happen in sleep without time relation."

"I have no difficulty with eventless time," said Darby. "I have the feel of that, but . . . the time you suggest," continued he, "would have to be felt in one's inner core as a time that is distinct from or above the feeling of *duration!* The sort that recognizes Being as a constant, not a variable."

"Yes," assented Betty, "it has no division, neither by hours nor by memory of events. The cat, the dog, the new-born child live in that time. This time — while *we* are conscious of it, and *you* at least recognize it — is still for you an X. A child is perfectly conscious of it, and he must develop before he gets out of living in that time. Yet you have always projected your individuality over into my time. You are always doing it; everybody does. Recognizing, to use your terms, the constancy of Being. That is the time your scientist would tell you has neither past, present, nor future. It is a co-existent. Whenever they tap that, it is *there*."

"Getting a notion of time's collapsible quality through the instantaneous transmission of radio may be a glimpse of how these people act in this third kind of time," suggested Darby.

"Let's get together," urged Betty, "because this time business is the common factor between us. It is the one place we *can* meet with understanding. You can be aware of my time much better than you can have an awareness of my kind of unobstructed space. Space, as you know it, is a series of obstructions."

All she expected of us, at this stage of her argument, was that we should have the *feel* of it. Later, she promised us, we should know what it is all about.

CHAPTER XIV

SPACE

1.

THE next job proved quite an assignment. We were to gain a feeling of space similar to what we had come, at least partially, to sense as a *feeling* of time. And after that of motion. Of their character, that is, in our obstructed universe and in Betty's unobstructed universe — sidereally and orthically, in short. These three, the great trilogia, said Betty, were the basic concepts of her new divulgence. Once we possessed them — and that means *possessed* — she promised us plain sailing and fascinating landfalls of new adventure in this strange land of hers. But we must, we simply *must*, do the drudgery of building these three concepts into our mental structure. So we heaved a sigh and tackled space.

This was, as Betty had predicted, a much more difficult subject than the last.

"You can be aware of my time much better than you can have an awareness of my kind of unobstructed space. I have already conceded that space, as you know it, is a series of obstructions," she said at the start.

"That's right," agreed Darby, "no obstructions; no space. Science measures from one limit — one obstruction — to another."

"Sidereal space is divided and obstructed as is sidereal time. They are alike. What about your psychological space? You must have it, as well as psychological time," commented Betty.

"I suppose," mused Darby, "that the difficulty in getting the feel of pure space lies in the fact that we have no instinct for it as we have for time. We can easily feel an eventless time. We do not feel as easily, if at all, placeless space. Could you give me the same feeling of placeless space as I have of eventless time?"

"Well," Betty attempted, "the whole difficulty is that two things have happened. First: long before you were born it had been discovered that your material earth, instead of stretching out flat to infinity, was round and turned back on itself. So you have the knowledge, as far as sidereal space is concerned, that if you go far enough on the earth's surface, you will come back to the *place* you started from. On the other hand, you can never return to any of your starting points in sidereal time.

"The other difficulty is that your sidereal space is not only measured obstructively, but it is measured muscularly. You cannot sit down inactive, and without motion of some kind — either by your feet, or the feet of a horse, or an auto or a ship — have a definite spot in space come to you. In your universe, for that spot in space and you to come in contact, *you* have to have a motion. On the other hand, with sidereal time you need do nothing about it at all. Ten o'clock will arrive for you, whether you lift a finger or not. Your office will not arrive for you, unless your body, in some kind of motion, covers the miles.

"Now those are the two handicaps you have to overcome in comprehending orthic space. So it seems to me that the best way for you to try to get it in your mind is to look out and up into the universe where you have, as far as your personal experience is concerned, no muscular obstructions and no limitation. The trouble is that you have been educated out of your sense of orthic space, and have not yet caught up with your sense of orthic time."

"On the round earth you deal with two dimensions only," objected Darby, irrelevantly, I thought. "I don't see how plane, or even solid, geometry will help."

"Oh, I used the image of the globe only as an illustration of a difficulty," returned Betty with a touch of impatience. "But remember this — you *had* the feeling of orthic space originally; only you were educated out of it — even more so than in the case of orthic time. Still, I recognize your problem, so let's try time-space, and see if that will help. That is one of the new playthings of your mathematicians, isn't it? It is a makeshift, but at least it expresses their dissatisfaction with their present working hypothesis and a groping after a new."

2.

Now I felt we were getting somewhere. Hooking time and space together made a new springboard. All three — time, space *and* motion — are hooked together, Betty somewhere reminded us; they *are* the trilogical co-existents of consciousness. In our experience they are more or less set apart from each other, and for analysis and understanding must be completely separated. But now she recalled to us what she had said some evenings before about the malleability of time and space, even with us. And of what Stephen has told us. He had popped in for a moment when Betty was floundering a little.

"What Mrs. White wants you to understand," he had said, "is that recent discoveries have made it possible for you to have a better understanding of our time ratio than any other of our shared characteristics," and promptly withdrew.

"To what discoveries was Stephen referring?" I asked Betty.

"He meant the radio and the various new light beams as affecting the ratio of time and your geographic space," she answered. "You have, because of them, a new ratio between your time and your space."

"In other words," I contributed, "the same amount of time does not measure the same amount of space."

"That's it!" she cried enthusiastically. "So many hours between New York and San Francisco instead of so many miles! You listen to a baseball game over the radio. It is a fact that you hear the crack of the bat on the ball before the people in the grandstand do; you are 3,000 miles away, and the people are within sight of it. Just as you have always been able to see the puff of smoke before you heard the gun fire. This suggests that your preconceived ratio of time and space, even in your own field, is variable, malleable, and is in the process of reestablishment.

"You know that we here, to use your terminology, travel far — call it spatially; yet you call me, and I can immediately come. The wave — conductivity — that is used by you now to transmit vibrations resulting in sound at the receiving end of a radio, is a part of our natural habitat. With your radio you are isolating, for a single use only, a medium in which we dwell. This is your next 'glimpse' of the relativity of time and space, something you yourselves are using. Now, since man has developed a mechanical thing through which, by turning a couple of knobs, he can make a new ratio actual, it ought not to be too difficult to conceive a different ratio of time and space for us."

"You must be able to slow down and to expand or otherwise to control that ratio in order to make it usable," I suggested.

"We can control time and space relative to our individual needs, precisely as you do," Betty agreed to this. "Man has himself developed a control. You can speed up or slow down, not to the same degree as ourselves, but much more than you were able to do even two decades ago. You are beginning to control the ratio of time and space — sidereal time and geographical space. Your spatial conception of yesterday is not your spatial conception now. So you see that, even with you, there is a variability and malleability of space. Nevertheless the geographical actuality is the same. It is variable and malleable only because of your new time-space ratio.

"Now we have here a parallel. These parallels are so important. Our orthic time and orthic space are in relationship to each other, as are your sidereal time and geographical space. You are able to control to a higher and higher point the time consumed to cover your space. We control our psychological time more fully than you. By the use of our psychological time we control our orthic space. It is simple here; but they tell me it's important for scientists, for it will change the whole idea on your plane."

"One of the first things you told us," said Darby, "was that our best approach to an understanding of orthic time was our sense of psychological time, which proves to be true. I feel that for us to get the *feel* of orthic space we shall have to explore psychological space even as we did psychological time. So why not broaden our conception of psychological space?"

"Well," assented Betty, "we'll take the stretch of road

from the foot of that hill to the postoffice. Now try to dis-associate any idea of time from this. We take your car. We drive up. We are there, and of course you have covered the ground to get there. But what is your *recollection* of it? It may be a complete blank.

"But wait until it snows, and you slip, and you slide back on the hill, and you start again. Now what will be your recollection of the same sidereal *distance* — leaving out time?"

"Or," I suggested by way of supplement, "suppose yourself in a brown study during the journey. Suddenly you find you are there. You have no sense of *either* space or time in getting there."

"Yes," Betty accepted this.

3.

We agreed that we had at least a working glimpse of psychological space.

"I have such a big job. I have to make you understand this afternoon," Betty sounded a trifle helpless, "the ac-tuality of space, plus its indivisibility, as respects the ob-structed and the unobstructed. In other words, your space and my space are the same. Their point of indivisibility is in orthos, of which you are somewhat conscious. In the obstructed universe the line of demarcation varies back and forth."

She cast about for some moments for a starting point.

"When you look at the stars you know that they *are*; and they are so far away that there is actual space you cannot possibly travel, which only light can travel."

"That isn't orthic space — unobstructed space," one of us objected.

The thought attempted seemed to be that we could not get at such space to handle it mechanically, as we handle the space within our reach.

"Of course it is obstructed, in a way," she admitted. "But to your comprehension it just looks like *out*."

Darby had an idea.

"Does orthic time, perhaps, debunk space completely? Is it possible that space might be a phenomenon only of sidereal time: and to an extent, of course, of psychological time? In the upper reaches of ourselves we do find a sense of orthic time; but we find no corresponding sense of orthic space. That suggests that there is no orthic space."

It was a grand idea, and if it could have been adopted into our philosophy it would certainly have simplified the universe. At the moment both Darby and I took it as adopted, for Betty merely remarked: "I have told you that space is a series of obstructions. Now our space is your space. You have manifestations that are obstructions to you. Those same obstructions, to you, are not obstructions to us. There is only one universe." This was one of those delphic statements that can be taken either way, and closed that session.

"I ask you to use your own minds to aid me in clarifying," began Betty, next session. "I want you both to attempt to conceive a limit to space. Or could you conceive time and space as being the same thing?"

"Pretty difficult. The rate of motion is one thing, and that equals time: the direction of motion is something else, and that equals space." Darby and I both thought up to now she was talking of *our* space. In our conception, at that moment, that was all the space there was! Darby had debunked orthic space. Nevertheless there must be a parallel.

"We agree that obstructions make our space in our obstructed universe. What analogous to obstructions makes your space in your unobstructed universe?" I voiced this.

"I don't want to disturb your sense of the reality of my unobstructed universe," Betty was hesitant. "Well, let's reduce the problem to the walls of this room. Suppose that inside this room were all the space in the universe, and we're all here. All this space is created for you by obstructions — that is, the chairs, the desk, the lounge and so on all make distance points of so many feet apart.

"Now the contour — the limitation — the boundary — of this arbitrarily restricted space is as real to me as to you. I am being and thinking in it. Yet inside this space these things are to me no obstruction.

"Suppose you took the infinity of the universe. The universe as such contains all the stars, nebulae and so on. You call that the universe. Your limited conception and perception of it is all made up of obstructions. But there is orthic space, just as there is orthic time, and we are all Being in it."

"Hold on!" I cried. "I thought Darby abolished orthic space!"

"Your difficulty is this: despite the fact that you have divisions of sidereal time, those divisions are not *material* things. So you have retained a qualitative conception of orthic time. Now your earth experience with space is materially obstructive. Your own physical habitation, your body, is itself an obstruction; and that obstruction is in turn hampered and obstructed by those form attributes of lower consciousness that make your material matter. Because you *bump* into that, you cannot conceive of my space as easily as you conceive of my time. You cannot have *either* time *or* space *or* motion alone in your obstructed universe. But by the same token you cannot interchange one for the other. Each stands on its own feet with you, and so do they with me."

Darby threw up both hands; another bright idea gone wrong!

"Very well, let's restore orthic space," he conceded resignedly. "We live in a spatial universe based on obstruction; she in an unobstructed universe where space is not relative!"

"Darby," she consoled him, "the thing you were groping for and misstated was that you know matter is the form attribute of consciousness and as such it is an obstruction with you. We have defined your space as a series of obstructions. But these are only form attributes. They are not obstructions to me. Space exists for me in essence."

"And are there no boundary lines?" asked Darby.

"Points only."

"Do they serve the same spatial purpose as our obstructions do — as markers?"

"Of course they do. But I have told you that in my universe we do not have obstruction. We do have space. Space with us is no more static than with you. It expands and contracts, according to its ratio with time. Let's discuss."

Darby was doubtful.

"To hook up space with obstruction in such a way as to contrast it with your space without obstruction is not accurate, because you must have the thing that causes us to *think* we have obstruction," he objected.

"Correct," approved Betty. "The degree of your awareness of my orthic time is the measure of your individual awareness of the unobstructed universe, or of the actual indivisibility of the universe as a whole. Space, as you conceive it, is the antithesis of space as an actuality. My space is the actuality; your space is only a conception. Living not only in the unobstructed universe, but in the obstructed universe as well, since they are one and the same of a whole, I manipulate what you call space — and I call conductivity — by means of what you call time — and I call receptivity. Nevertheless, our space is an existent of Being. It is no less a fact than your space."

4.

We agreed that our gallant philosophical attempt to abolish space, *per se*, in the unobstructed universe had failed. Betty had space; and as she dwelt in the unobstructed universe — in orthos — it must be orthic space. But what was it? We had no feel of it. That, said Betty, was exactly what we must try for, rather than complete understanding — the *feel* of it. As with orthic time. She back-tracked to a previous discussion, when she had pointed out that we had "contracted the space" between New York and San Francisco from nearly a year by ox cart to less than a twenty-four-hour day by plane.

And I had contributed:

"Continue this contraction to a logical conclusion. It has been brought about by the removal of obstructions. Contract it, by the same process, beyond *all* obstruction, and you would have your placeless space."

"Try this," she suggested. "You put in a telephone call

to San Francisco. You hear the voice. Where is the space between New York and Pittsburgh, and Cleveland, and Chicago, and Denver? It is not there."

"Then the nearer to complete instantaneity of time you get, as with radio, the nearer you come to instantaneity of space?" I asked.

"In other words," Darby caught up the thought, "if you postulate two separated places in any given field, as the broadcasting and receiving apparatus of radio transmission, then in *that particular field — radio transmission —* the two places instantaneously become one place."

"*Or any other field, with a high enough degree of frequency.* It's the extension of that field in frequency that is going to establish the existence of the universe as one," cried Betty, jubilant.

As a conceiving station Darby was going strong, as his next contribution proved.

"Take the psychic condition," he suggested. "Observe Joan — the feeling of obstructed space seems lost with her. How about that, Stewart? Did Betty seem to experience that when she was working here?"

"No sense of space. 'I'm just *there*,' she often said that," I replied.

"In your subconsciousness there is no awareness of sidereal space," Betty now helped further. "Take even your own thoughts. You can picture in your mind's eye any familiar place, or even an imaginary place, without any relation to sidereal space at all."

"Any different feeling of space in flight? Of leaving sidereal space?" asked Darby.

"Definitely," agreed Betty. "You leave the obstruction of the earth. Of course there are atmospheric obstructions, which on earth you knew nothing about. But granting that, and assuming a smooth easy flight, you have a definite sense of having eliminated obstructed space. You have a sense of being yourself a part of space. If you fly high enough, and don't look down, and don't observe the obstructions — which are divisions of your habitual space — you get the sense of the identity of yourself with space, just as you have admitted a sense of your identity with time."

"I believe I can carry that illustration a little farther," I interposed. "As you have said, our space is made by obstructions. The more obstructions we manage to remove, the nearer we come to a sense of orthic space, since, by definition, orthos is a condition of *no* obstruction. Now let's make your flight a night flight between Salt Lake City and San Francisco. We are enclosed in a dark cabin. The only space we know anything about is the little space in that cabin. We and that space are near enough the same for the argument. There are practically no obstructions, as far as we can sense. We assume a smooth flight. Indeed, the only obstruction of which our senses *can* be aware is the slight sound of the propeller against the air. So — as far as we are concerned — we are all the space there is. Nevertheless we start at Salt Lake City, and find ourselves in San Francisco. We have passed a lot of sidereal space. But without sensing it. The only space we have sensed is the space in the little cabin, but that is practically identical with ourselves. How is that for a *feeling* of something like orthic space?"

For once I had made good. Betty acclaimed this enthusiastically.

"I asked you to use your minds," she cried. "Now here's one other illustration of stripping down space. Take the last message of Edward VIII, when he abdicated.

That voice was heard more widely than any other in all of history. As he spoke in London, people in every portion of your world heard his voice, *simultaneously*. There was no sidereal space."

We did not have to understand it fully, as yet: that would be attempted in later discussion. It is sufficient for now if we get the *feel* of it, she reminded.

CHAPTER XV

MOTION

1.

"ONE of the great glimpses of the mad scientists," said Betty, "is perpetual motion. That is one of the truths that man has glimpsed and attempted to accomplish, but failed; the dream of the mad inventors — perpetual motion!

"For motion is a co-existent of Being. There is motion in everything that exists. Time and space are co-existents of the reality of Being. I am: Time is: Space is. If there is Being, there is Time and Space. And if you have the Time-Space combination, you are by way of having Motion."

Here we were again, back at "the new plaything of your mathematicians" — Time-Space.

"All right," said Darby. "We accept time-space, hyphenated for the sake of the argument. Let us suppose an object in motion between two points. In a sense, that is only another way of saying time-space. Now we speed up the motion. Exactly in proportion to the speeding up, we shorten the time and contract the space. Thus we telescope time-space."

"Exactly," said Betty. "But just what does that mean? We have learned that both time and space are malleable. Already your obstructed universe commonly measures the distance between two points (space) by so many hours (time). What makes that measure possible?"

"Motion," we agreed.

"But not what you call the *rate* of motion," warned

Betty. "That is something else again. That is the specific measure, what you can count. But it is just motion that makes the count possible — motion; the last, and the first of the three inseparables."

2.

Now we have here also a trilogy of aspect. We have motion-in-relation, with which we are most familiar: we have psychological motion, a fact which we did not apprehend until almost the end of the divulgence, and motion-in-itself, that is, orthic motion.

When I finally sat down to study the record as a whole — after the returns were all in, so to speak — I realized that in the discussion of motion Betty had deliberately reversed her method of procedure. In dealing with time and space she had used the same sequence, beginning with our everyday sidereal experience and then leading us on through our psychological *feel* and understanding, into her unobstructed universe aspect or orthos. But with motion she plunged us directly from sidereal motion into orthos, deferring discussion of psychological motion till close to the end. We had not much noticed this, and when we did we thought it an oversight, though by that time we felt we had arrived at a fairly clear conception of orthic motion. So, while not sensing any great need for a discussion of psychological motion, still we asked for it just to keep the record intact. And Betty was more than ready for us.

Naturally we were prepared for a discussion of psychological motion on the analogy of psychological time and psychological space. But Betty had her own viewpoint, the difficulty seeming to be that any exposition on those lines would be just a repeat of psychological time and psychological space as she already had explained them. It was, therefore, somewhat of a jolt when she pried out of us the idea that *thought itself might be psychological motion.*

I doubt if we could have accepted that as the next step beyond the in-relation-to, measurable motion that is so major a part of our hour-by-hour living. I think she, and those working with her, knew this; which is why Betty went about the subject of motion in another way.

Motion-in-relation, we can dismiss in a few words. It is the ordinary motion we know; and, as Mr. Einstein has emphasized, it exists in any object only as related to some other object.

"There is atomic motion," Betty opened the subject of orthic motion. "You don't see it, but you know about it. That is not orthic motion. And celestial motion. Neither is that orthic motion, for it is relative — measurable; always you relate it to something else. But it is in the concept of celestial motion as an inescapable, always functioning characteristic of the heavenly bodies that we may find a stepladder for the understanding of orthic motion."

"All right," said Darby, "we're pretty familiar with our measurable motion. So trot out your stepladder. Let's see if it will reach to orthos!"

"Well," continued Betty, "can you imagine anything that is *not* in motion in the universal sense? The earth turns, the grass grows, light travels, wood decays returning to dust, water evaporates into vapor and vapor condenses into dew. Something happens to carbon and you may get coal that can be turned into heat and gases, or you may get a diamond hard enough to cut glass — brilliant enough to set in a king's crown! You in your obstructed universe are aware of *something* that impels, energizes — even sustains. A sort of purposeful core common to all that you know.

"You see," she complained, "every word I use in your language is so surrounded by meanings you have attached to it, that it is almost impossible for me to explain. Now don't take this too literally," she begged, "but back of the motion you know — measurable — has to be the impulse, that aspect of consciousness which *is* motion; a motion back of the motion that manifests. Now the highest expression of orthic motion in your obstructed universe is life. Yet if there were no time or no space, life could have no form.* Perhaps if I said orthic motion is the evolutional impulse, that would suggest something to you."

"Speaking of time and space," Darby took a new tack, "assume an auto running at a hundred miles an hour. Speed it to two hundred, and then four hundred, and so on up. Its motion is measured against time and space. Now speed it up to infinity and it has nothing to be in relation to: it comes close to 'absolute' motion. Would that be orthic motion?"

"It is possible," supplemented Betty, "even in your universe, to speed up such things as a motion picture or a wheel so high that you cannot see them. They have gone beyond your sense of sight. It is possible to speed a twanging wire so fast that its sound goes beyond your sense of hearing. As distinct from obstructed manipulations, orthic motion is the *fact* of motion as you know

---

* More fully explained later. But, briefly, if there were no space for a thing to occupy, and no time to give it duration, it could not exist as an entity.

it in the lower degrees. One reason why the concept is difficult is because motion *per se* is something which you yourselves can create, operate and control — and thereby make it relative. It is an obstruction, as space was a muscular obstruction. But you *use* it. It is too familiar to you."

"It is even worse than that," complained Darby. "We have to analyze space quite consciously to see its relativity. But motion is the acme of relativity in our minds. It is immediately relative; we do not have to analyze it. In fact, we know it *only* as relativity. And I don't think merely adding speed answers the question."

"But conceive of yourself," prompted Betty.

"Myself," Darby slowly reflected aloud, "distinct from my members. Is that myself in motion? I haven't the feeling of it."

"Have you the feeling of being static?" countered Betty.

"In my inner self, yes."

"How about your relationships; to your mind, to the whole of consciousness, of which you are part?"

"Well —" Darby shook his head.

"Take it on the basis of a physicist's knowledge. What creates any motion at all? Why is motion?"

"It is a postulate of physical science that everything moves straight ahead until it is deflected or stopped." Darby obeyed. "Then it simply reacts and you have a resolution of forces, a change of direction but no actual loss of motion."

"How is this?" I proposed. "Take it from the other end. Motion is Being. And it is orthic motion that starts all obstructed universe motion."

"Getting warmer," encouraged Betty.

"We might say, then, that what we call motion ordinarily is after all just a segment, a little slice, of a universal orthic motion," contributed Darby.

Now it was my turn.

"A while ago," said I, "we conceived of a moving picture running at normal rate; and we gradually speeded it up. Then we noted that we completely altered the ratio between time and space as depicted on that screen. It took the actor less time to cross the stage-set, and therefore it became not so far across — space was less. And vice versa. Remember?

"Now speed it up until it completely blurs out into nothing. What have we got? No picture: just motion. Apparently there's no space or time in it at all. There, by way of illustration, is a glimpse of motion, orthic motion.

"Now start from there and begin to slow it down again. What are we accomplishing? We are bringing back space and time to the screen. In other words, we are bringing motion into relationship with time and space. And because of that fact it differentiates from pure motion into limited motion. And it has entered the obstructed universe."

"I *knew* we would get it over!" cried Betty in high jubilation.

It was, as I said, much later that, reading back in the records, we discovered there had been no concise discussion of psychological motion. So remembering Betty's law of parallels, Darby asked:

"We have had psychological time and psychological space. It logically follows that there should be psychological motion. Is there? Tell us something about it."

"Yes," said Betty, "there is. The highest expression of it in the obstructed universe is your awareness of self.

You know, for instance, that you were yesterday; you are today; and you expect to be tomorrow. The continuity of the I-Am."

"That is to be distinguished from time?"

"Possibly I should have said, 'of the I-Am's being.' You see, the I-Am is made up of frequency, which is the essence of motion."

A point, indeed, toward which science has reached in reducing all the material with which it works to protons, electrons, neutrons — all rates of motion.

"What you have said," commented Darby, "is that psychological motion is that rate of motion which one recognizes as his own vibration; recognizing also that back of that is the orthic rate of motion that one knows is the I-am."

"Take the subconscious activity of your own body," suggested Betty; "that is motion. Your sense of it could be as psychological as your psychological sense of time. Let's start there.

"Psychological motion is of complete importance because the individual's way back into orthos is through his own frequency. His recognition of psychological motion, therefore, is of greater importance than his recognition of psychological space and psychological time. It is through that recognition he touches the Whole and becomes a part of the Whole in his own sense of it."

"Would James's* old phrase 'stream of consciousness' mean anything here?" Darby enquired. Betty assented. "Actually we recognize ourselves as distinct from that flow," he continued.

* William James, American psychologist and philosopher, 1842-1910.

"You recognize yourself as an individual station in that stream," Betty amended.

"I recognize myself as distinct from the flow," insisted Darby. "I am close to orthic in that distinctness."

"As you consider the psychological importance of what you call the stream of consciousness, your own awareness will not only become more acute and individualized, but it will also become more consciously a part of the Whole, or the universe, or orthos. Because, you see, it is *that* which stays put. The only change that happens to it is its relation to space and to time. Your own rate of motion, vibration, is *yours*."

"In the phrase, 'my thought'—" began Darby, and stopped short. "Why," he cried in sudden illumination, "thought itself is psychological motion!"

"That was very bright of you," Betty applauded. "That bald statement will do for our purpose now, though it should be much elaborated — the statement that *thought is psychological motion*."

FREQUENCY

WE TOOK up time first, then space, then motion, not as indicative of relative importance, but only for logical convenience. However, in dealing with their essences it will be best, I think to reverse our order of procedure. This was, in a way, Betty's own idea of a point of departure. At our very first meeting she popped in the word frequency, all by itself, without relation to anything else; but her emphasis made a paragraph of it.

"Frequency — frequency!" said she, and let it go at that.

"Frequency of what?" I asked when, days later, she repeated.

"Of consciousness, the one and only reality. It is what controls. Consciousness is in evolution. Therefore it is in various degrees. Each degree has its frequency. That frequency is a — well, I'll have to call it a sort of magnetic energy. It is a vibratory emanation of the vital force; the thing that is; the individual rate."

"Apparently," observed Darby after we had discussed this matter a great many times, but loosely, "we're going to use the word frequency a lot. I'd like to know just what frequency is."

"Frequency," said Betty, "is the essence —"

"Don't say 'of motion,'" interrupted Darby. "You have told us that. And anyway, such a definition is merely restating motion in the terms of one of its characteristics or properties."

"Frequency is the essential characteristic or property of motion," insisted Betty. "I am not talking about *rate* of motion, which is the property or characteristic of motion most familiar to you in the obstructed universe. What I am talking about is that essence of the orthic trilogia which *results* in motion.

"Your individual frequency and your degree of consciousness are related," she continued. "There is, for example, a degree in the evolution of consciousness that we will call treeness; and in manifesting it becomes a tree. Now to that there is a corresponding frequency. And you have an electrical spark, and that is a degree of consciousness, and to it you have a corresponding frequency. There is an actual difference in vibration. Motion *is*. Frequency is an essence of consciousness, an actuality. What you call motion is really only one aspect of frequency."

She refused to consider vibration a synonym.

"Take the simplest thing we can call a frequency. Take a tuning fork. Its prongs move in space at a temporal rate." Darby was groping.

"That is motion, as *you* know motion," said Betty.

"The motion is simply the motion of the fork," continued Darby. "The frequency is the number of times the tine moves in relation to sidereal time. It makes a frequency in the air; a high tone is rapid, a low one is slow. Or take the pendulum of a clock. It is in motion. Now, the essence of the motion is frequency. The pendulum swings back and forth so many times in a given amount of time. The radio wave is no different. Any object, moving back and forth in space at a certain rate of time, equals frequency. Now, from that definition how can we build up the larger conception of frequency?"

"You remember," obliged Betty, "that I told you the

old hooted-at idea of perpetual motion was one of the great glimpses. The entire universe is in perpetual motion. All manifestations are the results of various degrees of frequency. To use your own terms, the rapidity of molecular frequency is one thing; the rapidity of light frequency is another; the rapidity of that frequency that manifests itself as life, as you know it, is another. My body that I have here is very close to pure frequency. It has frequency, true; but it is in orthos."

"The division into time, space, motion, I gather, is only for our understanding. Actually they are only aspects, there is no sharp division between them?" surmised Darby.

"Not in the orthic," agreed Betty.

"Time and space," Darby pointed out, "more or less stand on their own legs: we can conceive of them separately. But when you get to motion and frequency, they won't stand by themselves. You must have time and space or you can't have motion."

"Oh, yes, you can!" asserted Betty. "Because you *are* frequency. Go back to matter as a stress point. Conceive that the stress point of matter is an arrested frequency. The matter can be taken apart into flame, or smoke, or gas — all frequencies. There you have the material concept of frequency in a pluralistic universe.

"But step from what you call matter into what you call life. There you have your essence, the self, the I-Am frequency. You see perpetual motion is a fact in the sense of perpetual frequency."

"You mean to say that a frequency can exist without spatial or temporal —" Darby was incredulous.

"Yes," she interrupted positively, "if consciousness is the one and only reality. It has aspects. It has essences in those aspects, manifested in the obstructed universe as motion, space, time. Your trilogies are inseparable in actuality. That I have told you."

"Frequency means to me motion in time," insisted Darby.

"Frequency means to you a rate of vibration, a setting of particles or things or your body into juxtaposition. But what is yourself?" probed Betty.

"Myself? The entire of my awareness of the outside and inside world," returned Darby.

"That is good. You have defined your awareness by an outside and an inside world. But what is your awareness?"

"I think I'll redefine self as my inward feeling of being as distinct from any feeling of awareness at all," amended Darby.

"That is much better. This feeling of being is cognizant of a physical limitation. You know that Being is housed in a body. You *learned* that; somewhere between birth and early childhood. Now this self that can take cognizance of an inside and an outside world we might define as Being. That Being *is* because a certain frequency has been arrested, and in the arrestment creates a human person with the essence of self that is Being. It is in that frequency that your 'aliveness' of consciousness to all things is."

We let it go at that for the moment, but we did not consider the concept tidied up, for Darby returned to it at the next session.

"Frequency has been defined as the essence of motion," he began. "Part of our difficulty may be that we have accepted that, but we haven't related it up to consciousness. What we are talking about is frequency of consciousness, not of motion. Frequency is the unit of consciousness in motion."

"Consciousness is in motion," agreed Betty.

"And from the viewpoint of frequency, motion is the phenomenon," suggested Darby.

Whereupon Betty threw up her hands and Anne took a try at it.

"Take a seed in the ground," suggested Anne. "Now that seed bursts its shell and a shoot appears. But for that to happen to the seed it has to have the potentiality of grass, or a flower, or a tree, or a weed. Now that potentiality is its frequency."

"That means that frequency and quality are at least closely related," said Darby.

"What is that thing in any seed that bursts the shell?" Anne was not to be diverted from her line of questioning. "You know that there is a stir there. What word would you use to describe that thing-in-itself?"

She was referring to Kant's "ding-an-sich" over which Darby and Stephen had held many a battle royal.

"My answer would be motion," insisted Darby stubbornly.

"But," said Anne, "the motion does not start until after something else has occurred. Something must impel the motion. Frequency is more than a characteristic of motion. Motion *results* from frequency"

"Betty told us that," said Darby.

"She did," agreed Anne, drily.

"What you are postulating is that what you call frequency is a non-physical thing beyond motion — or certainly beyond motion as we know it," he argued. "And you can't use a physical term like frequency to describe a non-physical thing."

"An ye wad be doin' as ye be told," Anne came back tartly, her dialect broader than ever under her bit of impatience, "and strip the word down — *clear* down as Betty asked you — you would not find the term frequency entirely physical."

Then she relented and did the job for us.

"The word frequency," said she, "suggests motion to you over and above any other meaning because of its modern use in physics and especially in connection with electricity. Now, *any* term used to describe the essence of motion must suggest action. But it must do more than that. If you will make an analysis of the word frequency and clothe it with *all* its various connotations you will find — what modern use has discarded — two old meanings of the word which make it fit the present need quite perfectly. The adjective 'frequent' still carries them, though the noun 'frequency' has lost them. These two meanings are 'habitual' and 'persistent.' Habitual and persistent motion gives you sufficient content of frequency as an essence of the orthic trilogia."

"Well!" said Darby.

But before either he or I could begin discussion of just how much this idea of *habitual* and *persistent* action clarified our understanding of orthic motion Betty was back again.

"Impetus," she popped at us. "Remember, Stewt, how I always was bringing back — using — the word 'impetus'?* Well, I recognized what it meant then, but I couldn't explain it to you fully — not without this whole new interlocking concept of orthos and its essences.

* When as a receiving station here she was getting the material for *The Betty Book* and *Across the Unknown*. See both for her original use of the term.

And I couldn't get *that* until I *really* came here! Another way of saying it would be that *frequency is the habitual and persistent impetus of orthic motion.*"

It was my turn to exclaim, "Well!"

"Frequency is the eternal motion that never stops, and of which you are a part," Betty went on swiftly. "It is your bit of quality: it's your I-Am. You are that frequency of consciousness that is a man; oxygen is that frequency of consciousness which is oxygen; a tree is that frequency of consciousness which is a tree.

"It is difficult for you because you *are* the frequency; because the thing that is you is an arrestment of motion. Your duration of motion, your frequency, makes you what you are, just as another arrestment of frequency makes the tree. Frequency is the potentiality of immortal individualism. Everything is in motion. *That is why consciousness and the universe are in evolution.*"

CHAPTER XVII

CONDUCTIVITY

1.

BETTY made her approach to discussion of conductivity as the essence of space through Sir Oliver Lodge's ether of space. Until recently, as the reader knows, that concept has been considered sufficient and satisfactory to cover transmission of the finer vibrations — such as light — through depths of space where our ordinary well-known vehicles, like atmosphere, are lacking. A wave or vibration theory demanded some medium of transmission. The ether was invented by synthesis of all properties of matter necessary for such transmission, and a rejection of all other properties whatsoever. As a synthesis, of course, it is a highly theoretical assumption, that forced acceptance because it seemed to be the only thing that *could* cover the case.

The ether of space is, I think, still acceptable to a large proportion of present day physicists. At any rate it has not suffered any hundred per cent of rejection by the orthodox. But it is seriously questioned; especially by the mathematicians. The iconoclasts have as yet no satisfactory substitute; but they have established their case sufficiently for uneasiness; sufficiently for the creation of an impression that there may be a catch somewhere in this ether business.

The first intimation that our Invisible friends might share the latter view, was merely in the wording of a statement on quite a different subject. This was away back, in the course of one of our very early discussions on time.

"Time in your universe is in relation to your individual consciousness," Betty was saying. There followed considerable give and take wherein Betty tried to get into our heads the handling of psychological time; and was talking of the scientific discoveries that ought to help us to understand.

"There is a gentleman standing here," she said finally. "He thinks he might help."

The "gentleman" promptly obliged.

"Your scientists have accepted an hypothesis called ether as an actuality," said he, and proceeded with an illustrating statement relevant to the subject in hand. But what particularly struck both Darby and me was the caution of the opening phrase: "Your scientists have accepted —" Why the qualification? We fell into discussion of the scientific schism outlined in the opening of this chapter.

2.

"I think," began Betty, "the next subject for discussion is conductivity. You were speaking of the postulation called the ether, and of its present rejection by a certain school of scientists.

"The ether idea, as I understand it, is that in things like light and radio a series of vibrations are set up that travel, and produce another series of vibrations that a receiving end is tuned into.

"The difficulty with the ether postulate is that it is

conceived as a *material,* from the obstructed universe standpoint."

Scientists had to have, she explained, some vehicle of transmission: so they began with the material they knew, and from it stripped away all the qualities which either they did not need for the purpose, or which were actually antagonistic to the purpose. Such as friction and weight, for instance. But they still, as Betty said, kept it material; though they fined-out that material as thin as they possibly could.

"Don't you see," Betty pointed out, "that in thus discarding properties of the obstructed universe they are actually endowing it with the characteristics of my state of being in the unobstructed universe? They are making it as nearly unobstructed as they can!

"It's a great glimpse; but, being endowed with non-obstructive properties by science, it belongs thereby to the unobstructed universe. Consequently it cannot be material in the sense your obstructed universe conceives it. We must find a new name, because if we call it 'ether,' we get into the old wreath-hung terminology.

"This all-pervasive something is a co-existent of consciousness."

Now there, thought we enthusiastically, was in itself a great glimpse! And so simple! But we needed the implications.

3.

"It is perfectly possible for a vibration originating in San Francisco to be registered in New York, and for it to pass through this room without your being aware of it," continued Betty, after a pause. "Consequently you can see that the frequency of that vibration is higher than your awareness-mechanism can register. Now I employ frequencies that are still higher. You have not yet brought into general use a vibratory registration, from a mechanical standpoint, that can pick up my frequency. But it is reasonable that, if there are registerable frequencies beyond your awareness-mechanism — which man's ingenuity has mechanized — there are also frequencies beyond his present mechanization. It is perfectly true that so far it is he who has created — by means of isolation and utilization — the frequencies beyond the human awareness mechanism that he picks up mechanically. But it is also true that if a conductor were not there to carry those frequencies, he could not pick them up."

"It is, then, to a high degree, through the unobstructed universe they are transmitted?" I surmised.

"Exactly," said Betty.

"The difference between the radio wave you employ and the frequency we employ in parallel to it is that ours goes in a straight line: there's no conceivable obstruction to it. If you threw a ball, and there were no obstruction, by *anything* — gravitation, air, resistance, anything — it would go in a straight line. But the frequency of the thrown ball in motion is not high enough to escape these obstructions. So it falls to the ground. Radio, infinitely higher than the ball in frequency, is still not high enough to escape obstruction: therefore it is curved. And your present mechanisms can register it.

"The medium I postulate for conductivity is entirely unobstructed, and is therefore to be distinguished from the old theory of ether, which still has trailing to it a materialistic conception."

Darby summed up the scientific problem.

"The scientist," said he, "accustomed only to the concept of material conductors, but forced to postulate a conductor beyond known material, was obliged to endow his ether with properties beyond his physical knowledge, but still conforming to his materialistic conception of conductivity. Later certain scientists experimented for gravitational drift, with light, but found none. Therefore they discredit ether, and say the wave itself is all there is to it."

"Motion is a co-existent of Being," interpolated Betty. "That co-existence is a fact. But remember always you are conditioned by an obstructed universe."

"Displacement of waves in water is up and down, not forward. Do these higher vibrations, radio waves — of which we are talking — displace this new ether of yours through which they pass?" Darby went on.

"No, they go through it."

"But water is displaced up and down," objected Darby.

That, said Betty, is because water as a medium is an obstruction. The wave is obstructed because its frequency is low.

"Take the vibration of sound," she said. "You can measure on a machine* the up and down movement of the air. But, again, air is an obstruction. Your body frequency is so low that you bump against a tree; but the radio frequency is high enough to go through the tree. The higher the frequency, the less the obstruction."

"And the higher the frequency the less the disturbance of the medium?" Darby carried out the thought. "This 'new ether' of yours: what is that in your unob-

* She is referring to the cathode ray projection on a screen of sound as a line of light.

structed universe, what's the parallel to the purpose of the old ether? What function does that new ether serve in your unobstructed universe?"

For the time being Betty accepted without demur this suggestion, and this terminology, of a "new ether" to substitute for the old. She even used it herself. But as soon as possible she discarded it. It was for her a provisional hypothesis, so to speak, to avoid confusing us.

"It is," she answered Darby's question, "the medium for the conduction of frequency. The idea of ether was a great glimpse. But, just as your physicists thought it should have obstruction, and found out it didn't, so now they find that fact pointing to an unobstructed conductivity. That medium exists. At the same time, in your universe — which it pervades, as it does mine — there is obstruction in the frequencies of lower degrees. You yourselves can get vibrations so high — you have already created them so high — that they cannot be recorded or obstructed. When you *can* make a record of them, they are obstructed.

"We have communication with each other here. We have a parallel of sound. You can't hear us, and the reason is because our sound frequency is *above your* obstruction and hence your recording.

"We have destroyed the old ether — which I insist is a great glimpse. We are now postulating something that pervades the entire universe. It is the universal conductor. It is by means of that conductivity that you get light."

"— and all above the frequencies that can be conducted by matter?" I supplemented.

"Yes. One step further: so far the obstructed universe has not been able to record frequencies high enough to proceed in a straight line, that is, unobstructed frequencies. You will. The whole trend is that way. All lower frequencies are curved, but such things as X-ray, radio, and so forth, are far less variable than, say, the recorded sound of the voice."

4.

"Well, take sound," said Darby. "There's something that is conducted merely through atmosphere. In a vacuum the sound of an alarm clock simply doesn't exist."

"Not for you: but it's there. Your registration of sound is through your bodily senses. *I* could hear your alarm clock in the vacuum," stated Betty.

"Hold on," objected Darby. "Sound is a vibration conveyed by means of waves through the medium of air. Seems to me no ether is necessary; air is enough."

"Only the low vibrations are *recorded* in the atmosphere," Betty made a distinction. "Radio waves pass through the body, but the body does not record them. The atmosphere has a quality of obstruction. It is of the obstructed universe. Above that you cannot breathe, you do not exist. Sound exists, if you could register it."

Your own science, she protested, postulates that vibration, *per se*, continues on out indefinitely — or infinitely. Sound is vibration. On what medium does it continue when it reaches the limits of the atmosphere? A different one?

"Do you conceive that at the limit of the atmosphere the vibrations change cars?" she asked quaintly. "Or did they not start on the same vehicle that is to carry them on out?

"The atmosphere, or any other physical medium, is not the primary conductor of a frequency. If that were so, how, for instance, could the light of the stars, which you know emanates from far beyond your atmosphere, be conducted? *It is an obstruction that brings that frequency into the registration possibility of the obstructed universe.* Without what you called the new ether, no conduction; without the material, the obstruction, no registration by your universe.

"So while the atmosphere does conduct to you the frequencies you can pick up, and while the atmosphere is a necessary medium for your present registration of those frequencies, the sound in the vacuum *is* created. You stop hearing a tuning fork before it stops vibrating."

"Are you saying that, even though the transmission seems to lie in the atmosphere, it is even there conducted by the new ether, and that the phenomenon in the denser medium is a coincidental phenomenon?" Darby wanted to be sure.

"The sound you are making in this room is conducted over the atmosphere just as a telephone conducts over a material thing. But were it not for the all-pervading 'new ether,' the various types of material things like atmosphere could not register as they do. The atmosphere is required because you are still in the obstructed universe. But you have in your universe also the 'new ether,' just as you have in yourselves the beta body. *The 'new ether' is what makes the atmosphere a conductor.*"

5.

Our minds were not quite yet ready to abandon the idea of some material medium. Betty wanted to extend her provisional hypothesis of the "new ether," one step forward.

"It is," she said, "an all pervading absolute. But that," she added, of the latter word, "is *your* terminology, and so is the word 'ether.' However, I want to get into your minds the fact that this 'new ether' of yours is a co-existent of consciousness itself. A constituent," she added, "of the orthic trilogia. It is through it that our parallel laws operate throughout both the obstructed and unobstructed universes."

A day or so later Darby expressed himself as somehow uneasy about this whole 'ether' business; and I agreed that neither was I satisfied. This confession Betty greeted with a crow of delight, as at a symptom of mental convalescence.

The very next day Joan was given the 'essence' idea; and ether went out for keeps. We do not need it, or any other medium of conduction, for the simple reason that the *essence of space is conductivity*. Wherever there is space, then there *must* be conductivity; it is an inherent part of Consciousness, the all-inclusive reality.

6.

We took a long breath when we got this. But we were a little puzzled that it had not been said before. The simple statement would have avoided a lot of brain-fag on our part, and not a few of our interim misconceptions — with which, by the way, I have avoided overburdening this narrative. For instance, at one time — instead of the basic trilogia of receptivity (time), conductivity (space), and frequency (motion), we had one of time-space, 'ether,' and motion.

"This new material rather seriously revises material hitherto received." Darby was perhaps a trifle critical. "How come?"

At the moment he was talking to Stephen who, it will be remembered, came occasionally to help out.

"It was necessary to build up the concept," explained the latter. "If you will go back in the records, you will find that it has been done step by step, founded on your accepted knowledge. For instance, at first it was necessary to permit you to explore the time-space concept in order for you to encompass our thought at all. However, you will admit that it was not entirely satisfactory to you. As far as the ether was concerned, that was a confusion between the communicator and receiving station. The communicator knew perfectly that conductivity is the essence of orthic space, but to get the thought through the station she had to accept the old terminology of physics in the mind she was using. You must admit that we have been able to correct the erroneous statement quickly, and through the receiving station herself. Do not let her, in her conscious mind, be distressed over the understandable and quickly rectified mistake. Besides, it was not wholly a matter of error."

7.

"You tell us that the essence of space is conductivity. Let us see how that functions. Conductivity implies something conducted. What is conducted?" Darby opened a new phase of the subject.

"Various degrees of frequency," replied Betty.

"You must," she postulated, "conceive conductivity as variable. Suppose we take a pipe ten inches across and ten feet long. That would give quite a flow of conductivity. Now attach to the ten-inch pipe another, also ten feet long, but only eight inches across. Keep on doing that, reducing the diameter two inches at a time, until finally we get down to an infinitesimal opening, perhaps a molecular space. But it still has conductivity.

"It is obvious that, in addition to the bulk of any given ten-foot section of the pipe, there must be an *intensive* capacity, a *degree* of capacity. That is, it may have a slow or a rapid intensity, or a condition that is either heightened or lowered in sharpness and efficiency; for it is quite possible that through the smaller bulk of a given section there might be a more potent flow than through the larger bulk of another, according to what degree of frequency is conducted. For instance, in your physical world the flow of water through a ten-inch conductor, or pipe, would not have as potent a result as a flow of electricity through a two-inch conductor, or cable. Therefore you can see that conductivity, as such, *per se*, is variable. Conductivity itself is in degrees. You must not forget the basic concept. All consciousness is in evolution, hence in degrees. So, therefore, must be all its component parts — all its essences.

"I am hunting for a simple analogy. Suppose we take a road, any road. In your world it is a conductor. It is a space, and it always runs between points. It has location. The road is a direction. It constitutes a beaten path in your operations. Over this road people walk, ride on horses or bicycles, in slow-moving trucks, in fast-moving automobiles. In addition to that, this road often gives direction for a varied number of manifestations of motion, each of itself an entity, each producing a result, and each result different.

"The road, even when there is no visible motion on it and it is blank in the landscape, is still in and of itself a road. *It possesses the potentiality of permitting things to pass over it.*

"The purpose of the road is for easy travel and for the concentration of motion. Rather than going out on the sides, people go on the road. Now, this road has more than one lane of traffic; and since it has telephone wires and water mains, it has various types of traffic. One of the characteristics of the road is that traffic goes both ways. This also is an essential characteristic of the essence of space; you go backward and you go forward. Here again, in your own living, you have a manifestation of the malleability and variability of conductivity. It is true that it is not the road itself that removes back and forward, but it is its characteristic that anything that comes into juxtaposition with it *can* move back or forward — or stand still. The fundamental potentiality of the road is conductivity. If nothing moves on it, the potential is not used. But it is there.

"Conductivity is the essence of Space."

Wherever is Space, there, by the nature of its essence, is Conductivity.

CHAPTER XVIII

RECEPTIVITY

THE BARE statement—that the essence of time is receptivity — conveyed little or nothing to us. The explanation of mere meaning was much simpler than of the other essences. The extensions in implication were tremendous. To tell the truth, we did not follow them far. That may be for the future. Betty had a quip she used when we showed signs of getting off the reservation.

"Sufficient unto the day is the wisdom thereof," she paraphrased.

The first lead was given by Joan, speaking in her own person. Betty was "showing" her things, and she was reporting back. She did this conscientiously, but apparently without much comprehension.

"Motion," she told us the results of what she was shown, "has to have space to go around in. It is possible for motion and space to have juxtaposition, but, if not registered in time, the result is not an actuality. I don't get that.—If it doesn't get registered in time, it doesn't get itself born. Everything has to get born, all consciousness, to get quantitative development. It makes no difference whether it's an electric spark, or a baby, or a tree, or a mouse — everything has to be born."

The material world, both Betty and Stephen agreed, would probably give us the best hint.

"The easiest example is matter," observed the latter. "Let us reduce matter, *per se* to, say, gold. To you the gold is a form attribute of that degree of consciousness representing gold-ness. It is, to your sense-perceptions, visual. It is also tactile. You can feel it. You can measure the weight and thickness of a piece of it. You can melt it down and transform it into articles for your use. In other words, on your plane, it is quantitatively malleable and subject to your will. But the quality of gold-ness is always there.

"Now, whatever you do with the gold — whether you make it into a coin or a bit of jewelry — it remains objective to you. Your awareness-mechanism is aware of it. It is received in time, because it is in time that it, and its relationship to you, occurs. Your awareness of it from beginning to end is a thing of duration, exactly as would be your use of an electric current or a radio wave. As such it is observed, operated and established in your individual consciousness."

"You have in physics," Betty took up the exposition, "a law known as the indestructibility of matter. This covers energy. As to the indestructibility of matter and energy, you have the law pretty well understood. You can reduce your matter into various compounds; or strip it down to its elements; or you can bring two chemicals together and dissolve them into gas. But your scientist has learned that nothing is lost in connection with the element with which he works.

"All these things, all matter, all events, all thought, all ideas are received in *time*. *It is because of the receptivity of time that you have the law of indestructibility*."

"Matter that you see is a good symbol." She started to adopt Stephen's approach several days later, but switched quietly to one of her own which carried us straight to a broader viewpoint. "Man is the highest form of consciousness manifested in your universe," she began again. "He has the creative impulse, just as consciousness has the impulse to born things for the purpose of evolution. He makes things — whether a thought, or a cathedral, or a method, such as the way to use a radio wave — and he puts them into time. They are received in time. They stay in the obstructed universe, and other entities of consciousness use them and profit. Then man comes over here. The whole aspect of those things changes when he is here. They are no longer obstructions to him, though he did create that obstruction. Consciousness, *per se*, itself, the whole of consciousness, by its juxtaposition does the same kind of creation. I'm going to leave that now for you to think about."

"Time *is*, with us," she continued later, "just as consciousness is; space is; motion is. The trilogia is ever present with us — what we operate in. But it is in time that all the three-dimensional things of the obstructed universe are held and become realities. It is in time, too, that they exist, rather than in space and motion. They do have those essences, but they *really* exist in time."

"Time" — this was Anne taking a shot at it — "could be called passive. Motion and space are more active. Time does not create. Motion-frequency and space-conductivity — the balance of motion and space — they are the creative two of the trilogy. Yet they could not focus were it not for the actuality and the reception of time."

We were getting a pretty good idea of what was meant. Nevertheless Betty went back to her law of indestructibility.

"You have a saying that 'thoughts are things.' They are, in this way: they are received in time, and so are indestructible. You are having a bad dose of that in the world right now — retarding thought — and it's pretty much indestructible, and you've got to overcome it. If you ever think a thought or say a word, it is in time, and you cannot take it out. That law of indestructibility of matter goes clear through.

"You people haven't made much of my statement that the indestructibility law is possible because of the essence of time, which is receptivity," she complained, "but your physicists are going to!"

"Well, all right," agreed Darby. "Granted that things are received in time, it seems to me that things are also received in space. The physical world is 'received' in space; it exists — for us at least — in space. Tell us what is *not* received in space. How much do we reserve receptivity for time?"

"I suppose one answer would be that psychological frequency is not received in space. Your thought is not received in space, but it is in time. We have told you over and over that thoughts are things —"

"— and over, and over, and over, and over," we gave her our usual chorus.

"— and over." Betty was undisturbed. "There are psychological influences received in time and not in space. Ideas. Theories. As I said, you're getting quite a dose of that right now. Take history. The facts and conditions resulting from 'wars and rumors of wars' — any happening — remain in time, though the acts as incidents have vanished from space. What is your present? A condition created by the happenings — and thought being a thing, it, too, is a happening — received in time in the past. And on top of this past you, in your present, are conditioning the future. All that you think and do is received and remains in time, though your physical bodies and acts vanish from space. Research, invention, material catastrophes, like earthquakes uncontrollable by your free-will, or the beneficence of a season producing big harvests — all are received in space as incidents that pass. It is in time that they remain — to condition and influence your present and the present of all coming generations.

"Receptivity is the essence of Time."

CHAPTER XIX

ANNE SUMS UP

WE HAD now, apparently, surrounded Betty's basic concepts. And this gave her, and Anne, and the others working with them in the background, enormous satisfaction. Indeed, they pulled off a sort of jubilation, and told us we should "keep the feast of the Fourteenth of October as the birth with you of the *reality* of immortality."

"I will be talking to you a bit," said Anne.

"In the first place, consciousness is the one and only reality in both universes. In my universe and yours there is consciousness possessed of awareness-mechanism. With you it is entities, with form attributes. With me it is entities, with form attributes. You live in your world, you work with your world, you conceive your world. I live in orthos, I have to do with orthos, I conceive orthos. Orthos is only a word: world is only a word. There is but one universe.

"You have in your world what you term sidereal time, sidereal space, sidereal motion. These constitute the co-existent trilogy of your world. All that you have, has to do with them. You operate with them. Each has its own essence — motion, frequency; space, conductivity; time, receptivity. They are in degrees, and are therefore variously manifested. But they are in your world.

"Furthermore, they are in your world as obstructions. The world is an obstructed state. That is what makes it the world.

"In orthos we have orthic motion, orthic space, orthic

time. We operate in them. Consciousness operates in them, in our state, precisely as consciousness operates in your state. The only difference is that you operate in degree-manifestations that constitute obstructions, and we in degree-manifestation which overcomes your obstructions. Your world is our world. Your laws are our laws. The only difference is that our individual development, of our consciousness as a whole, is orthic.

"In other words, you exist in a world and we exist in orthos. You have the same degree-manifestations, after a fashion, in your world. The awareness-mechanism of the bug is to your awareness-mechanism as yours is to mine.

"Do not try to make the conceptions difficult. They are very simple. *They are only extensions of your own acceptances.*

"Now, you well know that there are about you things of which you have no sense perception; indeed, of which you are in no way aware. Of many of them you will be in time aware; or those who come after you. For, just as you are reaching after the awareness-mechanism that is beyond your sense perceptions — by invention and research — so are we reaching down with invention and research.

"Postulate orthos merely as a convenience in terminology. Orthic motion, orthic space, orthic time, are all contents of each individual consciousness as they are of the whole of Consciousness. If you will examine your own bit of individual consciousness, you will find this true. It is *so*, through the great trilogia, that you gather to the real You all that you take in.

"The vital difference between the world in which you exist and the orthos in which I exist is your conception of matter. This is true, because matter is always an obstruction to you, though degrees obtain in this case too. Some are not so great an obstruction as others: there are solids, liquids, gases."

Anne ended abruptly. She did not proceed, as one might have expected, to discuss what she had called our "vital difference" — matter.

"Well," said I to Betty finally, "you have your three central concepts. What are you going to do with them?"

"It is the meeting of the three that creates the objective in your universe," said Betty. "I think we should find out how that is."

PART III

CHAPTER XX

MATTER – ARRESTMENT

1.

WE HAVE, then, Consciousness, and in it three basic aspects — Receptivity, or Time; Conductivity, or Space; and Frequency, or Motion. These are the co-existents of Being.

"They," said Betty, "are the actualities we live with, work with; as do you. They are just as necessary to our operations as to yours. You can't do anything without time, space and motion; nor can we. Consciousness controls your fundamental trilogy — time, space and motion — just as consciousness controls the essences of our trilogia — receptivity, conductivity, and frequency. We here, because we are free-willed I-Am entities of consciousness, control — no, let us be more accurately correct and say *manipulate* — our trilogia. You there also *manipulate* your trilogy, but not as much — not to the same extent — as we do. However, the three great co-existents of consciousness are constantly, enduringly, uninterruptedly with me precisely as they are, and as you know they are, with you.

"The three," said Betty, "are co-existents in their own right. And the orthic trilogia of them is a co-existent of consciousness. The term 'co-existent,' it will be remembered, was defined as an all-enduring and inclusive aspect.

"Consciousness," she summed up, "is the one and only reality. The great trilogia is orthic time, space and motion. This trilogia is the co-existent — or constitutes the three co-existents — of consciousness. All are observable and operate in the obstructed universe, and all three are co-existents of your obstructed universe. All the familiar things, occurrences, beings and happenings of your obstructed universe are subject to the great trilogy co-existent of consciousness; time, space, motion. That is all there is. Now discuss it."

"I want to avoid the danger of setting out these three co-existents as actual *entities*," said Darby. "And also of setting them out as mere *attributes*, in the heretofore use of that word. It helps me to free them of these conceptions by considering length, breadth and thickness — in analogy only. By them I mean nothing separate from the object under observation. Hence I mean no entity, *per se*. Neither a mere property — attribute in that sense — of the object. I mean a mental conception I have of the *aspect* of things only. Cannot we conceive of length, etc., as *abstracted*, as it were, from the object? So, too, with consciousness; in one aspect, we conceive it as spatial; and in still another aspect as receptive and in another as movable. The co-existents comprise an *aspect* of things, rather than an entity."

"Go back to my definition of a co-existent," advised Betty, with vast irony. "Didn't I *say* aspect? 'Co-existent, an all-enduring and inclusive aspect,' " she quoted herself.

"By Jove!" Darby was both astonished and dashed. "You did say aspect, didn't you!"

"The three are co-existents of consciousness, but only co-existents," continued Betty. "You see, *consciousness* is the reality. It is with you: it is with me: it is. It is the power, the impetus, the thing that is, the Being. The co-existents of consciousness are what consciousness *operates* in. Consciousness is in motion; all the time. They — the trilogy — are not attributes; but various juxtapositions of them make various kinds of attributes. Now, in the light of this talk, could you define matter for me?"

We tried various definitions of matter, but none of them proved to be "in the light of this talk."

"Taking into account what your physicists have discovered and are postulating," said Betty, "would not matter be defined as a trilogical length, breadth and thickness of orthic motion?"

We agreed that it might; but added that she'd better explain what it meant.

"But, how does the physicist define matter? As charges of force in motion. Now read my definition of matter. The physicist does not understand yet, quite, the actuality of his so-called force in motion. It is orthic motion. Matter is the form attribute, in the obstructed universe, of orthic motion."

Well, anyway, we agreed, time, space and motion are always with us, and we have to have all three; and matter is somehow an attribute of orthic motion. And orthic motion is really frequency. So matter is really a product of frequency. That's all right; our own physicists tell us that.

2.

But before we go on to Betty's exposition of Matter there are three terms properly belonging to this portion of her "divulgence" which should be called to the reader's attention and defined for the sake of clarity.*

They are:

Arrestment: An incidence of frequency, conductivity

* See Glossary.

and receptivity that results in individualization in the obstructed universe.

Juxtaposition: The manner in which frequency variably collides with conductivity and receptivity to result in an arrestment producing manifestation.

Intraposition: As juxtaposition is the manner of arrestment, so intraposition is the status of relationship that obtains so long as that arrestment holds.

"I wish," said Betty, "that you could talk this out with some one of the bright youngsters at any of the electric research laboratories. It would mean something to him when I said that the radio beams, waves, electricity, light, all of which you are beginning to handle, are degree manifestations of only one reality; and that the highest manifestation of that reality, of which you are actually aware, is consciousness.

"As to matter in the *unobstructed* universe, it is a question of frequency. Matter — and by matter in your world I mean obstructions — in the obstructed universe is also a question of frequency. This is all very difficult even for me to understand. Individuals here, who in the obstructed universe made a special study of physics, tell me that your matter, like our matter, is a question of frequency."

All right, we agreed to that.

"Matter, and force and all of the things you handle in your chemical and physical world are the result of the juxtaposition in orthos of the three co-existents," stated Betty. "Matter, the form attribute of consciousness, is a frequency of orthic motion; conducted in orthic space; and received in orthic time. For earth perception, registration results as the consequence of obstruction."

"It always finds expression in one of these co-existents?" we asked.

"In all of them," amended Betty. "They interlock. Between the essences of the trilogia there is always a ratio of interdependence. Fix this fact of interdependence in your minds. When you take your obstructed universe and strip it down to the scientific, in so far as your material trilogies are concerned, and metaphysically, in so far as your psychological trilogies are concerned, you will find that everything is based on the great co-existent trilogia — orthic time, orthic space, orthic motion.

"Now the trilogy is the same with us as with you. It is motion, space, and time. With us it exists in orthos as frequency, conductivity and receptivity, and does not constitute an obstruction. With you it exists as an obstruction. It is this obstruction that you see, that you use. You yourselves are obstructions.

"Now it seems to me that it would be a good thing if we took some of these intrapositions in orthos and analyzed them. Suppose we take electricity, or water, or gas, or anything."

"I don't quite see yet what you are driving at," said I, "but let's take something simple — like water."

"All right," she agreed. "Water is one of your trilogies. It is a solid, fluid, gas trilogy. Now there is one common aspect, or one common terminology, we have to accept in connection with the three essences of the three co-existents in any discussion of matter; and that is frequency. And it is variable. In a chemical laboratory, if you combine more of one acid with less of another acid, you get one thing. But if you use less of the one and more of the second, you get another thing. The manifestation that results in water — H_2O is your symbol — operates the same way.

"It will be a long time before science has gone far

enough in the measurement of the frequency of motion and the conductivity of space to be able to segregate the essence of each to the point where they can tell how much of frequency and how much of conductivity results in the one case in water, and in another, earth, and in another, air. But you see that they are degree-manifestations of the same thing, only with different frequencies."

Darby caught here a possible point of confusion.

"You mention, or at least imply, a frequency not only of motion, but of space," said he. "You said before that frequency is the essence of motion. Was I wrong in thinking frequency the exclusive property of motion?"

"Frequency *is* the essence of motion," replied Betty, "conductivity of space; receptivity of time. But matter, as you know it — in any form — is a degree-manifestation, in time, of some *balance* between frequency and conductivity. It is no more split than is consciousness."

"Let's get this quite clear," said I. "Would you say that for the functioning of these essences they must be intermingled proportionately?"

"The orthic trilogia in the obstructed universe has to interoperate in its essences."

"And," I continued my surmise, "the nature of the functioning is dependent on the ratio of each that is used in the interoperation?"

"Yes. If frequency comes into juxtaposition with conductivity at one point, you get one thing; if at another point, you get another thing."

"Here's a frequency that is electrical, a volt," Darby contributed. "If it collides with a copper wire, a good conductor, you get a certain amperage of current. If with dry wood, a poor conductor, you get appreciably nothing."

"Illustrating Betty's last statement," said I, "if you send

your electricity through a copper wire, you run a motor. If you send identically the same current through an iron wire, you get radiant heat."

"Good!" she cried "The thing we've been trying to say is that the orthic trilogia is all you have to operate with; it's all there is. Certain juxtapositions of these essences produce different types of energy, force, matter, and so forth. That is the way the essences function."

3.

We had the subject pretty clearly, as far as our own obstructed universe is concerned. How about her state of being? Did the same principles obtain there?

"In this universe of ours," Darby worded this question, "we never have frequency of motion except in time and space. Now, in your universe is it otherwise? Is there frequency of orthic motion without its being in orthic time or orthic space?"

"No. You see, there is only one law," replied Betty. "It is the meeting of these three in your universe that creates the objective. The obstructed universe is for the purpose of birth, of the individualization of consciousness. All matter is born in your universe. Nothing is lost. Individuality is not lost; though in its lower forms matter can be burned, turned into gas, or what have you. Yet it is all kept. It is the highest form, the soul, that goes on undivided. But we have the same universe.

"Carry back into orthos the concepts from their intrapositions in your world. You must see that some place between that intraposition and orthos there is a point at which your awareness-mechanism stops registering them.

That point is variable with different people, and it is controlled for the human consciousness by the senses. You know how the senses vary in individuals — artists seeing color and form, musicians hearing sound. That can be shown mechanically, but we have no physical laboratory, so all we can do is to state the law to you. But after we have done that, it can be placed in the knowledge of men by means of a physical and chemical laboratory; and then science can extend the law, follow it through."

"Then you have 'matter' — or at least what corresponds to matter?" I asked.

Decidedly, Betty assured us; but added that she was, in the present discussion, more or less restricting the term to physical matter.

"Our matter is the essence of form, which is an accompanying attribute of consciousness individualized. Just as I am now the essence of my previous individuality. *Esse* — to be — essence. Our matter is not an obstruction to us.

"You have accepted the beta body.* I had it when I was visible to you. Then when the I-myself left my physical, or alpha, body, it was the form attribute of my consciousness — my beta — that went on with me. That form attribute exists in the unobstructed universe.

"Your scientists have accepted the law of the indestructibility of matter; but I say to you that this law is only a corollary of the indestructibility of consciousness. You have long known that all consciousness has form. It is a fact. Now, matter in the unobstructed universe is the essence of a form attribute. It is not broken up, as on your side. Primary entities are indivisible. Matter, as you know it, is not a primary entity: it is made up of primary en-

---

* See Glossary.

tities. My physical body was made up of a lot of little cells. My beta body is single, atomic.* All matter is atomic here, and of course it has form."

"Does such matter furnish points in space, as does ours?" asked Darby.

"Points in space; but not stress points, not arrestments.

"My awareness-mechanism registers and verifies an unlimited concept, which is my matter. Your awareness-mechanism registers and verifies a limited concept, which is your matter. Your matter, therefore, being limited, is an obstruction. Mine, being unlimited, is not an obstruction."

It is only, she said, a difference in rates of frequency. We have that relativity in our own universe, even before we escape into unobstruction.

"For instance, you know perfectly that there are vibrations so rapid that none of your senses can segregate them, and yet they remain obstructions. An example: you could cause a flywheel to be turned so fast that you could not see it, but if you put your hand against it the hand would be cut off. In other words, the obstruction is still there. This is true also in your simple understanding of an electric current. You can find plenty more such examples of the relativity of frequency. Moreover here we have matter which, because of our ratio of time and space to frequency, is not to us an obstruction; any more than, from a solid standpoint, gas — which you utilize — is an obstruction to you. Nevertheless you *do* use gas. Now, by this I do not mean that our matter is formless. All consciousness possesses the attribute of form, irrespective of

---

* Betty's use of the word is not scientific, but follows Webster —"not cut. indivisible."

what its frequency is in ratio to either the obstructed or the unobstructed universe."

She went into that aspect more fully later.

4.

"So," said Betty, "*the co-existent of consciousness that you call motion,* I call frequency. Individualism, in the material world, is caused by an arrestment of frequency. Thus all manifestation that is man has a common frequency. You do not raise or lower your own frequency. The manifestation that is a tree is the arrestment somewhere else along the line of frequency. The arrestment is what makes individuality."

"I don't like the word 'arrest.'" I interpolated, "and I don't believe you mean arrest. That means 'stop short.' If a frequency is to remain a frequency, it's got to wriggle a little."

"By arrestment I do not mean stoppage," said she. "The potentiality of evolution is still in the arrested frequency. It is held in suspension."

"It functions, but it functions in proportion, or at the rate of its suspension," suggested Darby.

But she clung to the word, possibly because she could find no other; with, however, the qualification to keep in mind. "Call arrestment a suspension of potentiality, if that pleases you better,"* she conceded.

Later, however, she gave us the idea of "arrestment" as "a sudden interruption in progress," which is the definition of the verb "to check," at the same time indicating that it is in the sense of this synonym of the verb "arrest" that she used the noun "arrestment."

* See Glossary.

"Aside from frequency," she resumed her argument, "take the supposition that matter is a rate of vibration. As there is only one reality, and since matter is one thing and you another, you and matter must have different rates of vibration. The essence of both matter and you is consciousness. The differentiation between you and matter is the rate of vibration, or frequency.

"My beta body is of my frequency. My stepping up process, as far as I am concerned at the moment, is the release of my beta from the lower frequency of my human body. The only reason you cannot exist and operate in the *entire* universe, as I do — for I operate in our universe as well as in mine — is because you are not able to step up your frequency."

"Matter, you tell us, is an arrestment of frequency," interposed Darby, "that is, an incidence of motion, space and time. So is consciousness of man. There must be some difference between these two arrestments."

"Assuredly. There is a ratio difference. It's a mathematical progression. Both are manifestations of consciousness. I don't want to use the phrase 'rapidity of vibration'; that gives a false picture. But man is a higher frequency than the matter he observes. He is closer to the orthic than the matter he observes. In this frequency band, that is conducted through space and registered in time, are innumerable very high frequencies that man is trying to observe. Not so high as his own frequency, but very close to his own."

5.

"Betty has encouraged two viewpoints," observed Darby reflectively. "The first is that the difference between her time, space and motion and ours is a difference of concept, a difference of aspect; and the second is that more or less she lives in an actual space, time and motion."

"Both are true," Betty assured him. She paused. "Now I want to do this carefully. We will take first the difference between my time, space and motion and yours, as to our individual concepts of them. It is difficult because you deal with the material *result* of receptivity, conductivity and frequency, and I deal with the actuality, the essence, the *real* receptivity, conductivity and frequency. Now there is no less receptivity, conductivity and frequency in your time, space and motion than in mine. But you deal with an arrestment of it, which is the obstruction that makes your obstructed universe, and I deal with the actuality."

"That is to say, with the unarrested actuality?" asked Darby.

"Yes."

"The fact that I am an arrested —" began Darby.

Betty chortled over this phrasing.

"Well, *I* have had no ticket!" she chuckled.

"The fact that I am an arrested frequency —" repeated Darby, determined not to be put upon.

"As long as you're not frequently arrested," prodded Betty.

"The sentence of the judge," Darby yielded to the conceit, "is a certain concept as to time, space and motion. Now you, as yet, are an unarrested frequency."

"I told you I had no ticket — as yet." Betty was unsubdued.

"So actually you roam the world quite free of my misconceptions." Darby was not to be deflected. "It occurs to me that time, space and motion are all concepts of relationship. Now, *if* our universe were *not* one of pluralistic monism,* there would be no need for time, space and motion. If there were just consciousness, and it were monistic only, and not in evolution, then there would be no time, space and motion. The point I'm trying to make is that time, space and motion are concepts of relationship between the individual parts of the whole."

"And something else. Fill it in," urged Betty.

"Can't. Think tank empty," confessed Darby.

"They are really the relationships between the orthic and the obstructed aspects of consciousness."

"Come again; don't get it!" cried we.

"How can I make you understand? In the obstructed universe all of the individualistic particles of consciousness that are manifested arrive with a set quality. This quality, as you know, is of varying potentiality with respect to each. You also know — now — that each unit of this varying potentiality is itself, in a generic sense, an arrested frequency. In the material world this arrested frequency, that is manifested either as organic or inorganic matter, has the potentiality of gathering what we call quantity.

"In terms of science, quantity means physical or material growth. In the spiritual sense it is a growth of character, say. The thing to keep in mind is that each of these individualities or entities of which you are cognizant is an arrested frequency, the essence of motion.

"Now I said to you that you, the observer, are cognizant of these arrested differences as entities. How come? Only because you have — yourself being an arrested frequency — established, by your own consciousness, the

* See Glossary.

measuring stick of the great trilogy on earth. It is *you* who have made a mile, created a clock, observed the varying positions of the stars.

"It is your knowledge and use of time, space and motion that links together the two universes into one!"

6.

"About this arresting of frequencies: what does the arresting?" I asked.

"The juxtaposition of different degrees of frequency in space and time," Betty replied. "You could perhaps illustrate it by algebra. Z plus Y plus Z equals a stone. X plus 2Y plus Z equals a weed. 2X plus Y plus Z equals a flower. And so on. X is a frequency; Y is conductivity; Z is receptivity."

"That describes a process, but does not say what does the arresting," I objected.

That was rather stupid of me, I now see. She had just said that juxtaposition had to do with it. But the question at least gave her material to develop the subject further.

"Here is a line coming down on a slant this way: call it receptivity," said she. "Here's a line coming down on a slant *this* way: call that conductivity. And here's a line slanting in still another way: we'll call that frequency. Now all three are in evolution. They are of consciousness, and consciousness is in evolution. If the lines of frequency and conductivity strike receptivity together in one place, one manifestation occurs. If you move the angle they make so it strikes in even the slightest deviation from the first angle, then you get another manifestation. But always all three must come together at a single point. They are variable, malleable and in evolution."

"Then would you say that frequencies coming into time and space are arrested by the very nature of that situation?" I enquired.

"No. It occurs because there is a stress point created by the juxtaposition of the three. Varying angles of incidence; various stress points."

"Then could you say that when the three get together it is in their nature to create a stress point?" I carried my suggestion a step further.

"Take an icicle." This was Darby. "It is none the less water with all its potentialities. Yet it is arrested. What caused that?"

"Being arrested means that definite, concrete, measurable form is being given. In the obstructed universe. That is the borning place. It is only arrested for a certain period. If heat comes to your icicle it will return to water, then to vapor."

"What happens to receptivity when an icicle is formed?" asked Darby. "I should say it is considerably slowed down."

"As is also conductivity and frequency," added Betty. "That is why you have your icicle. Your orthic trilogia comes into arrested juxtaposition. Which is what I was saying."

"Well," said Darby, "I must say your statement about conduction of sound was a good one! * I want to point out that it is immensely helped by the arrestment concept.

* "The atmosphere, or any other physical medium, is not the primary conductor of frequency. It is an obstruction that brings frequency into the registration possibility of the limited universe."

"Now there's another thought that occurs to me. What is conducted: frequency. What is received: frequency. When frequency is conducted and received, we observe motion. Certainly that constitutes a unified field. A unified field is what Einstein and all those fellows are after."

CHAPTER XXI

PARALLELISM OF LAW

So YOU see — was Betty's thought — the processes and laws and methods of creation work the same for both the obstructed and the unobstructed universe. This, of course, is only to be expected; and is really what we were talking about when we discussed parallel laws, and the like.

She carried us on a step further. She — and those with her in her state of being — live, not in one aspect only of the universe, but in the entire universe. It must follow logically, then, that she must be in our obstructed universe as well as in her own unobstructed aspect. Such, she assured us, was the case.

"Naturally!" said Betty. "Once you accept the un-limited action of the co-existent trilogia, you tear down completely any real wall between an obstructed and an unobstructed universe. Founding his researches on this formula, the scientist can go forward to prove, not only that supposed limited laws are in reality unlimited, but to discover many new laws and project their operation and beneficence into your limited field.

"One of the most important things, as I told you, is the parallelism of our laws. There is only one set of laws; but they are conditioned in two ways. Now, just to see how well you are getting this, I'll ask questions. The laws are conditioned in two ways. How? For what?"

"As to the material they work on, and the intention," I suggested.

"That's it. The material is the obstructed aspect; the intention is the unobstructed aspect."

Stephen, on one of his rare visits, made an epitomization that led up to this same topic. He covered much previous ground, but I include it all here, as refreshment of the subject.

"Consciousness is the reality," he began. "It is in degrees. It pervades the entire universe. Because it pervades the entire universe it has both quantitative and qualitative development. Evolution is a fact. Consciousness is in evolution. The highest expression of consciousness metaphysically is man.

"Now the manifestations of consciousness in the universe are in degrees because the whole of consciousness is in evolution. The degrees are the evolutional advances of consciousness. Consciousness being in evolution, and consequently in degrees, is individualistic. The individual manifestation, no matter what the degree, is an evolutional expression of consciousness. The entire universe is in degrees of expressed consciousness. What is an obstruction for one degree of consciousness may not be an obstruction for another degree. This law proceeds beyond my present knowledge.

"What you call earth, material matter, the obstructed universe, exists for the individualization of various degrees of consciousness. In a word: birth.

"Now, we gave you a new term — orthos, which is the Greek word for true. The term orthos simply means the true, co-existent characteristics of the reality, consciousness. We have told you that there is an orthic trilogia; in other words, three characteristics of consciousness that always obtain. These three are orthic time, orthic space, and orthic motion. They are — whether you realize it or not — the three greatest familiars of your obstructed universe; and also of the entire universe.

"We have chosen the word 'essence' as a term in this

new exposition, to be used in its basic meaning. The essence of orthic time is receptivity; the essence of sidereal time is receptivity. The essence of orthic space is conductivity; the essence of sidereal space is conductivity. The essence of orthic motion is frequency; the essence of sidereal motion is frequency.

"The new thought that has been growing in your minds is the fact that the three essences of the orthic trilogia — receptivity, conductivity and frequency — have been manifested in the obstructed universe as time, space and motion, precisely as consciousness itself has manifested in the obstructed universe as man, energy or force, and organic and inorganic matter. Or, in reality, life and matter.

"Every manifestation of consciousness operates in the trilogia essences. Your laws, which before were termed parallels, are in reality an extension to the obstructed universe from the unobstructed universe of the same law. However, there are many laws operating in the entire universe not yet discovered by individualistic consciousness in the obstructed universe. There is a whole field yet to be developed."

The disconcerting conclusion we drew from these and similar discussions was that there is no such thing as an obstructed universe — except for us! And when Betty says she lives in our universe as well as her own, she is just being polite. She "lives in the entire universe"; she told us that often enough. We live in it too, after a fashion, much as a blind and deaf man might live in our world. We are obstructed because we are ourselves obstructions, as one might say, so long as we are here on earth.

"But," insisted Betty, "this unobstructed universe is

part of *both* of us. The difference between your existence and my existence is that what is an obstruction to you is not an obstruction to me; and that you could not, in your present state, eliminate the obstruction."

All right: we agreed we would admit all that. Nevertheless, here we were, considerably obstructed; and after all we were the ones she was trying to make understand; and it is a condition, not a theory, that confronts us. Some time before, we reminded her, she had expressed the purpose, among others, of getting to us the actual interfusion of her state of being and ours. Perhaps we could best get at that by knowing more about her present state of being.

CHAPTER XXII

INTENT, EVENT AND THE EGG WOMAN

1.

WE ENJOYED considerable idle-curiosity give-and-take from time to time.

"Do you play games over there?" I asked, half jokingly. "Or is your work so much like play that you don't need games?"

"Of course we play games! We're human!" said Betty.

"What kind of games?" I was skeptical. "Trying to see who can hurl the best frequency?"

Betty refused to joke. She considered.

"Well, not unlike your games — in principle. We tackle something just a little too big for us."

That sort of thing was both interesting and amusing to us. We did not want to press details, but there were certain things having to do with fundamentals of Betty's present state of being that we desired mightily to explore further. How does she handle her time and space, for instance? We had already gathered that, to her, both were highly malleable: and we had been given certain analogies, as has been set forth in Part II. How completely could she escape from that trilogy of time, space and motion by which we are constrained?

She could not escape completely at all, said she.

"Neither motion nor space could impinge on your awareness-mechanism save in ratio to time. The same thing is true of me. The potentiality of all of these three is in consciousness. All I can tell you is that they operate in the two worlds," she answered. "You must keep clearly in mind the difference: that the obstructed universe has a limited frequency, and that the unobstructed universe has an unlimited frequency. But it is the same frequency. It operates in the same way. You have a frequency that permits your senses to be aware of the entire universe, up to a certain point. That point varies with the individual. Our frequency in the unobstructed universe is the frequency beyond the highest point reached by that variation.

"Let us take time in your own universe. Examine the various conceptions of time held by individuals in your own universe. What is time to a dog, to a child, to you? It is different to each. Time, in your obstructed universe, is in degrees. The nearest that you can now conceive of our orthic time, space and motion is your psychological time, space and motion. They are obstructed only by your degree of conception."

Her "degree of conception," she implied, is higher than ours; hence her psychological command is greater. This thought was at first a trifle obscure, though it afforded a glimpse.

"You manipulate time, space and motion — after a fashion — in your obstructed universe," she pointed out. "So why should not conductivity, receptivity and frequency be subject to manipulation?

"Our method of contracting* time is our individual attitude toward it. What may be a long time to another in my degree, may be a short time to me, and vice versa.

* And expanding?

We, because we *want* a given period to be long or short, make it so. Various persons in your degree of consciousness approach this power."

That gave us another idea, or rather another glimpse, but the subject was still not at all clear.

"The trouble is that you are *measuring* time," said Betty. "You get up in the morning. You have a sidereal day before you. For some reason you wish it were the end of the day. You don't want to endure the hours. In order to pass them quickly you put into them content of interest. You have to cover the sidereal measurement of the day. Twelve hours have to be filled — a duration. Our time is not divided in that fashion. But we can extend it in that fashion! I can live here, hour by hour, with you. Or if I want to leave you and go home and come back to the sidereal time I left, I can do that. You can't. You have only psychological control of time, that's all.

"You have developed in your world a greater control of space, mechanically, than you have of time. We have here a control of time comparable to that control you are developing of space. I realize that your control of space is only a time measure, but it is not the *time* of which you get final mechanical mastery; its the space. Our mechanics are yours — frequency.

"The best thing I can do to make you understand our apprehension of time is to liken it to a map. It is there. We encompass it. Time, whose essence is receptivity, is experience. It is all the empirical knowledge laid out for us to use. That does not mean that it is static. The future is there too, and if we have the impulse to pick out of it some particular potential, we can do so. The future is to us much as the past is to you. You can go back in history or emotion or·research or memory, and pick out any bit of empirical knowledge that you think will'serve you.

"Now, in addition to this aspect of time as a measure, you use time as a duration. So do we. But because we have the psychological control of the map -- we can see all over it -- we can pick out what we want, just as you can go *back* over it and pick out what you want. We can control the duration of it. Without your knowledge, you do the same, to some extent. You do it psychologically. One of the reasons why it is possible for me to be telling you these things today is because in the past couple of decades your man-degrees of consciousness have so much advanced in the control of the relationship between time and space.

"We can go backward or forward in time in the unobstructed universe. Time *is*. That is probably where the Old Testament writers got their idea of a God in the heavens, and the last is first, and rolling out like a scroll, and all the rest."

This too was at least thought-provoking; and it raised a lot of questions. We agreed with Betty that we would probably understand it better if we would go into it in connection with her kind of space, but some of those questions clamored in our minds for immediate discussion.

There was Betty's statement, tossed out in passing, as it were. "If I want to leave you and go home and come back at the sidereal time I left, I can do that. You can't."

And her remarks as to her command of knowledge of the future seemed to carry implications of predestination, of fatalism. And where did the power of prophecy come in on that? I had had some queer experiences with prophecy lately.

2.

The matter of what might be called Betty's fleet-footedness did not prove to be as difficult as we had feared. Betty left its solution to us; and we managed to wangle it out. She approved of my final statement as at least sufficient.

"Between the sentences of this very conversation," I proffered, "are a few seconds of sidereal time, a very brief period, nevertheless *time*. However, this is sidereal time; and it is brief only by sidereal measure. In orthic time, however, it is sufficient for whatever purposes you desire to accomplish. By means of your control of psychological time, and your ability to fill it with content, you are able in it to give yourself 'elbow room,' so to speak."

That would do for the moment, said she. Later Stephen added something.

"The essences — receptivity, conductivity, frequency — are the reality," said he. "Sidereal time, sidereal space, sidereal motion are the manifestations in the obstructed universe. That is what explains the malleability of time, space and motion. That is what Mrs. White was trying to tell you. Yet she didn't know how she could stretch or contract time, space and motion. She doesn't. But she does stretch and contract receptivity, conductivity, frequency. She knows how to do that. She told you she used her time psychologically. A little unfortunate; yet it's a key to understanding."

3.

The matter of predestination, free will, prophecy proved even more interesting. It came very much into the front of our minds through an experience that Betty urged upon me. Taking time off, I had been visiting friends down on Long Island who had invited in one evening a physicist and his wife who, like themselves, shared my interest in psychic matters, academically at least. The special reason for the invitation was that I might be told, first-hand, of a local psychic whom the physicist had visited several times from a research viewpoint, and about whom he and his wife had told my friends. His name for this psychic was "the Egg Woman," and though his reports of his experiences and findings with her were unusually interesting, they were in the main an old story to me. I long had been a member of a psychical research group in California and as such had "investigated" mediums all up and down the Western Coast.* So under these circumstances, and as it was not particularly convenient for me to visit the Egg Woman, I stored the evening away in my memory as a pleasant social experience and supposed it so written off.

However, when I next talked with Betty she insisted that I make the arrangements required to interview this psychic. Therefore, on a subsequent visit to the Island, my friends, nothing loath, drove me some distance into the country to visit the Egg Woman. The wife of a farmer, she proved to be what is usually called a "fortune teller." My friends made quite an occasion of the trip — "going to have our fortunes told!"

We found her a personable Welsh woman, very self-possessed, quiet, and sincere in manner, with extraordinary dark eyes. She needed the self-possession, I thought, for the house was filled with the noise of children and two radios going at once. Fortune telling was a side line

* See *The Mystery of the Buried Crosses* by Hamlin Garland.

with her. She had no assumptions or trappings. She took us each singly, in turn, into her dining room. There she presented me with a glass half full of water, a raw egg and a spoon. Under instruction I broke the white of the egg into the water, and stirred it with the spoon. She looked into the glass and "read" the pattern made by the white of egg. That was her form of tea leaves, crystal ball, playing cards. It was her "signal."

She encouraged the taking of notes; and she was remarkable, for of course she had never seen any of us before, and had no slightest idea of our identity. Her statements were very definite: they required no interpretations. But the most interesting phase, as it turned out, was the accuracy of her predictions. She made a number of them, categorically; and as most of them were cast to occur in the fairly immediate future, they could be readily checked. All such turned out to be correct. Some are still in the future — supposedly. While she gave neither my friends nor me anything of world-stirring importance, she certainly impressed us as possessing a definite gift, of its sort.

But I was still wondering why I had had to see the Egg Woman. The reason soon developed.

"I think," began Betty, the first evening I was back with Darby and Joan, "it was suggested that we talk about fate, and the conversation at dinner" — I had been recounting my experience with the Egg Woman — "put in Stewt's mind the glimpse that is to be found in the old doctrine of predestination. Suppose you begin by asking questions."

"Well," obliged Darby, "Stephen says that your greater knowledge of cause and effect permits you to make better predictions than we can."

"I told you that we looked over all time like a map. The contours of the map we see. For instance, one of the contours of the future is evolution, a growth toward perfection. We know, for example, that in the immediate future in the obstructed universe, there will continue to be apparent deflections of growth and a seeming retarding of perfection.

"Your will is free, and you can choose according to your quality. My will is free, and I can choose according to my quality. I don't know that you call it precisely picking out the future. It is perhaps that I set myself to assimilate an aspect of the future that I am aware I need.

"The truth in the glimpse of predestination is the fact that the individual *quality* of one born to earth is fixed; and that it must return back to its own quality when it comes here. That much is law, and if you wish to call that predestination, you can."

"Could you," Darby expressed the thought that was troubling us both, "expand the concept of the future in view of our new ideas as to time? We gathered that orthic time is rather collapsible; that you could pass on into the future more or less at will. It is accessible by some orthic law you can operate and we cannot. I find in my time *feeling*, as such, that it is more or less futureless and pastless. If you include that, it does give you somewhat of an insight into the future. If you can see that a thing is going to happen, what can you do about it? That's predestination."

"Cause and effect," said Betty, "is one of the laws of time, just as it is one of the laws of motion. There are those here now who could tell you things that are going to happen. They have proved it. It is done in time's essence, receptivity.

"Take your own experience. You get up in the morning. Your *intent* is to go to the office. You foresee your arrival at the office. It's perfectly true there are things that could deflect that intent. And it is true you have to operate certain things in your present to make that future event become present. Nevertheless, you do foresee the *event*. That is a very simple example. You can will it not to take effect. There can be extraneous deflections that can stop the effect. That is a condition of the obstructed universe. Predestination is, with you, only a glimpse. It is much more than a glimpse with us, though it is not a complete reality. Ask another question: she's lost it."

"You can see this room as it is. Can you see it as it will be two weeks from now?" propounded Darby.

"Yes, conditioned by certain wills."

"Whose wills?"

"Yours, first, because this room happens to belong to you."

"At some unpredictable hour, something is going to change this room. Have you the ability to see that change?" asked Darby.

"Yes," she claimed.

"Does that extra ability of yours have to do with a property of time, of which you are cognizant and I am not?"

"Yes," Betty assured him.

"Can you go farther into that? Or can you only say that it is your appreciation of more causes than I appreciate? Or is it in the nature of your sense of time, and not of cause and effect?"

"It is in the nature of my sense of time. But I must insist upon your also understanding the evaluation of small events and the malleability of them, in contradistinction to great purposes."

"By that do you mean that small events are more easily disturbed by small causes brought about by free will than larger events? The latter are too big to be affected ordinarily by small divergencies of free will? Therefore the prophets might have more luck with the latter," I suggested. I was only partly right; but my question did lead directly into the kernel of the matter.

"The *intent* in time is one thing. The *event* in time is another," stated Betty; and paused to let that sink in. "You foresee your future, for the most part, by the event," she went on. "You condition your future on the present event. We look forward into time in both ways. We are cognizant of the *event*, but we immediately relate it up to the *intent*. Some of you, too, do that — a little," she conceded. "Some people have that broader sense of the meaning of events, as it were, the broader evaluation of the event.

"The evolution of time we see. That you call the intent. It is perfectly clear to us. We see also the event as it is conditioned by the wills of men. But we, knowing the intent of time, which is the future, can follow that conditioned event beyond your present, and see how it relates itself, individually, to the intent."

"I think we need some illustrations," said Darby. "How is this? Here is a river. That is the intent of time. Here is a log floating in the river, an event. You know there's a log jam down the river. The intent of the river will remain. You know that this log, both of itself and as implicated with the other logs of the jam, is not going to alter the intent of the river; and that ultimately the jam will break, and the event-log will be absorbed in the intent of the river. So that if we were to ask Betty *when* the jam is going to break, she might make an inaccurate prediction. But if we ask her *if* it is going to break, she will prophesy truly, for she knows the intent."

"That's good," Betty approved.

"Or take another example," said I. "Before they started work on the Golden Gate Bridge you could predict accurately that there was going to be a concrete pillar on the Marin shore. That was in the intent of the bridge; and you knew that a bridge was intended. And that intent would not be affected by the small divergencies and exercises of free will, as in a strike, or being lazy, or sabotage, or what have you. But those things would seriously affect your predictions as to the *event* or when the bridge would be finished."

"The whole point is to differentiate between the event and the intent. And to consider the juxtaposition of the two," agreed Betty.

"The prediction of the intent depends on the sense of time; of the event, on cause and effect. Is that the difference?" I asked.

"I think that the intent is in time, and the events are the way stations along the stream," answered Betty. "The intent does control the event to a certain extent, but the event is more controlled in the obstructed universe by the free will of man. But you cannot control the intent by the will."

"Then," said Darby, "intent could not be implicitly relied on because of the conflicting intents of different intruders."

"You mean the intents of various degrees of consciousness," Betty particularized. "The only intent that really *governs* is evolution. It is the primary characteristic of receptivity, of time. It is true that there are various intents, including individual intents, but the intent of quality of consciousness is more in a straight line than the intent of quantity of consciousness. Even in your obstructed universe you have intents of time, as well as events.

"Intents might conflict with each other, you say. What you mean is this: a high degree of consciousness-quality can set in motion an intent. A lower quality can also set in motion an intent. This is so because both are free wills. But the difference here is that the intent of consciousness is one thing; and the intent of an individual — any kind of an individual — is only an event.

"When you get consciousness divided into individuals, the intent of the individual may run counter to the evolutional intent. The difference between us and you is that with us events are more closely identical with intent.

"We can see into the future as far as intent goes. We can see event on the cause-and-effect basis with a broader vision than you. We can see the event in intent; that is, we *might*. But what's the use? A leaf falls off a tree, but what of it? It is unimportant, because it does not interfere with the intent of the tree at all.

"Now the Egg Woman" — we were back to the Egg Woman at last — "is what you might call a near-sighted prophet. That is, while she does see, partly, the short-range intent, it is mostly cause and effect she sees. She does not predict far ahead accurately. But her close-range stuff is so good because there the causes and effects are pretty well laid out, with only small chance of outside modifying or interfering event happening in so short a time. Besides, cause and effect gain more solidity, immunity, against outside interference as they approach culmination. A good deal as a stream gains acceleration and strength as it nears the edge of the waterfall."

Later Darby had an idea by way of illustration.

"Here's a thought on that future stuff," said he. "I look into a mirror in the adjoining room, and I see in it a picture on the wall that I do not see actually. And I won't see it actually until I get up and go into that room and look; and all of that action is not now, but in the future. Time, the mirror, does show me the intent of the picture, but not the event — until it comes into the present by my walking into the other room."

CHAPTER XXIII

BETTY'S WORLD: ITS FLUIDITY

1.

WHEN Betty and Joan worked together as stations, back in 1922,* each used her own method. Betty went exploring, in her own person; Joan stepped aside from herself to permit the Invisibles to say what they had to say. Betty often — when both were in trance — tried to induce Joan to join her, but Joan had always refused. Her few tentative excursions did not please her: and the interchange of persuasion and objection was sometimes very funny.

In rough outline, Joan adhered to her old method now. But with, apparently, a difference. Heretofore she had been "taken away" merely. Now she was "taken away," as usual; but was also herself under instruction.

"Joan," Betty confided to us, "has for the past three weeks been going to the same school I have been going to."

"I've been here lots of times, but it's only since Betty came to stay that I've been able to be part of the pattern," was Joan's first comment. "I have to learn to do what Betty did. If I can do it, with her to explain, I can tell you how it's done.

"This wandering around over here with Betty is so confusing," she complained, "because it isn't any *different.* Now, if it were only a kind of down-under-the-water place! But it's no *different.*"

"Well, who said it was?" retorted Betty.

* See Appendix of *The Betty Book.*

"You know, I've been here *before!*" Joan repeated. "It's so *familiar*. I didn't know what the difference was. I'm finding out. — The only difference is the degree of frequency. I just have more power over here than I have back with you.

"There are a lot of funny things. — I'm watching people. I'm not like them yet because I have to go back. I can only stand on the sidelines and observe."

Betty displayed an almost inordinate pride over this first success of Joan's. The experience was not often repeated, or at least not often reported back to us; and was usually intended more to clear our understanding than to convey anything recordable.

"Joan is here with us," Anne suddenly interrupted Betty's discourse one day. "Would you like her to tell you what she sees?"

"Very much!" we responded heartily.

"I've always wanted to travel; and now I can travel," began Joan. "I can go anywhere I want to go. There are no obstructions.

"It is hard to make you understand the difference. The only difference I can see is freedom, liberty and reality in the things we fight for on earth.

"One of the things that interests me most is the beautiful bodies the people here inhabit. My body is tied: I have to go back, I cannot stay. But if anyone likes light and color — the bodies of these people shine with light and color. I recognize them by their light and color, because the intensity of their color and of their light shows their frequency. You can almost *tell* their degrees that way. Certainly you feel the radiance of their individuality. They are *very* beautiful.

"I'd like to tell you how I see Betty; how she is with

me here. She looks just as she looked in her garden, except that she shines, and there is a soft rosy glow from her, and it is warm and sweet, and very, *very* comforting to feel. It is friendly and kind, and there is great strength in it. Her color is a beautiful new color I have never seen anywhere else. I cannot describe it, for it is out beyond the color-frequencies we have words for. But it is made up of gold, and rich deep rose, and a sort of heavenly blue, and it pulsates around her.

"That old saying, 'the music of the spheres,' is true too; and it's the voices of the people around me; and Betty's voice is a dear, singing, laughing voice. Everyone here who knows her adores her; and she is accumulating to herself a great deal of power and graciousness and strength because of the work she is doing.

"Why!" cried Joan, "it seems that we, you, all of us who have close ties here, can do a great deal to help them, just as they help us! Betty says I help her, and you help her, oh, so much! She says you are doing the earth half of her work.

"This place where I am doesn't look any different. It's just here. The only difference is that nothing obstructs. There seems to be a fluidity to endeavor, to space, to time, to everything. It flows, some way. The only difference is that it is unobstructed."

"But," she added, "it strikes *me* as a place where they haven't any solids!"

2.

"You want to know how I operate in my consciousness, which is just beyond yours," Betty took up the story. "We have postulated that there is only one universe. For purposes of evolution this universe has been divided into quantitative and qualitative aspects.*

"First let me get into your minds firmly the idea that your world is my world, and your matter is my matter. Now, just as in maturity you handle an automobile differently than does a boy learning to drive, so do we here differ from you in our handling of the same fundamentals handled by you. I am going to have to eliminate details because I am afraid of confusing you, but I am going to try to tell you as nearly as I can what my world is like.

"In the first place, when you come here, one of the things that astounds you most, as Joan said, is the lack of difference. Over and over Stephen told Darby that one of his first jobs here was to meet boys who died suddenly in the war, without the little interim between the two consciousnesses, and explain to them what had happened and where they were."

Of course Betty had already told us, incidentally, a good deal concerning her state of being. The reader has had some of it in Part I of this book. And a great deal more came to us at the very first, in unrecorded conversation, when Betty was giving assurance of her actuality. So I then wrote out a little epitome, addressed to her, of what, up to date, we thought we had been told, and the conclusions we had drawn from it. Here is the epitome:

3.

"In your body you have, through its perceptions the same relationships with your world as we have with ours.

"But your body is not multicellular, not composed of

* See Chapter X, Consciousness, The Only Reality.

numerous entities; it is integral, and expresses only your individual entity.

"You are able to see and touch our world. You experience the same reactions, subjectively, as you would through your physical senses. However, you add something to what you have perceived in the flesh; you 'see also beyond it.'

"You understand us when we speak aloud to you. I gather that an unspoken message consciously addressed to you is likewise heard. I understand that you do not read thoughts not addressed you; but also you could do so if necessary or desirable.

"The 'density' so much talked about as being between your world and our world is a density affecting our receiving function. Its penetration by you is a job. But the idea that it is dulling to you, that it hampers you as a drug might, is incorrect."

4.

The basic difference between her world and ours was, apparently, one of obstruction. What, exactly, did she mean by that? And what were the implications?

"Just what I said," was Betty's attitude. "Matter is an obstruction to you; it is not to me."

"Well now," said Darby, "the desk there is no obstruction to you. I suppose you can walk through the desk. You must then be of matter so attenuated that you leave on the desk's substance no trace. I was wondering —"

"You can send an electric shock through the desk, or an X-ray, and leave no mark," Betty interrupted.

"The consciousness of matter is a very low degree, and it is at the command of the consciousness of man," said Anne. "It is even more at our command in the unobstructed universe. However, there are limitations here.

"You must not forget that we enjoy your earth garden. There is truth in the statement that God walked in the garden in the cool of the evening. We love your earth and its beauties and grandeurs. It is very pleasing to us, and we see more of it than you, and so we love it that much more. It is a wonderful place, even in its obstructed aspects; and unobstructed, it is heaven to us who developed our quantity there."

"Do you actually see the desk, just as we see it who are here in this room, in our physical bodies?" we nagged Betty.

"Let me talk to myself," she requested. After a moment she began to talk in a low voice, with pauses between each sentence, as though she were actually doing things, and checking on them as she went along.

"I come into this room. I am living in the entire universe. However, I see the desk. If Joan went to the desk, it would be an obstruction to her. To me it is not. Of course, I can't live in those limitations. I cannot refocus my frequency to recover the old desk. But I could use that desk in *my* way."

"Explain a bit," urged Darby. "What is 'your way' with a mundane desk?"

"Well," Betty tried to explain, "the form attribute of the desk is what is real to me. Now, the form attribute of the desk, naturally, to you has a certain use. I could do all those things, *if I wanted to.*"

"Then," queried Darby, "your use for the desk corresponds to our use for the desk, as your beta* corresponds to the beta of the desk. The desk is an alpha in relation

* See Glossary.

to my alpha body, just as it's a beta in relation to your beta body?"

"Our 'intent' is exactly the same, as relates to the desk; but our 'event' of use is different," said Betty. "The intent is the making and storing of records. We make and store records. And even with you there are various intents for desks. Stewt has a desk for writing one kind of creative work; Darby has a desk for another kind of creative work."

We abandoned the desk as our illustration. Long since Betty had warned us against what she called "educating ourselves beyond understanding"; which is a good phrase to describe a very common human fault. And also she had warned us that we must expect no clear and detailed account of her world. Indeed, that warning had been given us many times by our Invisibles when Betty was working on this side.

Focusing down to exact description was what Betty called "getting Oliver Lodgish," in reference to the statements about brick houses, cigars, and such things in *Raymond*.* Too literal a translation of a parallel, said Betty.

"Sir Oliver is a very great and comprehending physicist," said she. "He understood in part what Raymond was trying to tell him, but he did not get it clear."

The best we could hope to do would be to get the principles of her life rather than the concrete details.

I tried a new tack.

"You say that your body is 'just as I used to know it,'" said I. "That, also, is difficult to understand. What possible use could you have for such a body?"

"I am as I used to be — you'd know me as you used

---

* *Raymond* or *Life and Death*, by Sir Oliver Lodge; George H. Doran Co., 1916.

to know me —" Betty's voice was doubtful. "I don't believe I can make you understand. It's that law of parallels again. My body functions for me — according to my needs —"

"Your development is qualitative," suggested Darby. "Haven't you new functions and faculties for that development?"

Betty approved the question, but felt we were getting Oliver Lodgish again. So we veered off from that.

"Now," Betty returned to the original subject, "I said that your matter is no obstruction to me. Neither is my matter, to me. *But*, neither is my matter to you. Now chew on *that*."

Darby had a horrible thought.

"Good Lord!" he cried. "When we run against each other I don't know who rambles through whom!"

Betty laughed.

"The fact is, we *don't* ramble through each other," said she. "*Entities*, primary entities, are indivisible. Your body, the 'temple of the body' that *you* — the You, the I-Am, the Being — inhabit for a period of sidereal time, is divisible; for it is made up of innumerable low degree entities of consciousness.

"I am not telling you anything you do not know. Our primary indivisible entities could not go through each other. I am calling all this to your attention for the better apprehension of the indivisibility of your conscious entity and my conscious entity."

5.

The only difference, she reminded us, is the difference of frequency. Recall her homely illustration of the flywheel moving so fast — moving with a frequency so raised that its spokes are invisible, so that we see right through them. "That is the only reason you cannot see me," she had said. "And there is a corollary difference in the mechanism of awareness.

"You remember what I said about the 'density' many people suppose we have to penetrate in order to reach you. There is a question in Joan's mind about that. When I used to visit here" — she was referring to her penetration of the higher consciousness when she was still on earth — "when I used to visit here, you will remember that I used the word 'density' to describe a condition, a difficulty of understanding, a degree of obstruction. Now, that is what density is. It is not an obstruction in the sense that your matter is an obstruction, but it is a lower frequency than we here operate in, and it is a condition of the obstructed universe that sometimes makes it difficult for us to communicate with you. But it is not matter, *per se*. It's a lower frequency. We have to tune it up to get through it to communicate with you."

"Then it is not a thing that hampers you in going about in our surroundings?" I asked.

"No. It is psychological, as it were. It's not matter. It has to do more — a sort of border line between your subconscious and our actuality. If you will go back in our old records you will see, with this new understanding of frequency, what the Invisibles meant years ago when they talked to us about 'density.'"

CHAPTER XXIV

BETTY'S WORLD: ITS SOLIDITY

"YES," said I, apropos of Joan's statement as reported in the previous chapter, that to her the unobstructed universe looked like a place where there weren't any solids, "that's a good point. You said you wanted to bring — and I mean *bring*, said you — a picture showing the oneness of the two universes; and that they are parallel; and all that. Well, I'll state flatly that our universe is to us *solid*. I've bumped my head on it. And that solidity is due to the fact that things are an obstruction to me. But you live in an unobstructed universe. What do you do? Just float?"

But Betty would have none of that floating business. In fact, I think she was a little indignant about it. The accusation that she was in any respect a "disembodied spirit," a "shade," or a harp-playing angel, always aroused her. "But I tell you, we're *human!*" she would protest.

"What is your idea of where I am now, anyway?" she challenged a visitor, on one of the rare occasions when we had added to our number.

"Why —" stammered the visitor, "I just think of you as suspended, somehow, in space."

"I am right here," she was most emphatic. "There is only one universe. There is no other 'heaven.' It is only that you can't see me. Your eyes are not attuned to the color, your ears to the sound. I am in an unobstructed phase of the one and only universe, that is all. It is only that my I-Am is separated from the obstruction that was my body. My world is your world *plus*."

"Your world vibrates at a higher frequency than mine?" asked the visitor.

"Yes, it does," admitted Betty. "Just think that it is only that you can't see me; can't hear me, unless the talent of someone like Joan lets me express myself through it."

"I have thought of you as a higher octave. Are you always near us?"

"Where else would I be?" Betty was almost impatient. "Space is not what you think it is. It is only your idea. Space is conductivity. You know from science that there are a lot of things in this room you can't see. An ordinary camera would see some of them. My awareness-mechanism is higher tuned than yours. That is part of my being in the unobstructed universe."

And that's what we wanted to know about. "The obstruction of this chair," Darby pointed out, "is what keeps me from falling into the cellar."

"It's so simple," replied Betty, "but sometimes the simplest things are the hardest to explain. Of course it's a matter of frequency; that is, the relationship between frequencies — the frequency of what you call matter as a solid, and our own individual frequencies. Your relationship in frequency to the frequency of your matter is what makes it a solid to you. — I think I'll have to get a clearer explanation for you.

"Here is this world as you know it. You walk on the earth: it supports you. I walk on your earth, and yet I do not need it to support me. Your earth is there because it is a nexus of certain frequencies. It exists for both of us. You cannot walk on your water. I can. But that is because the relationship of my frequency to the frequency that is water is different from yours. My universe and my degree of consciousness is yours, only the aspect is different."

Apparently, then, solidity *per se* is a ratio between frequencies. As far as we are concerned, according to Betty, the denser the solid, the lower the frequency. And it is the ratio our own frequency bears to the frequency of the matter with which we are in contact that determines its character as a solid; or not, as the case may be. There are a lot of things in our own material world that are perfectly real, but are not solids to us.

"Suppose you are on a mountain," said she. "You see the clouds below you. They are objective. They have form, color, substance, and they screen from your sight everything below you. Yet you are aware that there is a world of action below the clouds. To the bodily you, and to your actual knowledge, those clouds are no obstruction. They are an obstruction to only one of your five senses — vision. You can eliminate that by projecting your body through the seeming obstruction by the act of walking down the mountain path.

"Or take a rock. You can *see* a rock, but you can't penetrate it. What can penetrate it? Solids can't; fluids can't; certain gases can't. But certain frequencies can. They can go through and be registered on the other side, without disturbing the rock's form attribute, in your consciousness. Like electricity or X-ray, or some similar force. Light cannot penetrate it. And yet your scientists and mathematicians use light as their yardstick of motion — frequency."

But, said Betty, *she* does not use light as her yardstick.

"Light," she defined, "is merely a degree-manifestation

in space. You know that both quality of consciousness and quantity of consciousness are in degrees; and you know that they have degree manifestations. Light is one of them. Now *we* take consciousness as in man as our yardstick, and that is a higher frequency. And I, in my present state, in orthos, as the highest frequency, can go through the rock. I am unobstructed by your matter."

All of which was interesting, but it did not meet our question as to her kind of solidity — if any.

"Now, if my frequency is great enough for matter to be nonobstructable," Betty sailed serenely on, "why does it not follow that this same frequency is great enough to be unneedful of support? I can walk *on* your matter, but the aspect of that matter is changed to me because I see it and deal with it in its essence, in orthos.

"Now I have told you that the individual in the obstructed universe has an alpha and a beta body. You can touch and feel your alpha body. It has a form attribute, as has all consciousness. The beta has a form attribute. This beta is so closely allied to the alpha in the obstructed universe that it would be recognizable to you, could you see it, and it is merely the extension into your obstructed universe of that degree of frequency that is the individual. I have begged you not to try to push this so far beyond human understanding as to make all of your hypotheses ridiculous. All the facts that you know in the obstructed universe are in the unobstructed universe. There is only one set of laws: only one universe.

"I have my landscape. If I wish to sit beside my stream on my bank of flowers I can, *by my handling of frequencies*, produce an *aspect* of my matter that will give me a perfectly good support."

"Somewhat like a man in water?" I suggested. "He

can float on the water, by taking certain measures; or he can sink down through the water by taking certain other measures."

"That's all right, as far as it goes," conceded Betty. "The thing that bothers you is that you consider matter as an obstruction, and as a solid. Matter isn't a solid; it isn't always even an obstruction to you. Matter may be solids, liquids, gases. You do not handle them the same way, and they do not affect you the same way. Are you near enough satisfied?

"The whole thing is a matter of relative trilogia," she added. "There are instances, therefore, in your everyday world experience of an approach to the essences of orthic motion, space and time. As Anne said to you, everything is fore-shadowed; it is a projection. Now it is easy for you to imagine the projection of many of your mundane laws into my awareness of the universe. It is not so easy for you to imagine the projection into your awareness of common ordinary laws in which I operate, but which you either have not discovered or are just beginning to sense. As, for instance, the thing they call now the radio wave; and the new stepping up of light frequencies through mechanics. Those are commonplaces with us."

CHAPTER XXV

THE HOMELY NECESSITIES

1.

THIS explanation of solidity was clear enough for the purpose at that time. It has become clearer since, the more we have thought it over; and that, I surmise, will be the reader's experience.

"All right," we agreed. "You have showed us that you live in a world that is solid to you — or of which you can make a solid aspect when you so desire by, as you expressed it, your handling of frequencies. And you have repeated in emphasis the old idea of parallels — or rather the idea of the identity of law in the two universes, yours and ours. In view of that parallel you must have the same basic necessities as ourselves. We don't want to force you to be Oliver-Lodgish, and indulge in exact descriptions, but could you discuss your form of such things as sleep, food, shelter, communication with each other? In principle at least."

"Well," said Betty, "what is sleep? Sleep, for the human body, is refreshment, replenishment of frequency. Not of the beta body — which, for a while, inhabits a so-called natural body — but for replenishment of the material body in order that it, being of a lower degree, may maintain the requisite ratio of frequency for your inhabiting it. All consciousness has its frequency. Now, in the intimate contact of the frequency of the beta body with the frequencies of the natural body, the lower frequencies drain on the higher. They have to maintain a definite ratio."

"Is sleep, then, a stepping up of frequency?" asked Darby. "If in sleep we are more sensitive to the influence of the unobstructed universe, is that because sleep raises our frequency? Or *are* we more sensitive then?"

"No," replied Betty "Your frequency is not raised, but your receptivity is, because the contact between the frequency of your material body and of your spiritual self is lessened during sleep. That is, your physical body is maintaining itself without your conscious aid.

"You have rest," she continued; "so do we. The very idea of frequency implies go-stop, go-stop. You have two types of rest required: psychological rest, and the rest of the physical body which is dissociated from the I-Am. Our form attribute — which we had there and now reclaim — the beta body, has to be replenished, to rest, just as you psychologically rest; but not in the long, stated, static periods you have established for the lower degree you inhabit."

"We are unconscious while taking that sort of rest: we sleep," said I. "Are you?"

"Our awareness-mechanism is never dissociated from our form. One of the characteristics of my rate of frequency is a closer association between the I-Am and the form attribute. My form attribute is so much a part of me that it came along with me when I died. You could cut off a leg or arm from the form attribute I left behind, and I could still have inhabited it. But because my form here is integral, there could be no similar division of it."

"What is your form of rest, if you are not unconscious?" I asked.

Betty was doubtful. "If I said suspension of frequency, it would give you a false impression. Why not a suspension of projecting frequencies?" she ventured.

"A withdrawal of contacts," suggested Darby.

"I really do as you do, only in a higher form," decided Betty. "I withdraw into my inner consciousness, *and stop radiation*. It's a sort of limited static; a little space of static in frequency. You have it in sleep."

2.

"Now let's take sustenance," she proposed. "You eat food. By that I mean you absorb matter of a lower frequency than that of your natural body. Now, we have form, and we have to maintain form, the balance of frequency. You do it through air, food, water, sleep. We replenish our frequency, but not through any kind of food you are talking about."

She did not seem to be able — or inclined — to go further with that.

"After all," contributed Darby, "it isn't the actual food we seek. It's rather the stimulus of our bodily frequency by means of chemical reaction. The chemical formula is a frequency formula, not an inert material formula. That gives us a line. They do it with a frequency formula comparable to the chemical-reaction conception of food."

"Absolutely!" agreed Betty.

3.

"So much for food and sleep," said I. "How about shelter? Or don't you need it? I mean something comparable to our mechanical shelters, such as houses."

"Our universe, like yours, contains lower degrees of

frequency which we want to avoid. We have our insulations."

"Do you have insulations of different kinds for different purposes, as we have homes, churches, dugouts?" asked Darby.

"We are so much closer to the essence of consciousness that our form attribute does not need the same shelter as yours. Ours is a type of insulation from lower degrees of consciousness that would impinge on our own consciousness unhappily."

"Well, has this insulation a form attribute, like a house?" I persisted.

"Now you're trying to get me to be Oliver-Lodgish again!" protested Betty. "Just as matter is a form attribute of consciousness, so is my insulation a perfectly real thing to me. It is an individual thing, that belongs to me. It's a condition."

And after all, in principle, that is all our own buildings are for; insulation against lower degrees of frequency we want to avoid, the frequencies of cold, wind, rain.

4

And finally this matter of communication with one another, we ventured. There is, said we, a strong suggestion that you do so mentally, by a kind of telepathy.

"No, no," protested Betty. "I've told you of that before. We have a voice. Your voice — in ordinary physics — is nothing but an impingement on your atmosphere that sets up vibrations — frequencies — that produce what you call sound. We have exactly the same thing in a higher frequency. So high that, like the last vibrations on the tuning fork, you do not hear us speak. That is the only reason in the world I can't talk to you direct."

"Do you use lower frequencies for communication with each other there, as we use lower frequencies here: air, pencil, or what have you?" I asked "Or do you tune in to each other's frequency; or to a common communication band, so to speak?"

"The latter," she replied.

"So you employ lesser frequencies than your own for such things as —" I began.

"I am here," she broke in "I have a form animated by frequency, like yours. It is a higher frequency. Your obstacles are not obstacles to me.

"Instead of our having to create clothing mechanically, for instance, we do so by a diversion of frequency. We can create directly by an impingement of our frequency on a lower degree of frequency. We use degrees. Color is a manifestation of a certain degree of frequency. I want it in my clothes. I don't make the color. I impinge on that particular frequency, and call it to my frequency."

"Are you taught how to do this?" I wanted to know.

"Yes, we have to be taught. I can't tell you that I hit a key or touch a string to do it. It's a selective impulse. I start an impulse with a psychological selectivity."

"You fix your mind on a frequency you know, and give it an impulse?"

"The impulse is there," corrected Betty. "It is already in frequency. What I do is to direct the frequency, and I do impel it.

"I don't think I can take you any farther into my mode of life," she doubted. "You have come so far in already, that to particularize is only confusing now, to us both. You see there won't be much use in my trying to give you anything more in that connection, because you have so much you have not digested. It would be like overloading your stomach."

We yielded, of course.

"Well," said Darby apropos of nothing, "we've got one thing you haven't got, anyway."

"What is that?" demanded Betty.

"Antique collectors," he said, still prodding.

"We've got 'em: lots of them."

"What antiques are there over there for them to collect?" jeered Darby.

"Outmoded empirical knowledge," retorted Betty.

Darby abandoned that. "How's the cosmos?" he asked lazily.

"Gathering no moss," flashed Betty.

"Well, you must miss something over there," continued Darby, who is a glutton for punishment. "What is it? The days of the week? Three meals a day?"

"No." Betty turned serious "The only thing I miss is the use of the five senses in the obstructed universe for the expression of my love for people who are still there; and of course if I had that, I wouldn't be here. I miss their not recognizing me, not hearing my voice, not feeling and seeing me when I'm there. And of course I *am* there. I miss your response. And that is all."

CHAPTER XXVI

HOW BETTY HANDLES SPACE

1.

WE HAD already gone through a considerable course of sprouts on the general subject of space, as the reader saw in Part II. But certain aspects of relationship were still in the air. Sometimes over a quarter of the span of the earth, Betty appeared to have "gone to find out" the answer to some question, and had returned within the compass of minutes. How did she do it? Her discussion of her handling of time gave us a clue, of course; but we wanted to pin the subject down. What *is* her space? Where? How does she "handle" it?

"In the sense of extension, your space is our space. Space is a map too. Again our ability to 'collapse' space is due to higher frequency."

We had found it wise, in these discussions to keep a dictionary handy; and we had early discovered that nothing less than the unabridged would do. Darby reached for it.

"The dictionary says," he read, "extension; a drawing or stretching out. Distance, a standing apart, separate. Is your idea of space, not one of the distance between two obstructions, not the standing apartness of two obstructions, but rather of an elasticity?"

"Space isn't elastic," disclaimed Betty. "Conductivity is. You see, it is conductivity of space we deal with rather than the limitations of sidereal space."

"Your measure of space is conductivity?" I asked, for-

getting for the moment that she had told us just that —
"over and over."

The frequency of an electric spark is naturally high;
and conductivity, for it, is also high. The frequency of
a physical body is comparatively low, and the conductivity of space, for it, is correspondingly lower. You and
I cannot get there as fast as does the electric spark, but we
get there a lot faster than we used to. Why? Because we
employ frequencies to supplement our own. In plain
words, by our inventive faculty in removing obstruction.
Or in concrete example, by means of motor, telegraph,
airplane, radio.

"Until a few years ago air was an obstruction to man,"
said Betty "He could not go through it except on the surface of the earth. The earth was his only medium of tra-
versing space. Now you have eliminated that obstruction.
What did it? What is it that keeps a plane that weighs so
much suspended and projecting itself through the air?
The air was never an obstruction to a bird, or water to a
fish. But both were an obstruction to man, until his ingenuity built ships, and later planes. In removing obstructions through his own efforts, man makes his obstructed universe ever nearer like to my unobstructed
universe.

"The whole point is that, gradually, through your
science, you are controlling more and more obstructions.
You are reaching up into my universe. By means of ex-
tending your understanding and use of the law."

"Frequency implies a time element as well as a space
element," said she on another occasion, "Naturally, it has
to have space to move in; and if you call it 'frequent' it
must be occurring again and again, and that requires time.
Now, we are able to manipulate the ratio between these

things; and by means of that manipulation — which is a manipulation of frequency — we can give our state of being its spatial contours.

"It's a matter of will, and concept, and filling it. We *will* to fill it. You have granted you can handle your space to a certain extent. We handle space psychologically instead of materially.

"Now suppose I tell you what I do. I want to go home and see if the leaves are raked up in my garden." Ensued a pause. "All right; I have been home, and I am here again. You have part of the mechanism I have in controlling space — the wish, the desire, the will."

"But we have to overcome actual obstruction, and you don't?" I objected.

"We have, in a way, to overcome the same thing she overcomes — our own concept of time and space; and the reason we have to have mechanical means is because we have to overcome a certain conception of time and space," interposed Darby.

"You have overcome your conception by means of such things as radio, for example," supplied Betty, "but you also have obstruction, and obstruction because of its material nature, must be overcome mechanically. Ours is an unobstructed universe; and therefore we have no need of mechanics."

"You live in orthos," Darby pointed out. "Yet you say your time and space are malleable, collapsible, more or less. If so, your time and space are variable."

"They are in manipulation; not in essence," modified Betty.

"Suppose," she suggested, "we reduce the problem to sidereal space. The linear space between two points is actual. In the mathematical sense it is a 'constant.' In the psychological sense it is a variable. The essence of that space, mathematically, does not change. Psychologically you can change it. Mechanically it becomes space-time, and is changeable. Just as space and time operate for you, so they operate for me. I am not great enough to change the essence of time, space and motion; I can only readjust myself to them."

"I assume that I have time, space and motion so I can orient myself in a pluralistic universe," said Darby. "I see my universe through time, space and motion in their relationships. You must do the same."

"But my concepts are more closely allied to the trilogical *essences* of the orthic," added Betty.

"The fundamental with me is relationship of the three, one to the other. To what extent does the question of relationship enter into your state of being?" asked Darby.

"I can no more get away, in being, from the trilogia, than you can get away, in being, from the trilogy," said Betty.

"Never," she warned emphatically, "question the reality of time, space and motion. They *are*. Just as your own individual concept of time, space and motion is malleable, so is mine. The reality of time, space and motion is in the entire universe. The essence of them in orthos — or the qualitative universe — is free, or unobstructed; and in the quantitative universe they are obstructed, for the purposes of individuality. But they are no less actual, and the essence is no less present. When the beta body is released from the obstruction of the physical body, it is true that your aspect, or your conception, or your understanding, or your vision or use of time, space and motion becomes unobstructed. It is further true that the malleability of the time, space and motion concept of your own world which you operate, is extended for me in my present being. In other words, your recognition of a psychological time, a psychological space and a psychological motion extends over into my reality."

"Does it follow then," Darby asked presently, "that your time, space and motion are only nearer approaches to orthos than ours?"

"Let me see — I don't want to mislead you," Betty hesitated. "The unobstructed universe is in reality orthos, and we inhabit it, yet we too are in degrees. The obstructed universe is in degrees exactly as is the unobstructed universe. It is a law. All laws operate with us as they operate with you. I am many degrees beyond you. But don't misunderstand me: I am unobstructed. That gives me a comprehension of, a touch with, orthos that you have not.

"The thing you must always remember," she reminded us, "is that all consciousness, all awareness-mechanism, individualized, is in degrees. It isn't that we don't have matter: we do. We all have form; and matter is nothing but a form-attribute of certain degrees of consciousness. And it varies in form according to the degree. Our awareness-mechanism apprehends. A certain degree manifests to your awareness-mechanism as a solid. But not to mine, as you consider a solid, because with you a solid is an obstruction. This is because of the orthic quality of time and space and motion with us."

2.

"There is a little point of puzzlement in that degree thing as manifesting in an individual frequency," interposed Darby. "You say I cannot become aware of your world because my personal frequency cannot be stepped up to that point. But another time you told us that there are certain personal frequencies here on earth that are actually higher than the lowest personal frequencies there with you. There's a discrepancy in idea there."

"Not really," returned Betty. "It is a question of *degree* of consciousness rather than of frequency. Your degree may be as high as mine, but your frequency is arrested, held static — as is your quality — in the obstructed universe. It is arrested by your earth-body frequency. The I-Am frequency is much higher than the earth-body frequency. Yet the two are combined in the obstructed universe for the purpose of individualization.

"The handicap is simply the handicap of the *combination* of the alpha and beta bodies."

"Yes, I can see that," agreed Darby. "Now, here's another thing that occurs to me. When all obstruction is removed, there's a lot emptied out. My typical day, for instance, is occupied with handling obstructions. I'm largely engaged in overcoming resistances. I get out of bed, and from then until I go to bed again fully eighty per cent of my time is occupied in moving matter, in one way or another. You don't have to do that. You have eighty per cent more time to fill up. If I had eighty per cent more time, I simply would not know what to do with it. You have a lot to fill up when they emptied out for you the content of your human senses."

"Emptied out the content of my human senses!" Betty repeated the phrase. "That just isn't true! We bring them with us, only intensified."

Darby still indicated that something must be done about that extra eighty per cent of leisure.

"Would it mean anything," suggested Betty, "if I said we fill up the gap caused by the lifting of obstructions by means of our increased *acuteness* of perception. Our range of registration is so much wider."

"I think I see it," I ventured. "If you take a two-hour walk in the country with a dull person totally uninterested in nature, it seems forever; but with a naturalist, say, who knows all about the birds and pretty flowers and things, those two hours —"

I did not need to finish.

"That's it!" cried Betty.

A stray word brought up another loose end of thought. It really grew out of one aspect of the discussion on space. In the course of it, one of us propounded the question that someone invariably asks — about life on the other planets, or elsewhere in the physical cosmos.

"What I have been told," Betty replied, "is that there are other degrees of consciousness on other planets — on the other solar planets—but not quite comparable to man. They are borning places like earth for other types of consciousness, but what their degrees are I don't know."

It seemed to me it ought to be simple for her just to go and find out. Hadn't she command of space? But apparently that did not work.

"It has to do with frequency. You see, we come from the earth; and while consciousness is only one in the entire universe, sidereal and solar, there are varying degrees of frequency: and because I am I, I too have my limitations. It would seem possible for me to visit the sun, but I am not ready to do so because my degree of frequency is not yet suitable."

"Well, how about tackling the planets, then?" I suggested.

"I think that has to do with light," said Betty doubt-fully, "I know it has to do with coldness, with that frequency. I do go beyond your frequency in sight and sound and obstruction, but I am still close to you, comparatively. Let Anne talk about it. It's confusing to me."

Anne obliged.

"This is difficult for your understanding, and I don't think it will mean much to you; but I'll try," said she. "Too much detail would confuse your judgment. There is much I do not myself know.

"This is true: that in all the universe there are manifestations of degrees of consciousness. Many of them manifest as what you call light and heat. These constitute your solar system. We have told you that the entire universe is constituted of obstruction and unobstruction; and that both are operated by the same law. You can call it parallel law, or extension of the law. On all these planets there is manifestation of degrees of consciousness. On some of them, I have been told, there is manifestation equal to man: that there have been such, equal to man; that there will be others equal to man."

We gathered that Anne was talking of sidereal planets in general, and not merely of those in the solar system.

"The attraction of the earth's frequency holds those of us who developed our quantity on earth," she continued. "The other night you were talking to a scientist, and he told you that if you had two currents going into a bed of mercury, and you put one pole of frequency in one end and the opposite in the other, they would draw together. That is what happens to the obstructed and unobstructed universe that is surrounding this particular bit — earth.

"All consciousness is in degrees. I apprehend that the

sun and its other planets are degrees of material consciousness of such a type that the beneficence of the sun's heat develops lower degrees of consciousness, where the heat of light strikes.

"But I would be misapprehended if I tried to tell you anything about it. The frequencies are so different that we are held to our own yet. That is why we are so near to you. We call this an unobstructed universe, but it is psychologically limited. There is a difference."

"Limitations of your own individual development of consciousness," I surmised. "We here, when you get right down to it, are developed by our overcoming of the obstructions that characterize our obstructed universe. Since we acknowledge the parallelism of law, you must have something analogous, in order to develop. Do limitations of individual development supply that resistance to you?"

"Our limitations here have to do with ourselves, and are mainly psychological," said Anne. "They are inside of us? — well, yes and no. There are 'obstructions' of frequencies and degrees. I shall go on into a further degree of consciousness, but I must graduate to it. Our resistances are for development, as are your obstructions. We grow by overcoming, just as you do. You have to overcome definite obstructions, physically, materially. And also you have to overcome mass psychology. You have to overcome now this ideology that is growing up in a strip of Europe. It is a more definite obstruction than a mountain range would be.

"I would not have you think that in this mode of existence here there is lack of understanding of psychological obstructions caused by deliberate planning. The obstruction here is in the degree — the lack of development of the degree; and our job is to bring it up. We are still so close to you that such an obstruction with you also retards us; and we can garner here much quality by aiding you to overcome it. We do this also individually. I heard Betty say last night that you were carrying on her work. That is true: but also she is carrying on yours, and thereby she is gathering to herself strength and influence and understanding and wisdom. It is a good word: wisdom."

"I understand," said Darby, "that you deal in two types of frequency — your own, and others outside which you employ for specific purposes. Those outside might be compared roughly to our electric or radio waves. They are no obstruction to you; but are they not more analogous to our conception of the material than are those frequencies which are your own?"

"Aye," agreed Anne.

"We are not conscious of doing anything of the kind, but do you not, out of your own frequency, develop what might roughly be called forces, which you manipulate?" Darby continued.

"Aye. What about thoughts, force of character, decisions? You develop them. They are frequencies, and are more potent than many other frequencies. Thoughts are things. The hardest thing to wipe out of your world is an idea."

CHAPTER XXVII

THOUGHTS ARE THINGS

"I AM glad Anne brought that up," said Darby. "I suppose the statement has come to us fifty times, not only from Anne, but many others. Just how literally is thought 'real' — is it *literally* a 'thing'?"

We discussed that matter, pro and con, without getting much of anywhere. But some days later, Anne abruptly began the evening.

"I am here," she announced. "I would talk to you for a bit on the reality of thought. I have nothing new to tell you. Many a time we have told it to you, but we will try to point it up into an apex of understanding. I will ask a question; and it is not rhetorical. What, above all other things in the obstructed universe, continues after the individual who promulgated it has been dissociated from the material frequencies which were his body, and himself passed into the unobstructed universe?"

"Oh, we'll grant that it is thought," admitted Darby, a little wearily, "but that does not answer; it just restates."

"Thought," said Anne, "is an attribute of consciousness. Being an attribute of consciousness, it has frequency. It is received in time; and, according to its creative potency, it remains in time."

"It is," Darby pointed out, "received in time; but it is not received in space. In that respect it differs from ordinary material things. Yet you are continually telling us that thoughts are things."

"Thought is as much a substance as electricity and such things that you deal with," asserted Anne. "There is a statement I will make to you, that I have not made. It must be apparent to you that you live in two aspects of the obstructed universe. You have sidereal experience; you have psychological experience; and you have empirical knowledge of both. This is what I would tell you: that the psychological experience is and remains realer, more comprehensive, than the sidereal. And you can understand your psychological experience more basically, minutely. You feel more the actuality and reality of it than of your sidereal experience. Why? Because the psychological experience is that which is most closely related to the I-Am, whose form attribute is your beta body, and which carries on forever; the I-Am which is the core of you, the purpose of consciousness expressed in the individual."

Darby accepted this.

"Would it be correct, then, to say thought is a frequency, just as electricity is?" he asked.

"Aye," agreed Anne.

"Then thought is a force, rather than a thing," I argued, "and manifests itself as a thing only through its action. Like electricity."

"You cannot use the word 'force' as that word is used by the modern world," Anne objected. "We want to avoid that word. I gave Betty very strict instructions not to use that word. There is a borderland, a no-man's land, between the obstructed and the unobstructed aspects where is all that which Stewart calls force. That you realize and manipulate, but its form attribute you cannot see."

"Then I am to understand that electricity, *per se*, has a form attribute to its own?" I wanted to get this extraordinary statement cleared.

"Aye," Anne assured me. "You know it by its potency. You diverge the potency into different works. It is precisely the same with thought; only, instead of the thought-frequency coming out of no-man's land, it is *your* creative agent, and it is *there* you are like what you call God — or the devil!" added Anne quaintly.

"There is form," she continued. "All consciousness has form. It is not true that all consciousness is associated with other consciousnesses, as man with his body. Life: yes.

"There is a differentiation between what man controls and what he cannot control, or recreate. For instance, you can call electricity out of 'nowhere,' and pass it into a wire, then dissociate it from the wire, and pass it back again. You can dissociate the I-Am from the alpha form attribute, but you cannot pass it back again. That is so with all life, as you call it."

"Your statements are reasonable," admitted Darby, "but our question is still not completely answered. You say, 'thoughts are things.' Marbles are things, and everybody knows what that means; and I can put one in my pocket. And it may be lost or roll into a corner, and I may never see it again. But it goes on being a marble. I have a thought. It isn't a thing in the sense the marble is a thing, and it doesn't last. You seem to say that all our thoughts keep on having registration somewhere. I have lots of thoughts of no importance for registration."

"Your own thoughts are of importance to you," said Anne. "The stream of electricity and of thought are only comparable for the sake of illustration, and not really near enough alike for that. But the individual thought is not unlike a spark of electricity that flashes up. It can't spark outside its own source or substance."

"The electricity eventually and inevitably grounds

back to its source," Darby followed the analogy. "Does my individual thought similarly ground back into the 'substance of thought,' the source-thought?"

"Aye," said Anne.

"So that when you, speaking morally, continually tell us that thoughts are things, you literally mean our thought is indestructible?"

"Aye," said Anne.

"Do my unexpressed thoughts have objectivity?"

"They have more objectivity in you than they have in the general reservoir." Anne modified this. "When your electric supply is flashed without application, you call it a waste of energy."

"Is there not," I put in, "a parallel in our quality-quantity idea? Thought is in evolution: no doubt of that. Is not the individual thought a contribution in quantity, so to speak, to the quality, which is the source-thought, or substance of thought, or whatever you want to call it?"

"Aye," Anne agreed to this.

"Just to sum up" — this was Darby — "thought is a frequency analogous to an electrical frequency. Just as a fortuitous spark finds its way into the body of electricity, so even the unexpressed thought finds its way objectively back to the body of thought. And, like the fortuitous spark, might not add much."

"It gains its dynamics by expression, by manifestation?" I surmised. Anne assented. Darby went on.

"But," said he, "the fact that the thought was not expressed would not break down the potential of its objectivity."

"You say that 'a certain attitude of mind is in the air.' You speak true," said Anne.

"That might be explained by the process you are describing," conceded Darby, "but on the other hand, modern methods of communication are so widespread and rapid —"

Anne interrupted.

"I grant the communication, but I do not grant that it need be in words. If one man in an audience is discontented he may infect a whole audience, though he never opens his mouth. Man never has realized the importance of thought. I will give you a key. How far does your thought go?"

"Without limit; no, limited only by my degree," replied Darby. Anne continued:

"There is a definite frequency that goes out from the minds of men of which they have not taken full cognizance, and that is thought. As a man thinketh, so is he. But I would go one step further and say: as a man thinketh, so is his surrounding habitation, so is his influence on the other frequencies he comes in contact with. Especially human frequencies. Especially those of lower degrees than his own.

"You go to your daily work with a glad heart and a free mind, happy in your consciousness, and the day starts with a snap, and you affect everyone. On the other hand, you do not feel so good, and down goes the whole day; and those in contact with you get the reflex. That is a definite application of your frequency, for it's a *thing*. A man can have private moods of his own, certainly — like sorrow — but this is true: that every time you overcome, you have strengthened your frequency, and you have gathered unto yourself a bit more of the source material, and the thing that is You. Thought is a reality. Its potency in your world is very great — as you of this generation should well know. He who seeks wisdom, either as a protection to himself or as a service to others, must first of all recognize the objective validity of thought."

CHAPTER XXVIII

DO YOUR JOB!

1.

"You started out to bring us a picture of your state of being," I said. "I'm willing to acknowledge it's a pretty good picture. But it is not complete; and that incompletion is dangerous."

How was that? Betty wanted to know.

"It's too attractive. You've talked so much about your lack of obstruction, and your high-wide-and-handsome manipulation of space and time, in contrast to our hampered state of existence, that you are apt to discourage the average man here so he'll be inclined not to bother any more. He'd rather just sit down and wait. Or anyway, he'll lose his zest. That's a state of mind they had, more or less, in the dark ages; and which great masses of people have now in India and the East. And it doesn't work. I don't believe that is the effect you desire."

It certainly was not. Betty applied herself very seriously to getting rid of that possibility of misconception. What is the earth for? Certainly not a mere waiting room. And certainly, if wilfully we use it as such, we shall not become an easily and pleasantly functioning part of her unobstructed universe. If we want to keep really attractive that picture she had drawn — we must earn the privilege. We have responsibility.

"Why," cried Betty, "the fact that you *are* a bit of individualized consciousness is itself a responsibility. The old saw that a chain is no stronger than its weakest link is true as far as it goes. The chain may indeed break there, but it can be mended. The point is, no one should want to be a weakest link — the cause of a need for mending. We all know that in ordinary living, rightness does have a certain reward, and that there are penalties for the breaking of any law. In the greatest actuality, consciousness, of which each of us is a part, that is the truest of all. Consciousness is in evolution. There is no way an individual bit of I-Am can stop it. Each bit has to grow sometime: it has to keep up with the evolutional law. Consequently, the more quantity one attains in the obstructed universe, the more beautifully he will be able to go on in the unobstructed universe. Indeed, just that accumulation of quantity is the reason a long life is desirable. That is why we have to look on suicide as cowardice. The suicide is the fellow who is not willing to accumulate as much as possible.

"In older civilizations, where they have a closer understanding of the indivisibility of the universe, old age is greatly honored and much desired. As Stephen told us years ago, there is a germ of truth in any belief that has survived over long periods. The ancestor worship of the Chinese is a recognition, from one point of view, of the accumulation of quantity given to the whole of consciousness on entering the unobstructed universe. Too great stress cannot be placed on the responsibility of the individual, not only in connection with the whole, but especially in connection with his own I-Am."

"Quite true," I agreed, "and you have expressed the idea before. But it is, to the average mind, too much of an abstraction. It will get mental assent, but mental assent to an abstraction has not nearly the effect of a punch in the nose. If you could tell, concretely, what's going to happen to the fellow who lies down on his job, you'd be getting somewhere. There's considerable virtue in this hell idea as an influence."

"Free will creates its own hell with the widening of the arc of understanding," said Betty. "No person of any sensitivity at all lives in the obstructed universe without having acquired, by maturity, some regrets, either slight or deep, though generally those regrets come only momentarily, in flashes. However, they should make it perfectly possible for anyone to understand the acme of regret that is the portion of the individual coming to this place of perfect understanding who has either shirked or passed by his earth opportunities.

"There is a very definite reality in 'hell' and 'purgatory,' not precisely as the theologians have it, perhaps, but a reality. But no one comes to the perfect understanding without the necessity of a time of readjustment, and wishing he had done differently, and a girding of his loins for going on in the evolutionary process which he cannot escape, and does not want to escape, because it is the law. So it is ever good to pray for the easier girding of the loins, at least, of those who have gone on into the perfect understanding. Why? Because the universe is one. You pray for us: we pray for you. You can be, in a sense, our guardian angels, as we are yours.

"He who comes here without his full accumulation of quantity, cannot quickly assume control and manipulation of the law of the unobstructed universe. It is here exactly as in adultland. A child who is well trained steps into manhood well trained, and can leave childhood behind."

"Well," said Darby, "take a man who does all sorts of wrong on earth. How does he get by so easily over there? How does he so soon get control, and so readily?"

"The answer is, he doesn't; he can't. That's his hell."

"Then actual unhappiness does exist on your side, in certain cases? It must," reasoned Darby.

"You see, consciousness is its own judge. So there must be individual unhappiness — until that consciousness is appeased."

That, she explained further, is one of the great differences between her state and ours. A fundamental in her state — whether of saint or sinner — is a tremendous urge to go on. Some of us here lack that; others may have it, but can ignore or smother it. That is impossible in her world. It is a basic instinct, even more peremptory and compelling than our own basic instincts, such as self-preservation, sex, hunger, thirst.

"It is the same for all," said Betty, "so peace and rest and ease do not come to those individuals as easily. They have to acquire it, to make up for what they did not do there. Furthermore, instead of going forward quickly into a higher degree with its higher perceptions and pleasures, they have to linger in that low degree in which they were. Yet in them the urge is strong. They suffer — from frustrated urge. And when they get here, regret is no momentary flash, to be thrust down, as on earth."

Darby returned to the original topic.

"In the obstructed universe there are material values that can be obtained by stealth and cunning," he propounded, "and if a man gets away with it, he has at least the satisfaction of actual possession. In the unobstructed universe there are no such values. Appreciation of that fact is part of the quick illumination of those who go over there? Here's a fellow who robs some other person, on earth. He goes there. He is quickly illuminated. Now, what restitution can he make to the man he robbed, still on earth?"

"Sometimes he can make restitution. But more frequently he cannot; not in the obstructed universe. I know such a man, and he spends his entire existence futilely trying to rectify, in the obstructed universe, a mistake he made there. In consequence, he was not only retarded when he came, but he is continuing to retard himself."

"Suppose both the wronger and the wronged are now in the unobstructed universe?" asked Darby.

"That is a happier circumstance. That is where the 'seventy times seven' forgiveness thing comes true. They both understand: they both are free."

2.

I had, apparently, brought up a good point. There is, said they, no stability to "spiritual development" unless first a foundation has been established for it by adequate accomplishment of the ordinary things of the life in which we find ourselves. We may think we are making progress for eternity by "withdrawing ourselves from the sordidness of life." We may imagine we are getting somewhere by cultivating assiduously our "higher natures," either by our own inner meditations, or by following the practices of some religion or cult. And, indeed, we may gain by such conscious effort — but only if we have first done thoroughly and adequately the ordinary commonplace job of living out what is thrust under our noses. That is what we are here for. And it makes no great matter how sincere are our "higher" intentions. Betty had scant patience even with those who piously and consciously devote themselves to "service," if by so doing they leave their own backyards cluttered.

"When you make a cult out of service," said she, "you have eliminated service, and created nothing but egoistic satisfaction. And egoistic satisfaction is a straight road to self-adulation, and that leads to attempted dictatorship."

We raked these coals over pretty thoroughly. Charity building up vested interests; altruism so focused on correcting one corruption or negative as to undermine hardly acquired positives — both were uncompromisingly criticized.

"The simplicities of truth have been for too long overshadowed by idealistic thinking," said Betty. "That type of thing establishes vested interests for itself, and then rationalizes and propagandizes for the sake of protecting them. I am not talking about any such colossal systems as have sprung up in Europe. I am speaking only of the comparatively uncomplicated social systems of your own particular way of living. I am not denying democracy. Nor education, nor charity. I am urging them. That is what this whole divulgence, this philosophy, is about! But I am also urging a recognition of the inevitable and undeviating laws of consciousness: an acceptance of them, and a responsibility to and for them.

"After all, if consciousness *is* in degrees, it is in that manner that it has to operate, and it is in that manner it must evolute. You 'can't make a silk purse out of a sow's ear'; but a sow's ear is of itself a very beautiful and soft thing. As I said, the world has gone haywire over idealistic thinking. It's the same story as that of the Jews modeling a calf out of gold, and then being so enamored of the apparent realism of their creation that they set it up and worshiped it as God. Your idealistic thinking has run along the line of trying to force what *you* consider growth on all degrees of consciousness.

"Now I submit, Darby, that that man who was here tonight [a mechanic, who had been called in to make household repairs] is gathering more quantity unto himself by going his own free-willed way according to his degree of quality than if he had permitted you to force on him the reading of books he could not understand, the possession of things he could not afford, or attendance at the opera that would entertain him about as much as Chinese music would entertain the three of you. There has been too much holier-than-thou stuff, and not enough recognition of the genuine adequacy of growth.

"Socially, democracy is the closest thing to real evolution. And it worked very well in this country as long as it operated on the degree method. And whose fault is it that it seems to be falling down? It is the fault of the higher degrees of quality, because they have become so taken up with their own creations — their golden calf — that they have shirked their responsibility.

"You are your 'brother's keepers'; and that goes for high, low and in-between alike. No man — *no* man," she emphasized, "be he born with great or small quality — his individual potential ability — can get away from this fact."

"Now," Darby reverted, "take the person who has fostered or allowed in himself a gradual growth or accumulation of petty griefs, envies, angers, unkindly judgments, intolerances toward his associates, amounting finally to a complex that actually makes a character? How is that resolved in the unobstructed universe?"

"Those are the negatives that must be cradicated in

'purgatory,' if you want to call it that. Such a person must come to a complete understanding, complete selflessness, complete love. *And by his own effort.* Except it might be made a little easier, as we here help each other.

"It is only the emotional things that really count. If people are big enough to live right emotionally, the concrete things can be overridden. Because — and I want you all to get this — because *nothing that happens to an individual is as important as what that individual thinks about it.*"

CHAPTER XXIX

THE CONTINUITY OF EXISTENCE

1.

OCCASIONALLY, after a period of good hard work, Betty was willing to indulge our curiosities a little. But only by way of dessert, as it were. "What do you want to know?" she would ask. Generally these talks started on a more or less frivolous note, but were likely to lead into serious discussion.

"How about dogs? Have you got dogs in your world?" I asked.

"Of course I have my dogs; and I love them," she replied.

"Then they continue on individually as you do? As dogs, I mean."

"The individual is immortal. He or it brings back to its degree its accumulation of quantity, thus raising the degree level. Too bad if, when the degree level is raised high enough to require a new form, there should be no more dogs born!"

"Well, some dogs have been over there so long they ought to show the effects of change, if there is any. How about Moses' and Aaron's dogs?" asked Darby.

Betty chuckled. "Why, I don't even know where Moses and Aaron are!" said she.

2.

This was one of the occasions when our trivialities led into something more serious-minded. Betty's confession of ignorance must have bothered her, for the next session she returned to the subject in the first part of the evening.

"I couldn't find Moses and Aaron," she began on a facetious note, "so I went off on a still hunt for Shadrach, Meshach and Abednego. And I've been told things. Some of them I don't myself quite understand. You see, I went to school and tried to learn some of the things you want to discuss. We were talking about the continuity and persistence of the individual. It's an old story that all religions that survive have glimpses of fundamental truth, which through the years become distorted into dogma. One such glimpse is purgatory. The conventional purgatory does not exist. What does exist is the life immediately beyond death on your plane. During this particular life — my present life — there is very little difference or change.

"Now, the best illustration for the progression of life here is your own. Your life is in stages — early childhood, boyhood, young manhood, middle age, old age. They are all steps, and they are all different. Each one is dependent on its preceding phase and what has been accomplished by and during that phase. My present phase of life, just as yours, is not my last phase. I shall go on again; I shall evolute; and I shall do it as an individual.

"You have been thinking about the persistence of the individual through all eternity in all its degrees; and you were talking about personality, and the difference between the two. Personality is not a strong enough word for my side of the wall. Mere personality can linger and remain potent in your obstructed universe even after the individual has passed to my plane. The personalities of Napoleon, Henry VIII, Plato, Caesar, Confucius, Lincoln — and thousands of others — were so vivid and so expressive of their times that they have remained in the world and in the minds of men.

"Now, it is true that all individuality, on being separated from its lower degree habitat in the obstructed universe, comes back to the qualitative degree out of which it was born into the world for the accumulation of quantity. And it is also true that in this very close-to-you phase of life in which I move and am, there is very little difference. But even on your plane all consciousness is in degrees.

"The lowest degrees of consciousness come back to our plane without much individualization. An electric current is not much different here or there. The difference between your matter and mine is obstruction there and not here. The thing that does persist individually on this plane is that type of consciousness that on your plane has acquired volitional reasoning.

"By that I do not mean instinct only; it goes on through, I don't know for how long. Probably to a certain point of development, rather than for any specific length of time. But only the volitional reasoning creature comes back to its degree as an individual. An amoeba does not come back as an individual. It hasn't the volitional reasoning power, and is absorbed into its degree. The amoeba has its degree here, and it has its purpose, but it does not manifest quite the same here; is not individually immortal, the way I am. For that you have to get closer to the man-degree. Dogs — my dogs are here — they do have fairly high development of volitional reasoning.

"As for me, when I shall go on into my next life, I do not know. They tell me it will be something comparable, but not quite as I know it here. I know there are future manifestations of consciousness, but I do not know their characteristics. I know I shall go on. I have had the experience of transition. You have not. When they say to me that I am going to experience further transitions, but that I am only going to experience something familiar to my being, I believe what I am told. There is an ultimate or supreme degree of consciousness."

"What is the highest degree of consciousness of which you are cognizant?" I asked. "Are there any of which you are not cognizant?"

"I know there are degrees of which I know only a little more than you know about me. I don't think there are any of which I am not cognizant," stated Betty.

"Then I gather there are degrees of consciousness with which you have not come in actual contact," said Darby. "You say there are none of which you are not at least cognizant. What is the content of that cognizance? Have you seen them?"

"I have seen some of them. Some not. I believe what I am told of them, as you believe what you are told of the South Pole, though you have never been there.

"I do not understand all the process, and I do not believe that even questions will make it clear, but I do know that for an ungraspably infinite period the individual man, created in the image of the consciousness that has reached man's estate here, will go on as an individual. 'God made man in His own image,'" Betty quoted. "Human consciousness, the height of individualized consciousness, reveals itself in a form that is a copy of the actuality which is the consciousness itself."

"All consciousness is limited by its degree until it evolves into the supreme," said Anne.

"How many are there — in the supreme? How many have reached the supreme degree?" asked Darby.

Anne indicated that this did not, as yet, concern even her; Betty adding that the whole question was so remote we need not concern ourselves about it either. "Sufficient unto the day is the wisdom thereof," she quoted again, "and, anyway, I don't know enough about it to tell you."

CHAPTER XXX

IMPLICATIONS

1.

So FAR as a system of philosophical thought was concerned the "divulgence," Betty indicated, was complete. We drew a deep breath and relaxed.

"I suppose," mused Darby, "that Betty might sum it all up — in effect, I mean — by saying: 'There! That's how it is. That is how you *do* live with us, removed only an inch from us. Or at least that is how you *could* live.'"

"Well, yes," Betty conceded, "but that's the emotional climax. The real climax is, that here is a reasonable explanation of an unobstructed I-Am, and its habitat. And the startling thing is, that it is not merely logical; it is as you, and your poets and playwrights have most acceptably visualized it. Furthermore, here am I, a woman who is known to have done this work on your side, and who now — still doing the same work — has come back, and has been able to propound this philosophy."

"It's an explanation not so much of the *fact* of immortality, as the *hereness* of it," said Darby.

He was right. The "hereness of it" is what has come to seem most real. That is, to us — who experienced these forty sessions of communication with Betty; sessions vivid with her unseen presence, from turn of phrase and mode of thought to her own especial brand of fun and laughter. But to you who read, the *suggestiveness* of what we were told, together with implications thereon based, must constitute the greater value. The major implications were set forth at length. Others were outlined for us but briefly; just touched upon. A new slant on sociology was suggested; a revitalized and more practically operative code of ethics; an advanced psychology dealing with memory, genius and dreams. The last we were keen to pursue, but Betty would have little of it; and her reticence hinted at other fascinating topics, which, however, she has not yet taken up.

"The subject is an anticipation," said she. "It has directly to do with the Content of Consciousness. But I want to say this much more:

"We do creative things here. There is not much original genius on your side; sometimes there is, but more often what you call genius is a dipping into what individuals here accomplish. Great artists have dexterity; and as a rule they are also great psychics. Sometimes they get our thought without being able to produce it, and that is a real tragedy. Scientists work on what you call scientific discovery, and are subject to sudden solutions of their problems. As in sleep."

"Can you get at us better in our sleep?" one of us asked.

Sometimes, Betty agreed.

"Just as, in this communication, I use the released subconscious of this station, and its storehouse, to produce my message, so in your sleep — to an extent — is your subconscious released. And sometimes the impingement of our ideas is actuated in the same fashion — in sleep — by the stirring of a subconscious memory. Frequently dreams, stripped of their emotional content, are a direct contact with the unobstructed universe and with an idea being promulgated here. With this knowledge you could become mentally adept at using your dreams, and solving your problems during sleep.

"And do not think for one moment that high, low and in-between do not, at times, tap the infinity of our thought."

2.

"I am wondering," said Darby, "about the wisdom of using the word 'prayer.' It has such various connotations in people's minds."

"I think most people understand, dimly at least, what prayer really is," said Betty, "and I think that to most there comes, sometime, a pretty keen understanding. I don't think the exact meaning of the word is discarded."

"To most it means that you are trying to influence a power beyond you in your own behalf," pursued Darby. "It is directed to a god with magic power to answer it. That is not the conception we have. We need some different devotional word to indicate contact with unobstructed consciousness, do we not?"

"The majority of people cannot aspire to such contact," pointed out Betty. "Their degree is not yet high enough. The formulation of a need into a thought, a petition, with the sure submerging of self, that comes with prayer to what is higher and greater than self, is a beneficent operation to the individual, and is a definite projection into the unobstructed universe."

"It is a very good thing to teach children to pray," contributed Anne. "Prayer is an actuality and gives them a belief. The world has got along very well on a belief in prayer, for the voicing of a desire or an emotion makes it concrete. It clears it in your own mind, if nothing else. And maybe when you have formulated it, you find you do not want it; or if you do. . . . It was one of your own great countrymen who said, "God helps those who help themselves!"

"Well, now," said I to Betty, "you have always been beyond the anthropomorphic idea, yet you were always fond of repeating the Lord's Prayer. What did you have in your mind? To what or whom did you address it?"

"To consciousness," replied Betty.

"Did you think of consciousness with personality, warmth — such warmth as comes with personality, I mean?"

"As though I were drowning in a great sea, and there was a shipful of people, any or all of whom could help me," replied Betty promptly.

3.

Perhaps as advanced ideas as any were supplied by the Doctor. You will remember that the very first evening Betty spoke through Joan I asked her if she was "working on the subject of pain, its nature and the technique of handling it" — a message purported to have come from Betty to a friend, and relayed to me — and that she replied she was, under the tutorship of "the Doctor."

This Doctor, dead these many years, and a great friend of Betty's, spoke to us infrequently, but here is a sample of the sort of thing he had to say:

"All sickness in your obstructed universe existence is nothing but a maladjustment of frequencies. All consciousness in the entire universe has a degree-frequency. The individual consciousnesses of the various organs of the body each have their individual frequencies, since all consciousness has its degree-frequency. Now my point is this:

"In the obstructed universe I employed certain drugs, which were themselves really lower degrees of consciousness — each with its own frequency — to stimulate or retard frequency in higher degrees of consciousness as manifested in the human organism. I had, for example, something for a torpid liver, for a tired heart — digitalis — and so on, which should continue to be employed. But with your present concept and understanding of frequency and its relation to consciousness as the reality of which you are a part, I think you could, after a few trials, open your mind to the inflow of the orthic whole for restoring the depleted frequencies of your body. Use your minds! That is one of the truths that has made Christian Science live.

"The only difficulty with that system is that, having added the unobstructed universe's healing concept to earth's own restorative properties, they immediately eliminated the degree-frequencies of drugs. Now, both should be used. If a tool has been placed at hand, why disdain it, if it can aid you?

"When you understand illness and pain from this angle, you can see why the Science healer, not through the laying on of hands, but through the deliberate opening of the mind, does get results, as well as the practitioner of materia medica."

The Doctor in this life was a thorough-going allopath, and — though for his times he was unusually restrained in medication — his doses, when he gave them, were the bitterest of bitter!

More than once he talked to us on the modern use of radium, electricity, various light rays and the like in medicine; all based on the supposition of their being entity frequencies complementing the various degree frequencies of the function of the human organism. It was interesting and provocative but entirely too technical for us to comprehend. It did call to mind, however, recent successful experiments of forcing plant life by means of artificial light and electrical charges and keeping alive an isolated chicken heart through chemical stimulation.

Perhaps if, as Betty claims, they of the unobstructed universe "do creative things" in their celestial laboratories, some obstructed young medico may be "dipping into" the great reservoir of research Betty and her Doctor both insist "is all here waiting to be told" and discover for mankind new "frequency" in healing!

4.

Anne had a last word.

"Long ago I told you," said she, "that the greatness of communication is not the mere fact of communication, but the creation of new understanding. That is what is *real* for you — a new understanding out beyond the current conceptions of the obstructed universe. One of the criteria of your own existence is the endurance potency of new thoughts. Whom do you best remember in your own world? The same is true with us. If we, by any means, can create, for the entire universe, in either phase, a definite and concrete advancement of the experience and thought of that universe, we have shared in real Creation. And if you have wanted a proof that I, that Betty, still exist, better than all the so-called evidential we could possibly give, that proof is in our building up the foundation of your own empirical knowledge into new and advancing thought."

Also it is worth while to quote Stephen's comment when we had finished receiving all Betty and the rest had to say.

"We on this side are almost as much amazed as pleased over what has been done in so short a time," said he. "It has been possible only because, without exception, those involved managed an entire submergence of egoism. And the station has been remarkably cooperative. Her mind is much interested in this, and the natural wish would be to sit in on the party. But there has been as complete and definite a submergence of opinion, personal and theoretical, as one could find. So there has been little coloring. And she has thereby learned a great deal in manipulation of herself as a station. Much of that is due to Mrs. White.

"All this has taken a lot of work. For us, as well as you. Mrs. White has not been alone in it. Indeed she has never claimed to be, and has stated that she was not. But she was decidedly the best adapted to give this, both because of her work there and here. We have really had a pretty large group. Some had the sole job of attending the station. They treated her physically, for health of the physical body. They entertained her. They took her away for profound instruction of a type she has heretofore refused, or been unable to lose herself in. Her success in that was due to Mrs. White and their fondness for each other.

"Mrs. White herself is now getting her reward for not 'finding a place in the universe to slump!' as she expressed it in *Across the Unknown*. There are very few who are able to walk across the no-man's land as sure-

footedly as she. It was not new ground for her: it was a
road she knew. And now she comes back over it with
most unusual ease, and facility and accuracy. Those who
give largely, receive largely. She learned this and prac-
tised it of her own free will."

PART IV

PART II

CHAPTER XXXI

WHAT IT ALL MEANT TO DARBY

1.

I LOOKED at Darby, and Darby looked at me.

"Well!" we exclaimed in unison.

We sat awhile and smoked. We agreed that this had been a most amazing performance.

"To start from *any* premise — true or false — and build on it so inclusive a philosophical structure, so closely knit, so airtight logically: one that proceeds through so wide a range of subjects and interlocks them all so perfectly that not a seam shows; and, with all that, expresses it so simply and clearly —" Darby was overwhelmed, apparently forgetting that Stephen had put on a similar show, more than twenty years ago. "A man *might* do such a thing by his own processes and unaided," he conceded doubtfully. "But you can bet all you've got he wouldn't do it in forty days. Not by forty *years* he wouldn't. Why," Darby was warming up, "he'd get the germ of the idea, and he'd fumble, and he'd cut and try, and he'd go back and modify in the light of his greater thought, and feel about again, and restate, and when he'd got it really airtight — according to him — he'd have white whiskers, and they'd call him a Philosopher, with a capital P.

"And this thing has come complete, as is!" Darby mused a moment. "I'll tell you one thing I know!" he said with conviction. "Joan is out of it — except as the receiving station. She's gone to school, and she's a bright gal on her own, but she just hasn't the equipment. And I know I couldn't do it."

"That goes double for me too," said I. "And Joan has done a grand job as receiving station." A thought struck me. "That reminds me, Betty gave us a job too — as conceiving stations. Now she and Joan have certainly made good. How about us?"

"What do you mean?" inquired Darby.

"Just recall what Betty said when she appointed us," I urged. "We were not only to help develop her thought — subject," I added in rueful reminiscence, "to her correction and veto; but we were to 'reflect back' our understanding, so she could judge how much of her thought she had managed to get over to us."

"I got it," said Darby.

"So did I — I think," I agreed. "So let's do a little 'reflecting back.'"

"As how?" Darby was puzzled.

"Let's sit down and write out, in our own words, what we each understand to be Betty's basic concepts, or otherwise comment on them."

Darby nodded. "Good idea," he approved.

"That will sharpen our own mental picture, at least," I continued, "and I have a hunch that something of our own obstructed viewpoint might help all the subsidiary conceiving stations — may their tribe increase!"

"Huh?" grunted Darby.

"The readers of the book," I explained.

And then, characteristically, it turned out that Betty had intended this all along. She had hinted at a Part IV, for which we could see no material. We told her that henceforth we would utterly give over the hope of having original ideas. She did not like that, even in fun; but we reassured her by the promise of doing a bit of unimportant independent thinking from time to time. After which, Darby settled down seriously to compile his report.

2.

This is conceiving station D-A-R-B-Y speaking.

That there is psychological time as distinct from clock, or sidereal, time seems plain enough. No matter what the clock says, five minutes becomes sixty when you're waiting for a pot to boil. But I don't think Betty would have rung the changes on this obvious enough fact just for the sake of its own exposition. What she really attempted was to entice S E W and me — and you, too — out of our customarily static conception of time, out of the acceptance of an hour as a fixed length, unvarying irrespective of circumstances. That done, she sought to ease us into an appreciation of time's malleable character right here in our ordinary experience.

Yes, psychologically a day may be short or long. We can fidget during the fifteen minutes we wait for a train — bored, empty and bedeviled by frustration — and thus stretch a quarter of an hour into three quarters. Or we can be interested in our surroundings, speculate on where all the people are so intent on going and why, and — presto! — the train arrives before we know it; somehow fifteen minutes has been contracted to one.

So *that* is psychological time— not hard and fixed like sidereal time, but stretchable, contractible, collapsible, elastic, malleable. And all of this is in our daily experience.

I do not remember whether S E W has quoted the

statement, and I shall not stop to search through the record for it, but my recollection is that Betty called time, psychological time, the road by which our understanding might with the least sweat and strain penetrate into her land of the unobstructed. For a certain distance it is a road we know. But perhaps it has not occurred to many of us that, beyond the familiar portion, this road continues as a trail.

Here is a little-trodden path leading beyond psychological time, quite as psychological time carries on beyond sidereal time, to still another kind of time — what Betty at first, for want of the word "orthic," could call only third time.

Have we in our present obstructed state any perception, however elusive, of this third time? The chances are we do have, if the wall between our obstructed universe and Betty's unobstructed is as thin and fragile as she asserts. This much we can now infer: That third time is malleable as is psychological time — only more so; that like psychological time it expands and contracts.

And this must mean that the tenses of sidereal time do not survive wholly intact in the third time; surely they crumble in our daily experience of psychological time. It would seem that, in third time, present, past and future somehow coalesce.

Suppose you enter that railway station again, this time rapt in thought. It will be no unusual experience if you pace about oblivious of everything, finally boarding your train you know not when. In some stray corner of your mind you will have noted its arrival, of course, and you do board it. Nonetheless you were unaware of the passage of the fifteen-minute wait. Clock time ticked its way into a past that left no impression on you. And more ticks were just around the corner of the future, but they were unanticipated by you. Only the present registered. You were *in* that present. Or should I say you *were* that present, that one way or the other you and time, for the while, were one?

Betty's third time is like that. It stretches and it contracts; but neither the stretching nor the contracting can be defined in terms of a sidereal future or past. An odd kind of time, admittedly. But strange also is the malleability of our own everyday sense of psychological time. Look at it as we will, clocks are one thing; our internal timepiece is something else again.

So far, so good.

But I think we can do even better than that. I think that we can dig down into our consciousness, not mystically, but in a rather commonplace way, and find there an all-including present — a matrix, as it were, that receives and registers yet transcends events. Let's try.

There is in you, as I think there is in me, a final point below which there is no need of underpinning. That point is our ultimate foundation, supporting by its own sheer strength all the vast structure of our senses, emotions and thoughts — the manifold of our perceptions, instincts, tastes, our loves and hates, our very response, and even obligation, to the world of things, forces and people about us. It was called by the Jehovah of the ancient testament, "I Am." And after thousands of years, language can find for it no better word. "I Am" — not I was or will be, but just *I am*.

Now, in this deep-down, ultimate core of you do *you* find anything like the past and future that clocks record? I think not. Do you find there primarily just a *becoming*, such as might be measured by the standards of ordinary time? Hardly. I think you will find there, as Betty encouraged S E W and me to find in ourselves, something more fundamental than becoming, basic as that may be, something that after a fashion escapes the squirrel-cage of past and future: *Being* — being that is rooted in one tense only, the present.

You, the innermost you, *are* — co-existing with change and becoming, and so still in time, still a matrix for reception, though looking neither forward nor backward.

That kind of enduring yet malleable present you will find, I believe, in your own feel of being. At least, it is foreshadowed psychologically. It is the third time. It is the orthic time of Betty's unobstructed universe.

3.

If time has three aspects — sidereal, psychological and orthic — so too has space — or so Betty said.

I shall always remember my first automobile. One-lungers had disappeared some time before, but high-compression was still many years away. Tires carried seventy pounds of air and were about as unyielding as the bumpy unpaved roads, which, however undeniably they lured us, had to be negotiated with a fine skill. Differentials had a way of responding totally to every other thank-you-ma'am — they just up and fell out. Axles were always breaking and springs forever going smash.

With the requisite urging this automobile of mine could do twenty miles an hour. But, when on the open highway that speed was attained, farmers working in their fields would turn to see what all the din and uproar was about.

For at twenty miles Peggy (feminine for Pegasus) shook in all her parts, shivered and snorted, rattled and clanked — from radiator to tail-light. And I, with Joan holding her breath in the seat beside me, had a sense of tremendous speed. The rougher the road, the wilder was Peggy's career; and the more boisterous that career, the faster Joan and I seemed to be propelled.

"She certainly eats space up," we used to say affectionately of Peggy, as we bedded her down for the night after a fifty-mile run done in four hours and thirteen minutes flat.

So, right in experience, you and I know that a mile is not simply a fixed geometrical distance between two points. Sidereally it is all of that, but psychologically it varies. Long if we walk it, footsore and weary; short if we ride over a concrete road in a modern motor car geared to do seventy, eighty, a hundred miles an hour.

A commonplace, of course — this mental appraisal of distance in terms of experience rather than in geometrical feet and miles. Betty would not have labored the point, as without ulterior purpose she would hardly have hammered away at psychological time, had she not hoped that through psychological space we could get some inkling of a third space — the orthic space of her unobstructed universe.

As a rationalization, the proposition can now be stated. Betty's space, like her time, is elastic, malleable — in the same way that we know our psychological space to be elastic and malleable. And again it should be added, "only more so."

But must we stop at a mere rationalization?

Unlike S E W, I have not taken to the air. A Pullman compartment, usually entered at night to save a day, remains my fastest mode of travel. Invariably, when I turn my back on the lights and sounds of a busy railway station, board my train and close the compartment door, idling away then the few minutes till the train pulls out, I have this experience: It seems that space in its ordinary sense has vanished, that suddenly all there is of space has been squeezed into the four compartment walls. A feeling of intimacy with it comes over me; space and I are alone at last, and the world with all its places and all that intervenes is gone.

The train now moves, picks up speed; and still all space is compacted within my four walls, but with a difference. Now this intimate all of space has become *fluid*. Malleable? Of course. Has it not all been squeezed into one small Pullman compartment! But it is *flowing* now, and I with it. The two of us seem everywhere, yet nowhere. No longer for me does space mean just the distance between two points. Rather, it's a stream, without banks or landscape — a stream that flows in all directions out from a center which is no dimensional center at all but only myself.

Perhaps the telling of this recurring experience tends to trip and fall into the occult. Yet I have never felt any sense of mystery accompanying it. At least, there's nothing even slightly mysterious about the further fact that after a night's sleep I, who switched off the light just out of Elizabeth, wake up in Chicago, with no feeling of geometrical space traversed or of the places that dot that space. By availing myself of the mechanical help of a railroad I have traveled five hundred miles in less time than a good rider on a good horse could have run seventy, and with infinitely less pains.

After all, then, it is not the number of geometrical

miles that obstructs us, but our inexpertness in telescoping them or, if you will, flowing through them.

In the company of two friends I took an elevator the other day to the sixty-fifth floor of a certain skyscraper. Numerous stops were made on the way up, and finally we reached our floor, and that was that.

But, coming down, we made the descent without stop, clear from the sixty-fifth to the ground floor. There was no sense of speed and little of motion. Unprepared for the mental effect of the long drop, we stepped from the elevator into the lobby.

And — bang! — it was like that explosive recovery from nitrous oxide with which you crash back into everydayness after the dentist has extracted an infected molar. "Where am I?" you demand, faced with just the plain, familiar world, but now for a moment strange and curiously elfin. So my two friends and I felt as we stared about in the lobby of the skyscraper.

Through some trick of the small, moving enclosure called an elevator we had been loosened, maybe, from the space of good old Euclid and then, on reaching the ground floor, unceremoniously dumped back into it.

"Where am I?" I almost asked the starter in the lobby. More sensible perhaps would it have been to ask, "Where *was* I?"

All in all, third space was hard for me to get the hang of. For third time I seemed to have an intuitive feeling. But I could uncover in myself no similar spatial instinct. And Betty's introduction of the time-space concept as an aid to understanding did not help much, though in retrospect it becomes clear that all our modern control of space analyzes down to control of the time required to travel space. With me the time-space idea began really to click only after motion came under discussion.

But, whatever my difficulties, they need not be yours. For some ordinary experience of your own may so illustrate the malleability of psychological space that it will be easy for you to add Betty's new ingredient, the *flow*. Do so, and I think you will have glimpsed orthic space.

And now let's go back for a moment to consideration of unadorned sidereal space. Is there warrant in it, wholly aside from psychological reactions, for Betty's conductivity concept?

Look at the matter in this wise:

Your physical body is itself an obstruction, and as such it is in constant conflict with environing obstructions, the most deterring of them being solids. It is from these solids — the doors of our houses, their walls and floors and furniture; the materials of our handicraft and its tools, from lathes and drills to pencils and paper and even books — that we gather our more obvious spatial impressions. Everything is so long and so wide and so high; and that, we judge hastily, is all there is to space. But even sidereally this is only one aspect, and perhaps not the more fundamental. The other aspect tells us that space is that in which we *move*.

Space itself is not a solid. On the contrary, except as we meet obstructions, we pass right through it. Indeed, it is only because our bodies are material and must be moved about in such a way as to avoid, or utilize, other material obstructions that we are particularly aware of space at all. To the degree that our bodies are not hindered by other material objects, we pay but small attention to the length, breadth and height of things. But always we are aware that we move — through space.

Surely we do recognize the conductivity of space, even in this sidereal world.

So, to use Betty's phrase, *strip* space down. Strip off its three dimensions, and there is still left conductivity. Orthic space *is* conductivity — a fluidity of conduction, neither up nor down nor across, yet, because of its very fluidity, still definitely space.

4.

In presenting orthic motion Betty did not follow the pattern she had established for explanation of third time and third space. Starting with the motion of our obstructed universe, whether astronomical or just pedestrian, she could have passed glibly to psychological viewpoints. For motion — the uniform sway of a clock pendulum, for instance — does seem to speed or slacken according to the observer's interest; at a scene of disaster relief arrives with cruel slowness, be it rushed by horse or truck or plane.

And it was thus that I supposed Betty would postulate orthic motion: malleable, just as a given rate of ordinary motion appears to vary with the conditions under which it is experienced.

My questions led in that direction. Betty would have none of them. Once, if my memory serves me, she came close to denying existence of any such thing as psychological motion. Later she took that half back, with a ho-hum and a yes-no. And in the end she took it back with a vengeance. Thought itself, she announced, is psychological motion! Had this been an early statement, S E W and I might well be floundering still.

In any case, abandoned the established pattern was,

even at the risk of motion appearing for a while to be the ugly duckling of Betty's grand trilogy. Instead, we found ourselves plunged deeper and deeper into that hyphenate of the modern physicist — time-space.

First, let me say that Betty used this concept only as an aid to instruction. When it had done its work, she proceeded promptly to knock the hyphen out, ever so solicitously putting time and space back on their sundry and individual legs.

Several decades ago a search developed among mathematically inclined physicists for a fourth dimension. The length, breadth and height of objects in space, satisfactory enough in everyday thinking, had become inadequate. For it was being experimentally demonstrated that the innerness of all physical things was in flux — even inert matter. And how in the world could one go on charting a no longer static physics in terms of three-dimensional substance?

A number of dizzy books were written. But few, if any, of them tried to name or describe the needed new dimension. That is not to say it didn't exist. As a mathematical X, it opened fields of equations far beyond the ambition of a Leibnitz and his calculus. And as a convenience in accounting for the disappearance of lost articles it was *par excellence*. After a man had searched ten minutes under bed and bureau for his dropped collar button, he could dismiss the wretched thing with good conscience — somehow it had just rolled into the fourth dimension.

Finally something akin to common sense prevailed. By common sense is meant, I take it, the art of reasoning toward what one doesn't know from what one does know. If we can't find a clew to the unknown in empirical knowledge, we had best wait. Otherwise, we are liable to become spinners of remote and inapplicable theories, or, worse, mystics, or, more horrid still, cultists. Anyway, common sense found a fourth dimension, truly essential to the new physics of radiation and electrons and wave-lengths and what-not, in simple, ordinary experience — in *time* itself.

Let's explore the idea. There in the station waits our railway train. It possesses the traditional three dimensions; it is so long, so wide and so high. But now it moves, quitting the station; and, as it moves in the three dimensions of space, uphill and downhill and straight away on the level, it moves as well in a fourth dimension. It swings along in time — in time as in space.

And men say, as they have always said of such matters, that the train moves so many miles an hour, which is to assert that its rate of motion in space can be stated only in terms of time.

But suppose the train does not get under way. Suppose it continues to stand still. Nonetheless it moves, because it is part and parcel of an earth that itself is in motion.

So pertinent to any analysis of motion is this concept that one may well ask whether time-space is not just another name for motion. Maybe so, and maybe not so. This much, at least, the concept makes clear:

Without the time dimension there can be no sidereal motion, and, equally, there can be none without the dimensions of space. In other words, there can be sidereal motion only in time plus space.

But where does this get us in understanding orthic motion?

Betty says that her unobstructed universe is but an

extension of our obstructed. To use Stephen's language of some twenty-five years ago, the two worlds function under parallels of one and the same law. This being so, it follows that motion in the unobstructed universe is as inextricably tied into an orthic time-space as motion here is tied into sidereal time-space. If, then, we have learned anything of orthic time and orthic space, no matter how little, we probably have learned a like something about orthic motion. Let's see.

Sidereally, any really instantaneous transit is impossible. The train can move faster and faster as the engineer desires, but only up to a certain limit. There is a final maximum rate of speed beyond which it can not go. Light moves fastest of all, so fast that astronomers set down its speed in terms of years; but even in the instance of light there is always just so much movement in any given interval of time. Never in the obstructed universe is motion transmitted instantaneously.

In the same way, sidereal motion cannot escape the fixed distances of space. However fast the train, it must run the exact length of each individual mile traveled.

But orthic time, we have learned, is malleable, collapsible; and orthic space is a flow, a completely rarified conductor if you please. In such a time and such a space, the instancy of motion becomes conceivable or, if not quite conceivable, imaginable.

And that — instantaneous transit, with all the brakes of sidereal time-space released — is half, more or less, of Betty's story of orthic motion, as told through Joan.

You will understand now, I think, why Betty did not rely on psychological considerations to demonstrate the motion of her unobstructed universe. Sidereal motion, unlike sidereal time and space, is patently malleable here in the obstructed universe. It not only *seems* that way to us; it *is* that way. We can walk or we can run. By interest and anticipation we can speed the frequency of our very heartbeat. S E W and I knew that all along, and Betty knew that we knew it. But what about it? It helped us not at all to apprehend instancy, that is, motion unlimited by a maximum rate.

Our effort to visualize an infinitely accelerated flywheel did help — some — at the time. But this was largely an intellectual exercise. For myself I had no *feel* for that sort of flywheel, though at the point of infinity its motion would plainly imply instancy.

No, some other device was called for — and provided. The time-space concept, offering an everyday frame for sidereal motion and then argued from the obstructed to the orthic, turned the trick — for me. At least, I can state the proposition:

Motion in the obstructed universe is gripped in the vice of sidereal time-space. That time-space is fixed, and any motion through it is potentially limited. The parallel motion of the unobstructed universe is as unrestricted as the orthic time-space in which it functions. And orthic time-space is limited neither by tense, direction nor extraneous resistence. In orthos, motion is instant.

You may say, as I was tempted to say, that this annihilates time, that a truly instantaneous motion would have no need of time. But that is to think in terms of sidereal time, with its three tenses. Furthermore, Betty cautioned us again and again not to confuse the rate of motion with motion itself. Perhaps all this can be made clearer if we pause to answer the question asked a page or two back: Is time-space just another word for motion? The answer is, no.

I walk into a room, stumble and in recovering my balance knock a chair over. As it topples to the floor it is in motion; it moves through time-space. But time-space was there before my awkwardness upset the chair, as it will be after I put the chair to rights. Given time-space and it only, the world would lie as unruffled as the night before Christmas, when, as everybody knows, not a creature was stirring. A *stir*, an *activating* something must exist as a condition precedent to any motion.

It is that stir, orthic in the final analysis, which, colliding with sidereal time and space in the obstructed universe, sets up the phenomenon we know here as the time-rate of motion. The stir itself requires no rate.

And now to get back to earth, if only briefly. Let's reason out the second half of Betty's story of motion unobstructed. This exploration need not press beyond mundane frontiers.

In everyday motion we deal first with our bodily impacts. We hit things and they move. And so we are inclined to assess all motion in terms, say, of a billiard table. The cue strikes a ball. Immediately that ball leaps into motion and hits another, which in turn rushes off to hit a third. Finally all the balls are at rest again, and we say that the motion set up by the impact of the cue has spent itself. The fact, of course, is that that motion did not *spend* itself, did not cease, but was merely *distributed*, its big stream breaking up into innumerable small streams no longer apparent to us.

It is only on reflection that we note that motion never comes to rest. It may be transferred or transformed until it eludes our senses; but, on second thought, we are not deceived. It still oscillates, actually or potentially, in one wave-band, so to speak, or another.

Of course, then, orthic motion is perpetual, just as perpetual as is sidereal motion. And again it is well to add, "only more so." This is why Betty spoke tolerantly of the "mad inventors" who, glimpsing a truth, have labored honestly, if fatuously, to apply it. Their perpetual motion machines have not come off for a variety of reasons. Nevertheless motion itself is perpetual.

Perpetualness, demonstrated in the obstructed universe, is the other half of Betty's story of orthic motion.

We know now two characteristics of the orthic stir, the activating impulse without which time and space would be as dead as a herring — instancy and the state of being perpetual. And we know one thing that this stir is *not* — thought. For thought, says Betty, is *psychological* motion; and I suppose that psychological motion is as remote from orthic motion as sidereal is short of psychological. Yet, to use the word of children playing hide-and-seek, thought is "warm" — warmer than the sway of a pendulum or even the course of the planets around the sun.

From the very beginning of Betty's divulgence, it was a sidereal word that she used to express the essence of orthic motion — "frequency." This, I think, was because modern physics has gained wide acceptance for the word and given it new and flexible meanings. Also Betty may have been influenced by the fact that men know much about the deep inwardness of themselves and can tell little, while of the world outside themselves they know little, yet feel qualified to tell much. Pardonable, since language depicts the outer world more adequately than it does the inner.

5.

There remains a clump or two of underbrush to clear away, and then, I rather think, we shall be ready to make trial of what Betty, borrowing again from the Greek, called "trilogia" — her threefold frame of consciousness.

First, we must not be tempted to regard time, space and motion as mere attributes of consciousness, as one might say blueness is an attribute of the sea. Under shifting light conditions, the sea may be blue or it may be green or just gray; it is still the sea, whatever its color. Time, space and motion, however, are of the very fabric of consciousness. If it is correct to say that they exist no otherwhere than in consciousness, it is hardly less correct to say that consciousness exists no otherwhere than in them.

The second misconception we shall want to guard against is illustrated by the very emphasis of what I have just written. I seem to suggest that the sum of time, space and motion equals consciousness. Not so. Always consciousness works through time, space and motion, but their total is not consciousness, any more than leaves, branches and roots add up to make a living tree.

One thing more, in passing: The word trilogia could be applied, of course, to the time-space-motion complex in which we function here in the obstructed universe, as well as to orthos. Do not the obstructed and unobstructed parallel each other in all respects, existing under one law? But it was not the obstructed universe that Betty sought primarily to clarify. She was trying to rationalize the unobstructed. For the ends of language she reserved the term trilogia for the orthic complex, and it has seemed best to S E W and me to preserve that usage.

And now let's get on.

Consciousness has three co-existences. From the obstructed point of view this is not a difficult statement. You are constantly in time; you are constantly in space; and I suspect you are constantly in motion, or at least you are always in the midst of motion. It is not otherwise in the unobstructed universe, granted that time there is not measurable by clocks, space by footrules or motion by speedometers.

Betty's trilogia, co-existent with the consciousness that is she, consists of *orthic* time, the essence of which is *receptivity; orthic* space, the essence of which is *conductivity;* and *orthic* motion, the essence of which is *frequency.*

A day or two after the essences were sprung on us, without which I am afraid trilogia might indeed have proved just a verbal curiosity, Joan, S E W and I had occasion to drive sixty miles across country. As we climbed into the car, I had a big idea. For the purpose of this one ride, why not forget all our ordinary notions of time, space and motion and instead think only in terms of receptivity, conductivity and frequency? "A good idea if it works," agreed S E W.

Well, it worked and it didn't. Certainly the well-tuned motor fired with an unmistakable rhythm, and regularly this frequency was transmitted to the wheels of the car. There was conductivity too, such as modern road-builders know how to make; for we were being propelled *through* rather than *against.* And there was receptivity, maybe. S E W said the receptivity was good, meaning, I inferred, that, as the countryside was new to him, his mind was registering many fresh and interesting impressions. To Joan and me the receptivity was only fair; we had taken that ride too many times before.

"How shall we define the rate of this frequency?" I asked S E W.

"So much conductivity per so much receptivity," he replied with a twinkle.

"Hooey!" volunteered Joan. "Why not say a mile a minute and be done with it?"

Why not, indeed? For were we not right where we began — in sidereal time, space and motion? The plain fact was that we had never got out of them. And that, of course, was why the experiment had failed to work.

"But," I said, "it does help. Imagine a road of perfect smoothness, running through an atmosphere of no resistance. That road, that space would suggest just conductivity."

"A super speedway for a motor of unlimited frequency!" S E W contributed.

"Provided," said Joan, "one hasn't brought the wrong kind of receptivity along. I insist on the orthic brand."

I think Joan's insistence went pretty straight to the heart of things. The effort of our technical age has been to control motion, to speed it and so to collapse time. Thus stated, time shortens as an effect of speeded motion. But actually it is the other way around. You must tinker with time first, seeking to step up its ratio to space. Accelerated motion is the external evidence of how well you have done that tinkering.

Betty says she controls her orthic time, the essence of which is receptivity. How? By manipulating receptivity? How? I was in deep water.

To say that space, orthically viewed, is essentially a

matter of conductivity was becoming acceptable enough, because in ordinary experience space *is* a conductor; we do go through it. To say that the essence of orthic motion is frequency may require a deal of explanation, but it rings a bell, because even in the obstructed universe we are so accustomed to analyzing motion into vibrations, cycles, rhythms — in fact, frequencies. But to me time seemed possessed of other characteristics quite as essential as receptivity.

There was duration, for example. Had I been asked before Betty came what was the essence of time, I am confident I would have replied, "Duration." Surely so subjective a characteristic as receptivity would not have occurred to me; such is one's inveterate devotion to the working materialism of the obstructed universe.

And I was not content even after Betty explained at length how all things are received in time, and in time only, and how an event remains influential after its occurrence — as the influence of a man may continue after his death — precisely because of the receptivity which is time's essence. I was impressed, but not satisfied.

So I had to back-track. I had to remind myself again of what Betty was really trying to do. It was this: She was seeking to explain to us why her world is unobstructed and the how of it; she was trying to make her unobstructed state reasonable in terms of our obstruction.

All right, then, how do we *here* overcome obstruction?

The sixty-mile cross-country automobile ride is a good enough answer. We *mastered* space, because a mechanical gadget, our gas engine and its appurtenances, had put us in a position to take more than usual advantage of conductivity. But we did not really *shorten* space. As to time, that we *did* shorten, relatively. We traveled sixty miles in the interval it would have taken us to walk five. And how did we do that? By manipulating duration? Scarcely. For duration, I was learning, really was the thing shortened. We shortened time, because we had increased its receptivity — crammed more into it, as it were — thanks to our humming motor.

Orthic space is no obstruction at all to Betty, if she is in full control of its essence, conductivity. I had ceased to argue about that. And it now seems that there can be as little argument over the essence of orthic time, receptivity. For it is only in this characteristic of time, as we know it here in the obstructed universe, that control is to be predicated.

To the extent that Betty can increase receptivity, that is, fill time to its utmost, to the extent that she can increase conductivity, telescoping mere distance, to that extent she can step up, as she will, the essence of motion, frequency — all this simply on the basis of an altered time-space ratio. It is in this orthic ratio that motion becomes instantaneous; time becomes an all-inclusive now; and space becomes only a stream of non-resistance.

To assert these wonders of the trilogia would seem fantastic were it not that we find them grounded right here in the commonplace experience of our obstructed universe. After all, these are the very wonders that Joan, S E W and I worked in that sixty-mile auto ride — imperfectly. We shortened time by crowding its essence, receptivity. We overcame space by utilizing to unusual degree its essence, conductivity. And motion beyond the dreams of shanks' mare resulted. As Mr. Wordsworth might have said — Trilogia lay all about us.

6.

Speaking of wonderland, you'll recall that when Alice arrived on the other side of the looking-glass she was horrified by the persistence with which the people she found there attached strange and outlandish meanings to comfortable words that Alice had always supposed she understood quite well. So it had to be explained, and this is what they told her concerning one of their puzzlers:

"You see it's like a portmanteau — there are two meanings packed up in one word."

Betty's term "frequency," I take it, is a portmanteau word. And therein it differs from her other terms, receptivity and conductivity.

As a word, "receptivity" functions well enough whether applied to material or psychological processes. For instance, paper is receptive to ink, and likewise your mind is receptive to sensory impressions. In the same way, the word "conductivity" blankets both the objective and subjective ranges. A length of pipe is conductive of water; from the verbal standpoint, one can say just as reasonably that your mind is now serving as a conductor of the thought expressed in this sentence.

But with the word "frequency" it is different. There may be a word so descriptive of the essence of motion as to work both materially and psychologically. But I don't know it. Neither apparently did Betty. Anyway, it was a portmanteau word that she left with S E W and me — a word of two meanings. Rather, I fear of three and maybe more.

Frequency — what is it sidereally? On first consideration, only the number of vibrations in a unit of time. That's our take-off; and in these latter days we get off the ground quickly enough, leaving such old-time familiars as the oscillating clock pendulum and the vibrating piano string far below. For now the primary meaning of the word is no longer so simple. With the discovery and utilization of electricity, including in recent years what we have come to know as radiant energies, the connotations of the term have been vastly broadened. Now we talk confidently of radio frequencies. We never saw or felt one. But because of mechanical registration we know they are.

It is this territory of new energies — and of older but equally baffling ones such as light — which Betty (or was it Anne?) called "no-man's land." Scarcely nonmaterial are they, nor yet material in the old acceptance of the word.

A few pages back we tried to isolate two characteristics of orthic motion — perpetualness and instancy. As motion is perpetual even in the sidereal universe, further comment is unnecessary. But sidereal motion is not instant. Orthic motion is, says Betty. If so, perhaps the frequencies of no-man's land foreshadow orthic instancy. Certainly they should do a better job of showing the way than do the grosser vibrations of tuning forks and such.

The radio announcer, broadcasting miles off, says: "Eight o'clock by Fugit, the world's most estimable watch." And we, sitting at our firesides, haul out our own watches to see if they need resetting. So close to instantaneous is the transmission of the radio frequency that we ignore the lag between the announcer's spoken words and our reception of the impulse that reproduces those words in our own living rooms. This discrepancy never occurs to us.

Or we push a button in the wall and expect instantaneous response in the chandelier, and for all practical purposes we get it.

So our present-day experience does encompass frequencies approximately instantaneous. Suspect, therefore, the existence of really instant frequencies, as far beyond radio, for example, as radio is beyond a clock pendulum. Thus SEW and I were charged by Betty, through Joan.

In fact, one of these ultra frequencies men have known since men were, more intimately than they know land and sea and all that in them is. But, because they have found no way of measuring this particular frequency, they still swear by the gods of earth, air and water. Good, reliable old gods, to be sure! But their robust objectivity became measurable only when yardsticks were devised and applied by *thought*.

True, the energies of no man's land lift our understanding of frequency, the essence of motion, beyond the simpler mechanisms. But with the frequency we so intimately know as thought we climb high above no-man's land, high above wave-lengths, and quanta and what have you.

Betty did not ask us to conceive thought as orthic motion. For us in the obstructed universe it remains only a psychological frequency, still short of orthos, but powerful, *real* and pointing straight up the skyway in the direction of orthic frequency itself.

Let's test the proposition out. Assume that thought is a frequency, an ultra frequency, foreshadowing the orthic essence of motion. In that case you would not expect to find it in sidereal space. Do you? Obviously not. Nor would you expect it to be confined in sidereal time. Is it? The *act* of thinking may be in sidereal time, but thought itself jumps all sidereal barriers. The truth is, neither space nor time obstructs it. You can think of China, not as accurately, but as easily as you can think of the street you live on. You can think of 10 B. C. as easily as you can of 1940 A. D.

There was once a very great philosopher who, wishing to prove all things, began by trying to prove his own existence. And he proved it, in his own estimation, by saying, "I think. Therefore, I am." Critics ever since have been clamoring that Descartes could have said with equal sense, "I walk, or I talk, or I weep. Therefore, I am." But the critics, I submit, have been only half right. For, while it may be futile for any man, no matter how great a philosopher, to attempt to prove the only thing that he really *knows*, his own consciousness through which he infers all else, nonetheless long before consciousness walked or talked or wept or even rejoiced, it *thought*, if only amoeba-wise.

Another thing: Betty says that we here always confuse the obstructed manifestations of the simple mechanical world, and those of the more complex no man's land, with motion *per se*. We are made that way, it seems — with an exception, however, in the case of thought. Thought is a thing that we never confuse with objective manifestation. We may think to walk, but we do not call walking thinking. And there, too, thought is on the side of the angels.

Again, if thought previews the essence of orthic motion, we would expect it to be close to instantaneous. Is it not so? And we would expect it to be close to perpetual. Surely it is ceaseless in our waking moments; and we are told by psychologists that subconsciously it continues even in our deepest sleep. Betty is living proof — to me — that its activity survives bodily death.

In the same vein, thought does not vanish with the act of thinking; the thoughts of a thousand years of yesterdays color today, for better or worse, and will color tomorrows unnumbered.

Yes, I think thought offers specifications on which to build whatever lame conceptions of orthic frequency we denizens of the obstructed universe are capable of. It is the freest, the least obstructed fact in our experience. And, more, is it not the great creator? Is it not our world's biggest stir, its mightiest activity, its most potent impulse?

I make these observations on thought not to glorify it. There are negative as well as positive thoughts. My purpose is only to suggest some experiential basis for your and my understanding that the essence Betty calls frequency is the *activating* impulse, without husk, shell or wrapping — obstructed in this world, but with thought offering a glimpse of its unobstruction in orthos. There is nothing I can add to the phrase "activating impulse." We shall just have to let it go at that, with, however, a caution or two.

Don't think that by frequency is meant consciousness itself. Frequency, the essence of orthic motion, activates consciousness, and is co-existent with it, but not more so than is receptivity, the essence of time, or conductivity, the essence of space. All three together constitute the trilogia of consciousness. They are interfused and interdependent.

Nor should we vainly imagine that all orthic frequency

is of the same degree. As there are many sidereal frequencies, each differing from the other, so there are many orthic frequencies. Betty's world is as pluralistic in its monism as is our own.

For instance, there is in our world this thing we call electricity. We know that we do not know its essence; all that we know about it is the manner in which it behaves in obstruction. In the unobstructed universe the essence is known and dealt with. And that illustrates why, when we asked Betty if there were electricity and oxygen and bricks and sticks and stones in her world, she answered, yes — even at the risk of being Sir Oliverish. But always she added that she knew and dealt with these things, not in their obstructed aspect as we do, but in their essence.

Never fear but that Betty's unobstructed universe has all the infinite variety of our obstructed universe — "only more so," what with frequencies we here have not been able to reach up to, and she there, reaching down to us, is unable to bestow.

So the portmanteau character of the term "frequency" need no longer concern us, because it is clear that frequencies must be in degrees, as is consciousness itself. There is no difference·in kind between the essential frequency of ordinary visible motion and a radio wavelength; there is only a difference of degree. In essence, a radio wave-length and thought are alike in kind; they, too, differ only in degree. It is the same way with thought and the frequencies of orthos.

But Betty did not mean that all orthic frequencies are of a potential equal to that of thought. On the contrary, thought, even as it operates in the obstructed universe, has a potential far beyond that of many a frequency of the unobstructed universe. She meant only that in the unobstructed universe all motion is apprehended in its essence and that our feel of the freest obstructed motion, thought, gives us a clue to motion's orthic essence, called by her for the purpose of her divulgence, *frequency.*

7.

Still another of Betty's terms seems to warrant special attention — "arrestment." She had her bit of fun with me there, as I maneuvered this way and that to get at her meaning. But I forgive her. Certainly I had earned no "ticket" for speeding. I was guilty only of the common and relatively trivial offense of blocking the traffic. In the name of the unobstructed universe, aren't we all!

You and I — every mother's child of us — are arrested, joking aside. And so are all other frequencies manifesting in obstruction. Thus spoke Betty. Perhaps a moment's introspection will help us to understand.

We have all had the experience of being lifted out of ourselves by great music or perhaps just a good movie. Under the spell of art, we escape our encirclement. That is, we imagine we are escaping it. And then when the play is over, what do we do? Do we go out and crystallize the vague aspirations of make-believe into fact? Sometimes — if we have aspired quantitatively, as Stephen would say. But if we have aspired qualitatively, and often we do, it is otherwise. Here we are left to settle back as comfortably as may be into what we really are.

The point is that but slight self-analysis is required for each of us to recognize arrestment in himself. We know our arrestment unmistakably enough whenever we try to escape it.

But in the field of self-awareness, as elsewhere, arrestment of frequency does not imply obdurate limitation. That can hardly be, urged as we are by our deepest nature to break through whatever it is that confines us. And surely arrestment implies no dead stop. It means only a *suspension* of potentiality. Nonetheless, frequency as it manifests in the obstructed universe is arrested; it does have its point of suspense.

Take the electric fan that Joan was repairing one morning in the early days of Betty's divulgence. Let's say it was a fan of two speeds. The low speed we'll label 50 and the high speed 100. We set the fan revolving at 50. It will go right on revolving at 50 indefinitely, though its over-all frequency is 100. In other words, without disturbing the potential of 100, we have arrested the fan's motion at 50.

Now, forgetting about 100 being a potential, we'll push the control lever directly into high. With the fan going twice as fast as before, we note a curious effect — just as did Joan. Whereas at 50 we could see the blades clearly, now we don't see them at all. We look right through them at the wall behind.

It is easy for us to say that the fan is revolving too rapidly for our eyes to follow its motion, and that's true. But something else is also true, something that is independent of our eyes. It can be stated this way: At 100 the blades of the fan are traveling twice as far as they did at 50 — in the same unit of time. Into the same time interval we have packed double the space.

And this brings us to Betty's statement that matter as we know it in the obstructed universe is an arrestment of frequency resulting from a certain incidence of motion in time and space. This is not altogether a hard saying, if, for the purpose of illustration, you will assume 100 to be the essence of motion, frequency itself in its orthic meaning. To our obstructed eyesight the blades of the fan are invisible at 100 (essence); there is just the wall behind the place where the fan was. But now we pull the control back to the 50 mark of arrestment. Behold the fan again, safely back in the obstructed universe! All done by a simple shift of the time-space ratio.

Physicists have been telling us for some years now that there is no material substance as we have understood the term in the past; that instead there are only aggregates of energy. Matter, it seems, is the name that we popularly apply to those particular stress-knots that are three-dimensionally measurable. Well, it is the arrestment of frequency, if I understand Betty correctly, that makes that measurement possible. It is the arrestment, in fact, that we measure.

8.

The universe, Betty told S E W and me, is one and entire, despite its two aspects. Therefore this one and entire universe is *here* now, despite our obstruction.

Go into a dark room. You blunder around and see nothing. That's one aspect. Now find the electric switch and flood the room with light. You no longer blunder about; now you see furnishings and decorations, colors and shapes. That's another aspect. Yet both aspects are of the same room. And this is the room you were in all the time. You are still in it and will be in it. You perceive the room in obstruction. Betty perceives it in essence. The mental and actual. The astral altogether, as—

Did you ever see two sides of a coin at one time? You could do that only with mirrors. Yet, seeing one side of a coin, you do not deny the existence of its other side, or that both sides belong to the same coin.

It has not been my purpose, in this contribution to SEW's more detailed report, to tie Betty's divulgence down to hard and fast formulas. That I could not do, and would not if I could. For she intended her divulgence only as an aid to thinking, as suggestion rather than statement.

The truth never varies. Men's understanding of it does, and will for long, long ages to come. New knowledge brings new understanding. Hence it is that dogma dies. To me it seems that the fruits of Betty's divulgence are for those of us who are still willing to ask: "Where shall wisdom be found, and where is the place of understanding?"

This is conceiving station D-A-R-B-Y. I return you now to S E W.

CHAPTER XXXII

THEY SHALL BE COMFORTED

1.

"Now," said Darby to me after he had finished the foregoing, "it's your turn."

"It is," I acknowledged. "Only — what you have written so exactly expresses my own understanding that you've left me nothing to do! And I'm not saying that to dodge work, either."

"I hope it will help," said he, "for it does take some thinking out, I found. I wonder how many people will 'get it'?"

"More than you think," I assured him. "It offers as first concepts what anyone can understand, and what everybody wants. And it goes on to show that anyone can have it. An unobstructed universe," I anticipated the question he looked as if he were about to ask, "immortality; life beyond death. They'll get Betty's new terminology, and the reassurance that terminology carries with it, whether they get all the finer points of the argument or not."

"I don't know," doubted Darby.

"I do," I persisted. "Why, an eight-year-old child knows he lives in an obstructed universe. He knows because he bumps into it. So even the eight-year-old will understand that much if he is told. And a twelve-year-old, tinkering with his radio, has a glimpse, through it, of the possibility of unobstruction. And so on right along the line. Every man knows only too well that he lives in an obstructed world. Everybody has at least imagined a world without obstruction as the height of desirability.

It's an almost universal hope — more or less vague — but characteristic of man as far back as history goes; how things will be when he 'dies and goes to heaven.' So now if he sees a good chance that he's going to get some acceptable foundation for his hope; that this divulgence of Betty's gives good and acceptable reasons, not based on mere statement, but on what he himself knows and experiences in his everyday life . . . why, he's going to follow that argument even if it is a little difficult for him. But," I added, "I don't myself think it *is* difficult. I asked my typist to be a guinea pig for me and mark down any points that seemed obscure to her, but she found it clear enough, and she was busy typing, remember, and —"

"Hold on," Darby stopped me, "don't talk at me. Write it down. I've tried to give my understanding of the concepts as I see them. Suppose you give your understanding of the significances as you see them."

"I'll try," I agreed. "It's a large order."

2.

Mankind has always had the picture of two entirely different states of being separated from each other as by a wall — the "on earth" and "in heaven" idea. That division has been expressed, of course, in all sorts of terminology. But the concept is always the same; in every age, by every race, through every creed.

Betty called it the obstructed and unobstructed universes, but she denied the wall between. That was her mission in her present divulgence — to knock down the wall.

To accomplish this she pointed out, first, that there are

not really two universes, but only two aspects of one. We here live in the obstructed aspect, a proposition none of us is likely to deny. Given this fact, the logical deduction would be that she lives in the other, the unobstructed aspect. But that, astonishingly, she asserts, does not follow. On the contrary, says she, she lives in *both* aspects, in the *entire* universe; in the obstructed phase — that tiny percentage of the whole which we of earth inhabit — as well as in the vast and mysterious unobstructed portion she assures us science has glimpsed but of which as yet we know next to nothing. It is one homogeneous universe to her, simply because what are obstructions to us are not obstructions to her.

So we are forced to modify our earth-heaven picture. We must see ourselves as living in a minute segment of a "one and only universe," held within its confines by obstructions that affect only us. Those obstructions have nothing to do with Betty's state of being; they are inherent to ours, and even are, somewhat, of our own production. Furthermore they are, to a greater extent than we have realized, removable by ourselves — if we thought so, and knew how. That is one of the things Betty tried to show us; to what extent and how. And here we touch the practical value of her divulgence for us, right now, at the present time. Especially at the present time.

For she insists there is no wall! The two universes, or rather the two aspects of the same and only universe, are already so alike in texture that they interfuse. In fact, there seems to be a "no-man's land" in which even we of the obstructed aspect can scarcely tell which is which! But Betty defines first the one, then the other, in the terms of our own thinking, to show that the *only* difference between the "two worlds" is from our viewpoint, and is no more than that little business of obstruction. From her viewpoint there is no basic difference. Each removal of obstruction brings these viewpoints — hers and ours — closer together. And from the beginning of time man has been busily doing just that; removing obstructions and thereby eliminating, as far as he is concerned, some of the differences.

Betty's present effort is to convince us of this fact, of the gradual elimination of the obstructions; to prove to us that this underlying principle may be made — *and by ourselves* — even more workable for us, so that we may be less bewildered, so that we may proceed more confidently and understandingly and happily toward conditions of less and less obstruction. Personally and racially.

How she builds up to that great concept through analysis of the fundamental principles of the entire universe in its obstructed and unobstructed aspects — ours and hers — is the body of this book.

3.

Betty further says that the human race has come to a point in evolution where, as she expresses it, "consciousness must be ploughed." I believe her. It may suffice in our earlier and cruder stages to pattern life on mere self-preservation, with the accompanying greed, indifference to the other fellow, hatreds, cruelties and treacheries necessary to carry out that scheme of things. But civilization is supposed to be growing out of it. As individuals I think we are making pretty good progress toward growing out of it. But our collective policies have been too often based on the same barbarisms; and, in singular blindness to opportunity, we have recurred obstinately after each lesser ploughing to build anew the same old structures on the same old foundations.

Worse, we latterly have showed a tendency to sheer away from the straight path of such progress as we have made. We have gone far in our understanding and control of physical matter and force since the days when we lived in caves and did our controlling mostly with our two bare fists. Indeed, so far have we gone that we have lost sight of the two truths that are the underpinning foundations of all advancements in living: the creator is more important than the thing created: the end and aim of evolution is the perfection of the whole through the unretarded functioning of its individual parts.

Perhaps in ordinary course a swing toward materialism is normal. Any forward movement occupies a broad band of extremes. And it is the commonplace of commonplaces to say that we have not caught up spiritually with our scientific achievements — assuming comfortably that we are going to do so in due time. But unfortunately we have showed few indications of so doing. After every ploughing of consciousness — even those of more recent years — we have again set up things-created as the ends of desirability — as our golden calf to worship.

Now by that I do not mean merely the material "products of civilization." We might, with a little more growth, be able to handle them. To take them in our stride, as it were, and to control them. I want to include also the trend of thought that more and more subordinates the individual to the institution and the thing; a trend that reaches its logical and predestined end in totalitarianism. Which means only, "stripped down," that the state, the nation — man-created — is so much greater than the individual that the latter must be sacrificed to it. But do not mistake me: governmental totalitarianism is only the outward and visible symbol.

The same trend runs deep through all modern life, not only political and social, but economic, industrial, artistic and even the formal-religious. And in its pursuit, often sincere, men have been forgetting more and more the basic truth — that there can be but one Reality: that the Intent of that Reality, which is Consciousness, is Evolution; and that the one law of evolution which we of earth have established beyond question is that it proceeds exclusively *through the individual*. We are parts of a Whole; not alike, not even of equal degrees of capacity and potentiality; but no part is of lesser importance than another part, and no part greater.

Again and again during the forty sessions of her "divulgence" Betty insisted on the value of what she called "stepladders" as aids in reaching up to her ideas. Many such stepladders did she actually point out to us — though she seemed to find more value in teaching us how to recognize them for ourselves.

"Find one of your own stepladders," she would say when we failed to understand, "climb to the top of it, and reach from there."

Those she did indicate she brought to us from all kinds of sources; from science and the arts, from history, from fairy tales, from the Bible. The latter especially; because, she reminded us, "as an exposition of the human emotions" it is rich in stepladders. What worthwhileness Betty herself places on that record comprised of the Old and New Testaments I am going to let her say for herself later in this chapter. But I myself found so good a stepladder concerning our individual importance to the Whole of which we are each parts, that I want to call it to your attention right now. It is too long to quote. You can read it for yourself in the twelfth chapter of St. Paul's First Epistle to the Corinthians. I was particularly interested in the 12th to 26th verses inclusive. It is, beyond question, the simplest, clearest statement of democracy I have ever read. "For as the body is one and hath many members ... the eye cannot say unto the hand, I have no need of thee; nor again the head to the feet, I have no need of you. ..." But take time to read the entire chapter. A great metaphysician and a wise man — Paul.

4.

Now, as I hinted, a certain amount of calf-worship may be part of the method of progress, provided we balance it with proportionate spiritual expansion. Nobody wants to go back to the flickering of candlelight, and there is no reason, moral or material, why we should. In fact, there is every reason why we should not. But for the sake of the steadier, clearer light of a tungsten lamp we are not called upon to sacrifice the hard-won treasure of past spiritual attainments.

The creations of man's hands are cheap — cheap in time and sweat — as the creations of men's souls are dear in age-long struggle. Not through any one, or two, or even dozens of brilliant generations, but through age-long struggle has man attained the simple things of the spirit, what we call the homely virtues. The sacredness of a promise; the sense of moral obligation; common ordinary veracity; personal integrity, individual liberty, elementary justice...to mention only a few. And in the end — when all else in the world crashes about our lives — they are the things to which we turn; the things that count. The "homely" virtues. Spiritual values.

5.

This ploughing of consciousness is no affair of judgment or retribution, but of simple cause and effect, as natural as the reaction of the bodily process when, at a certain stage in hyperacidity, the body starts to produce its own correcting alkali. The present catastrophe in Europe is no product of proximate circumstance, nor wholly of any one race or cast of thought. It is, rather, that men's minds have more and more centered on the material world outside themselves, less and less have they looked within, until, at last, almost nothing of their attention turns to the inward searchings that alone maintain spiritual faith.

Now, the only way that an individual, who has so prospered in this world's goods that he has become wholly engrossed with them, can be made to look within is to take those things away from him. That, I suspect, is the real meaning of the story of Job. Sometimes it is necessary to take away from a man *everything* he holds dear before, in despair, he will sit him down alone to find that which cannot be taken away from him; that which, despite all, endures and lives within his own consciousness. It is no different with peoples.

Something of that sort, I gather from Betty and her friends, is back of the present world-wide turmoil. How much will have to be taken away from mankind before it sits itself down to its inner searchings, she cannot, will not, predict.

"That," says she, "is dependent on the free-will of man. Your wills are free. That is your heritage and your glory. That we cannot touch."

Only when the balance is restored will the storm die. Not because somebody decides that we have suffered enough, but because the cause and effect have worked out in restoration. When the Intent of Consciousness, which is evolution, again becomes an *event* in the hearts of men as well as in their research laboratories.

6.

"There was growing up in the world a definitely retarding influence," Stephen told us. "The best way a thing can be destroyed is for it to destroy itself. That so many, who are themselves individually positive, must be destroyed with this negative, is your side of the tragedy," he continued pityingly, "but you must remember that it is only one universe after all. And we know, *without a question*, that your world, which has forgotten the importance of immortality and the wisdom of recognizing the reality of the Oneness of Consciousness, is going to recover that knowledge. 'Where your treasure is' . . . remember? The world will recover that knowledge because so much of its treasure — so many of its individual loved ones — will be here, with us, in the unobstructed universe."

"The price is high," supplemented Betty, "but that for which it is paid is man's greatest good, and so no price is too high. The time has come for a distinct step forward in man's psychological and moral evolution, and sometimes it takes great shock and sorrow to force him to take that step."

What is that step forward?

Realization of the truth from which humanity was straying.

What truth?

Faith in the immortality of the individual, and the extension of outlook that faith implies. Not belief, but *faith* — as man has faith in his compass when he is on the high seas.

What extension of his outlook?

Knowledge that he, *himself*, is in evolution as well as being part of that greater evolution of the whole of consciousness that must go on, that *will* go on. That his own little segment, of an obstructed universe, and what happens in it, are only a part — though a vitally important part — of the greater whole.

"The actuality of that relationship is what I am trying to prove to you," said Betty. "It is what I want to make real by showing you — in your own terms that you understand and of which you can intellectually approve — that the universe is one, and that you and I are co-existent in it. So that," she pointed out impressively, "you may widen your thoughts, and so your actions, to that horizon, and by so much escape into the unobstructed.

"I am," she continued, "stating nothing new. The consciousness of man knows the truth. He need only be told the truth to recognize it — *if he will* — since the truth is in himself. And the only reason he has stepped aside from *living* the truth is because he has become too enamored of his own creations. That which creates, I repeat, is greater than the thing created, no matter what it is.

"Now man must be retold. Always in world crises he has been retold; always it has taken a world crisis to make him receive.

"Now, perhaps, he needs this stepladder I offer — this divulgence with its modern terminology — by which to climb back. In the crash and fall of ideals, in the chaos of a world new to him, he *must* have a beacon toward a wider outlook. He must have a significance to life, wherever he may be and whatever may happen to him. He must know that, however untoward or retarded the *event*, the *intent* of consciousness, which is evolution, is eternal; unchanging and unchanged.

"So many stepladders by which to get back," she went on. "So many stepladders the human race has accumulated, if only it could recognize them. They are recorded in all languages and in all sorts of ways; in folk tales and the picture writings of the savage tribes; in the various bibles of the various races; in poetry, in music, in sculpture, in painting. In fact, all humanity has been reaching toward the *unobstructed* ever since humanity was.

"Above all there is the Christian Bible. All faiths have in them truth. Indeed, *any* system of thought that has lived and continued from generation to generation in the minds and habits of peoples, has some element of truth in it. Otherwise it could not have lived. It may not contain all the truth, and its element of truth may have become overdecorated by what Stephen called 'emotional hypotheses' — in other words, the elaborations of dogma. And, again, what may be truth for one age may not be truth for a succeeding age. But so long as a man seeks truth and keeps his path straight, his own *seeking* makes it true.

"Of all the faiths that have lived, Christianity has done most for the world; in envisioning individual and collective liberty, in belief in self, democracy, education, real freedom. It was first expressed in terms needed for understanding at the time, just as I retell the truth now in the terms of your times. It is the same truth, whether you call it the brotherhood of man made One in a fatherhood of God, or the individual degrees of consciousness operating in evolution toward the perfection of the whole of Consciousness, the Reality.

"And I want to call your attention to the sweep of the Christian Bible as a whole. It is the historical record, not only of events and the rise and fall of social orders, but of human emotions and — most of all — spiritual evaluations. In the Old Testament there is a happiness, and references to joy and singing that you do not find in the New. True, you have Job with his troubles and Jeremiah with his lamentations, but you also have David with his psalms and Solomon with his songs. Now, if you read carefully you can find, in this gradual getting away from happiness, story after story of the ignoring of the Oneness of Consciousness, the rejection of what they called 'the fear of the Lord.' So when the Jew, Jesus, came to preach his doctrine of brotherhood, one of the first things he did was to scourge the money-changers out of the Temple. The things he had to say were pretty much paradoxes to them — so captivated were they by the things they had created. But these paradoxes, or parables, need not be such for you.

"The Christian Bible is full of stepladders," she repeated. "They merely need restatement, or perhaps reinterpretation, in modern terms. For instance? Why, for instance, the second of the Beatitudes? 'Blessed are they that mourn, for they shall be comforted.' What could apply more directly to the world today?

"What was meant by these words then? and what is meant by them now? I have said to you more than once that the thing most needed by the human race is a renewal of faith in its own immortality.

"All that was meant two thousand years ago was that people who mourn seek after the truth of immortality for the sake, first, of those they mourn, and, second, for their own sakes. And that is what is meant again, today. And the promise is, remember, 'they shall be comforted.'

"*If* your life on earth is all, why bother with it? Why bring children into the world? Why plan ahead for coming generations? Fundamentally, you know that the I-Am of man is in evolution, and must go on. But man has become so engrossed in the wonders of his own obstructed universe — allowed himself to become so confused and overawed by things outside himself — that he has broken away from that simple, early faith. The world is mourning now. And it is going to mourn. It is losing much that it has valued, emotionally and materially. It is only when people who have become stiff-necked and proud in their own self-sufficiency are forced by sorrow to take time to seek after truth — when they themselves *want* truth — that truth can 'comfort' them or again make them free.

"If you search, you will find many such stepladders to a clearer understanding of the things I have been permitted to tell you.

"I gave you the other day," concluded Betty, "the symbol of a wheel, and the hub of the wheel is truth, and the spokes of the wheel are the various paths leading to truth. Now, no two spokes are identical, and no two start from the same place on the rim, but in that they all run straight and bind the rim to the hub they are alike, completing a perfect whole, each spoke strengthening the hub. So if one man, starting from one place, reads one meaning into this divulgence, and another starting from another place reads into it a little different meaning, it can make no matter."

GLOSSARY

CONSCIOUSNESS: The one and all-inclusive reality, in evolution. Man's self-awareness is the highest expression of this reality.

ORTHOS: (Greek, *orthos*: true.) The operation of consciousness, through co-existent essences, in its unobstructed aspect.

ORTHIC: Adjective. Pertaining to orthos.

UNIVERSE: The total of all manifestations of consciousness.

OBSTRUCTED UNIVERSE: That aspect of the whole universe which man knows through his senses, including their mechanical extensions.

UNOBSTRUCTED UNIVERSE: That aspect of the entire universe ordinarily considered to be beyond the limitation of man's sense perceptions and their extensions.

TRILOGIA: The threefold aspect of orthos, consisting of receptivity, conductivity, and frequency.

ESSENCE: (Latin, *esse*: to be.) The co-existent and co-efficient actuality of orthos, manifesting itself in the obstructed universe as Time, Space and Motion.

RECEPTIVITY: The Essence of Time.

CONDUCTIVITY: The Essence of Space.

FREQUENCY: The Essence of Motion.

TIME: The obstructed manifestation of the orthic essence, receptivity.

SPACE: The obstructed manifestation of the orthic essence, conductivity.

MOTION: The obstructed manifestation of the orthic essence, frequency.

ARRESTMENT: An incidence of frequency, conductivity and receptivity, resulting in manifestation in the obstructed universe.

DEGREE: Consciousness, being in evolution, is in degrees. Each degree represents a specific manifestation.

QUALITY OF CONSCIOUSNESS: That aspect of consciousness resulting in species manifestation, as electricity, gold, tree, antelope, man, etc. In the unobstructed universe Quality is in evolution, and therefore in degrees. In the obstructed universe it is of fixed potentiality in its given degree.

QUANTITY OF CONSCIOUSNESS: That aspect of consciousness, in the obstructed universe, capable of, and subject to development by the individual, in evolution and therefore in degrees.

MATTER: In the obstructed universe matter is that arrestment of frequency which manifests itself in a three-dimensional extension; in the unobstructed universe it is the form attribute of any aspect of the trilogia.

MATERIAL FORCES: Those arrestments of frequency expressing themselves through matter.

AWARENESS-MECHANISM: That equipment of self-aware consciousness whereby the individual perceives that which is objective to him.

PARALLEL LAW: The term connotes the interextension of principles operating in both the obstructed and unobstructed universes.

BETA BODY: The form attribute of that frequency which is an individual consciousness, an I-Am. It is integral, atomic and noncellular.

ALPHA BODY: The form attribute of a combination of frequencies, constituting the physical housing in the obstructed universe of an individual consciousness. Such as the human body.

PLURALISTIC MONISM: Connotes one reality expressing itself in individualization, alike in kind but different in manifestation.

JUXTAPOSITION: The manner in which frequency (motion) variably collides with receptivity (time) and conductivity (space) to result in an arrestment, producing manifestation.

INTRAPOSITION: As juxtaposition is the manner of arrestment resulting in manifestation, so intraposition is the status of relationship that obtains as long as that arrestment holds.

CO-EXISTENT: That which is united in Being with something else for the production of an effect.

APPENDICES

APPENDIX I

Reprinted by permission from

WHO'S WHO IN AMERICA

Reference Service, January 1940

WHITE, Stewart Edward. In his first biographical sketch for insertion in *Who's Who in America* — published nearly 40 years ago in volume 2 — Stewart Edward White listed himself as unmarried and the author of two books, *The Westerner* and *The Claim-Jumper*. When volume 4 went to press he had married — Elizabeth Grant, in 1904 — and there were seven books to the list, including *The Blazed Trail*.

By the time volume 19 of *Who's Who in America* was issued, Mr. White's list of books had grown to forty — and all forty of a type so related one to the other that even the titles carried a common thread of romance and adventure. However, when a proof of his sketch for volume 20 — the current *Who's Who in America* — went to Mr. White for revision he added a forty-first book, the title of which at first glance hardly connected it with this thread of pioneering and new frontiers.

For the title of this forty-first book was *The Betty Book*. Surely only those who by one circumstance or another were led beyond the title discovered that in it Mr. White as a matter of fact still held to type, and actually recorded astounding adventure on the greatest frontier of all. And probably very few of those fortunate enough to go beyond the title, knew, if outside of Mr. White's own circle, that

"Betty" was Mrs. White, the Elizabeth Grant first appearing in Mr. White's second *Who's Who in America* sketch, published thirty years earlier in volume 4.

The facts are that Mr. and Mrs. White have been exploring the most challenging of the frontiers for many years. Several thousand pages of closely typed records have been assembled; Mr. White's brother Harwood was contributing much of his time in collaboration.

When Mr. White received the proof of his *Who's Who in America* sketch to revise for volume 21 — to issue in 1940 — Betty had crossed the frontier that she and "her boy" now knew so well; this time not to return as she had in the course of many previous adventures along it. Also, a succeeding volume to *The Betty Book*, and one under a more revealing title, was in the printer's hands — *Across the Unknown*, now available.

The research editors came to Mr. White's biography in the course of the careful checking all sketches in *Who's Who in America* undergo, including the comparatively few which, like Mr. White's, have appeared regularly for decades. It was immediately noticed that while Mr. White had added *Across the Unknown* (with Harwood White), 1939, as the forty-second entry on the list of his books, he had not altered the line "m. Elizabeth Grant, of Newport, R. I., April 28, 1904." The usual notation was about to be inserted in the sketch, when one of the editors recalled that he had only a few days previously received a copy of *Across the Unknown* as a gift from a friend. He glanced through it. His eye was caught by the final chapter — "I Bear Witness."

Before he had finished the four pages of the chapter he understood why Mr. White had not himself altered the reference to Betty. And he had reached a decision — he would suggest that the usual notation be not made.

His suggestion carried — and the chapter, "I Bear Witness," was the deciding factor. There will be no change in Mr. White's sketch other than the addition of his forty-second book: Elizabeth Grant and Stewart Edward White will continue to be listed in *Who's Who in America* exactly as they have been since April, 1904.

There results a "first" among the 433,050 sketches published in *Who's Who in America* since Mr. White's sketch first appeared nearly four decades ago. A waiving of accuracy to make possible a gesture recognizing the beautiful chapter in an unusual book. No doubt justified on that score, but have the editors of *Who's Who in America* for the first time actually waived accuracy to any material extent? Perhaps *The Betty Book* and *Across the Unknown* should be read before answering.

THE SEVEN PURPOSES

THE remarkable series of psychic communications relayed in the spring of 1918 through Margaret Cameron by a company of the Unobstructed under leadership of her deceased friend "Mary K.", and published as *The Seven Purposes* by Harper & Brothers in the following autumn, ended with this statement: —

"Two things only we have striven for through you: to prove to a group of intelligent persons that this force [the motive power employed in communication] exists and may be practically applied between your plane and ours, and to warn mankind of the nature and eternal import of impending struggles.... Upon the choice of them who hear this truth the immediate progress of the world depends. It is a warning to unite and prepare for combat. This is the truth. Heed it." (June 13, 1918).

In the shorter ranges of human affairs, it would appear, much that is wise goes to waste. Bread, cast on the waters, returns. But not always is it so with wisdom. While *The Seven Purposes* was widely circulated during the years after its publication and has exercised a continuing influence since, its acceptance was largely among those interested in personal proofs of individual survival after death. That the book was of equal significance this side of death, economically and governmentally, seems to have been overlooked. Certainly its "truth," which one can now see offered the design for social living then required by events, has not been heeded.

"The forces of disintegration," said Mary K., in course

of the twelve brief "lessons" that serve to focus the broader narrative of the 314-page book, "have made friends with the poor and the needy, and have fed them husks of brotherhood. They have made friends with the powerful and rich, and have tempted them with earth and its kingdoms. They have fed the artist falsehoods, and the writer fear of fear... These are the works of the purposes we fight, and thus do they disguise themselves. Unless this can be brought home to the souls of men, the fight will be long and bitter." (March 26, 1918.)

If these were words of today's writing, they would be without portent. For already the prophecy is fulfilled. All too apparent is the present debauching of the needy by specious promises of security and of the rich by empty assurances of controlled profit. Force now has followed propaganda. The "long fight" is upon us. But they are not words of 1940. They were communicated through Margaret Cameron in 1918 and were immediately passed on by her and her publishers to the public.

One is reminded that prophets, so-called, were as natural to the ancient scene as they are strange to the modern. Then popular thought accepted a priesthood whose function it was to confer with divine oracles. Vague were the findings at times and clothed in imagery more metaphorical than factual. Yet did the seers of old venture to prophesy; and their words still ring in our ears — true in the main as to intent, however wide of the mark of event.

But the compiler of *The Seven Purposes* had had no thought of consulting oracles. A gifted author in her own right (see *Who's Who*), none was as astonished as she when overnight she discovered in herself a talent for what psychical research has called automatic writing. She had knocked at no door; she had gone up into no mountain; she had encountered no burning bush. Without asking for the communications later assembled in *The Seven Purposes*, she received them just because they came — free of obscurant symbolism. Nonetheless the twelve lessons were prophetic. Consider the following, also from the material received March 26, 1918:

"This is the second lesson.

"The forces of distintegration are gathering for a titanic struggle, of which your Great War is only the beginning....

"Germany...chose to follow the forces of destruction, and they will surely destroy her. But the forces she followed are uniting for a fiercer fight, more subtle, more deadly, more furious. Hidden beneath the garments of peace and good will, they make ready to poison the minds of men before destroying their forces and delaying their purposes.

"This is the battle to which we call you and all who are for progress. This is the message you are to give the world, to warn them of the danger at hand. The time has come when men must choose consciously to fight for or against the forces of construction. They are confused from the conflict within themselves, running hither and thither, calling for help from the gods they have made unto themselves, but looking only to the present good, perceiving only the present purpose, fearing only the present defeat. They will find no help from these gods, for they have impotent feet of clay....

"The forces of light are positive. Shun negation. The forces of freedom are individual. Shun dependence. The forces of progress are fearless. Shun fearful combinations. Work together as individuals, consciously cooperating, not as sheep....

"The forces of disintegration are wily, but fearful. Bullies and cowards. But when they are united in sufficiently strong numbers, fearless and unscrupulous. They fear the reawakening of the forces of progress in your life. This is the reason they gather now, to smite while the world is weary. Disguised as purposes of light they hope for welcome."

The deterrent saviors of mankind, who leave no man, rich or poor, free to create his own freedom! They have indeed found a welcome. The name of the deluded who hail them is legion. Legion too is the name of those who hail them through fear. Nor has the welcome been solely of Europe and Asia; and that, in this year of disgrace 1940, is the bitter lesson.

Perhaps America, at least America, will listen now: —

"Free development demands free purpose and concentrated force. Wherever two or three are gathered together to follow the same purpose in free and conscious cooperation, there force is multiplied. Wherever a hundred are assembled to be led like sheep by the bell-wether, there force is debauched and disintegrated.

"Because men have huddled together in fear, destruction threatens them. Because free speech has been debauched to fell purpose, free men distrust it. Men, forces of disintegration, but possessed of glib tongues, have played bell-wether to the multitude. Priests of purpose, whose counsel was inspired by the Eternal, have been thrust aside... Better were it for the immortal man to follow his purpose to death and mortal oblivion, than to lose his force to the bell-wether..." (April 1, 1918).

Is a vivid description desired of the pressure groups that have bedeviled American politics for the past ten years? Read this, received by Margaret Cameron April 3, 1918: —

"Brotherhood, to one class, is a defensive organization, for protection. Brotherhood, to another class, is an offensive organization, for pillage. Brotherhood, to another class, is an organized attempt to preserve the unfit. Brotherhood, to another class, is a dream of unorganized following of untried theories. None of these know that all men are brothers."

Such is the brotherhood of disintegration. And the brotherhood of construction — how is it described by Mary K.?

"A great brotherhood is possible only when its component parts are great. Strength lies not in numbers, but in purpose. The fit may not lie down with the unfit, and their progeny survive. The strong may not yield their purpose to the weak, and their force remain. . . .

"Brotherhood is purpose of progress, not purpose of profit. Brotherhood is made beautiful by unity, not by schism. . . All build together the common home of all.

"Seek ye those of your own purpose. Unite together all who fain would build. Master and man, architect and mason, financier and farm laborer, all work to the same end, and this is Brotherhood.

"To work to the same purpose, in whatever capacity may be necessary, this is the only Brotherhood." (April 1, 1918.)

Again: —

"Today, the first essential of brotherhood is freedom. Freedom to think, freedom to believe, freedom to strive, freedom to develop, from highest to lowest. And the employer who refuses this opportunity to the men who work under him is no more truly a force of disintegration than the laborer who refuses to cooperate with his employer and thus proves himself unworthy of a place in the procession of progress. . .

"There can be no society that will withstand disintegration that has not labor, capital, and market. When capital oppresses labor, forces of disintegration are freed. When labor dominates capital, forces of disintegration are freed. When the people forget justice, forces of disintegration are freed. And the destruction of one is the destruction of all.

The rich man who denies his brother freedom is a destroyer. The poor man who denies his brother freedom is a destroyer in no less degree. Each is a part of the other, and each follows eternal purpose to one end — construction and progress. . . .

"There are seven purposes. Progress, Light, Truth, Healing, Building, Production, and Justice. Equally great, save Progress, which moves them all. One of these each man must serve, if he proceeds toward the Great Purpose. . .

"Give unto each his opportunity to grow, and to build for progress. Freedom to strive is the one right inherent in existence, the strong and the weak each following his own purpose, with all his force, to the one great end. And he who binds and limits his brother's purpose binds himself now and hereafter. But he who extends his brother's opportunity builds for eternity." (April 3, 1918.)

Aside from the reasonableness of the argument it makes for personal survival, *The Seven Purposes* stands as one of the truly important books of the twentieth century; because (1) it clearly foretold, twenty-two years ago, the plight in which the world and its freedom find themselves today, (2) it forecast the cunning disguises of good-will, peace, prosperity and security behind which the powers of bondage would plot their victory, and (3) it carried assurance that in the end Construction, not Disintegration, would win through, despite all — if and when men cease to huddle, cease to hesitate, and choose.

As important as the first two, more so, is the third, phrased thus by Mary K.: —

"All men aspire. Some with reluctance and halting, but all feel the purpose of progress working within them. They may mistake its nature and deny its power, but no man lives who has not felt its prompting. This is the purpose beyond all others, the Eternal Purpose of United Construction. No man can thwart it, no man can evade it, no force can defeat it. Why, then, oppose and delay it?" (April 9, 1918.)

This Great and Eternal Purpose is defined by the lessons of *The Seven Purposes* as unity — united construction. Betty would broaden this definition a bit, as did Stephen. Unity of what? Her answer: Unity of Consciousness, the one and only reality. In the oneness of the whole of consciousness all men must needs be of one flesh, one blood and one soul — not figuratively, but actually.

The Great Purpose is served first and best by the purpose of Progress, said Mary K. Betty would give progress an inclusive connotation. She would call it evolution. But really the two names have but one meaning.

There are disintegrating purposes as well as constructive, insisted Mary K.; and all men know that this is so, though Betty, one imagines, would prefer the word "deterrent." It, too, was sometimes used by Mary K.

Supporting that preference are statements such as this, taken, not from the lessons but from the body of communications reported elsewhere in *The Seven Purposes*: —

"The individual whose purposes are fundamentally destructive is not damned nor lost. He is just delayed. Sooner or later he must work his way up, and it is entirely up to him whether he does it sooner or later — after he reaches this life, especially. In your life, he is sometimes confused and misled. He pays for that, too — not pays, but makes good for it, by working here for the development he had not sense enough to take there."

It must be remembered, however, that a prime aim of *The Seven Purposes* was to arouse, to realization of new and more perilous dangers, a world that believed that the defeat of Germany in 1918 would bring a final peace to all peoples. Accurately to characterize the hands and minds from which renewed and greater violence — material, intellectual and moral — was to come, required strong words, particularly as the tools of that violence would be brute force last, but first envy disguised as justice, doubt disguised as tolerance, cupidity disguised as building, destruction and nihilism disguised as progress.

Surely the following prediction, made by Mary K. in March, 1918, and now fulfilled, called for uncompromising words:

"The forces of disintegration are gathering for a tremendous fight. The Great War is one of the crises of civilization, but the battle to come still is one of the crises of eternity."

And now as to the word "purpose" itself — just what did Mary K. mean by it? From the positive, constructive viewpoint, simply those great inexorable currents that have controlled mankind's development from cave to culture. It is these trends, inherent in consciousness itself, that keep the ideal of man's destiny ever in his heart — a whole of brotherhood perfected through the free service of individuals.

These are the purposes of consciousness that, like hounds of heaven, will not down. Betty has called them intents. But the sweep of Constructive Purpose as set forth through Margaret Cameron needs small re-enforcement beyond the pages of *The Seven Purposes* itself.

— **D.**